C000242456

# Magical

## A Life in Football

## Paul Fletcher MBE with Dave Thomas

## Vertical Editions
## www.verticaleditions.com

Copyright © Paul Fletcher and Dave Thomas 2012

The right of Paul Fletcher and Dave Thomas to be identified as the authors of this work has been asserted in accordance with the Copyright, Designs and Patents Act, 1988

All rights reserved. The reproduction and utilisation of this book in any form or by any electrical, mechanical or other means, now known or hereafter invented, including photocopying and recording, and in any information storage and retrieval system, is forbidden without the written permission of the publisher

First published in the United Kingdom in 2012 by Vertical Editions, Unit 4a, Snaygill Industrial Estate, Skipton, North Yorkshire BD23 2QR

www.verticaleditions.com

ISBN 978-1-904091-70-7

A CIP catalogue record for this book is available from the British Library

Cover design by HBA, York

Printed and bound by MPG Books Group, Bodmin

# Contents

This book is dedicated to my wife, Sian, and all my family for the magical times they have given me.

Paul Fletcher MBE

# Foreword

I first met Paul in the 1990s when I was chairman of Sheffield Wednesday and he came to Hillsborough to speak at a Sportsman's Dinner. We sat next to each other that night and our friendship was sealed. At the time he had just joined Huddersfield Town FC as their new commercial manager and we debated the possibility of The Terriers moving to a new stadium.

Over the next decade I followed Paul's progress with interest as he masterminded the project to relocate Huddersfield Town into the Alfred McAlpine Stadium. This was one of the first new stadiums and became a blueprint for others to follow and I was not surprised when it won the 'Building of the Year' award in 1995.

I also watched his progress at the Reebok Stadium Bolton and, as I was becoming more involved in football's hierarchy, I recommended Paul for the commercial director role at the proposed new Wembley Stadium. He contributed well to the project even though, in its early days, it was dogged by delays and bad publicity.

At his next project, The Ricoh Arena Coventry, he was able to bring together all his stadium experience to develop a commercially driven building which included a hotel, exhibition hall, health and fitness club, office accommodation, casino and has become a major rock concert venue for the Midlands. It also featured in the 2012 Olympic Games.

I was delighted to see that in 2007 he was awarded the MBE for his services to the football industry and I was pleased to provide a letter of support on behalf of The FA Premier League.

Paul is one of the few ex professional footballers who has made the transition from a player to successful businessman and to this day continues to be on the lookout for new initiatives like StadiArena and UCFB, for the benefit of the football industry, which we all adore.

I was not surprised when Paul returned to his beloved Burnley Football Club in 2007 and even less surprised when, as chairman, I welcomed Burnley back into the Premiership in 2009 making Paul the only employee of the club, who, over the last 130 years has won promotion into the top division in English Football as both a player and a chief executive.

At Melton Mowbray when he and Burnley chairman Barry Kilby met up for the first time with all the other Premier chairmen and chief executives they received a standing ovation from everyone who was there. I was genuinely sorry that their stay in the Premier League lasted just the one season.

He must also be the only chief executive in the history of the game to be a member of the George Formby Appreciation Society. His rendition of *When I'm Cleanin' Windows*, I'm told is memorable.

This is much more than just a Burnley book and I am confident that his recollections of his 'Magical Years' will be a great read for not just Clarets fans but everyone with an interest in football, its development, and its wider world.

Sir David Richards, Chairman, FA Premier League.

# Introduction

I started this book some time ago when Burnley were in the Premier League in 2009. Then it got put on the shelf when Owen Coyle left the club. There didn't seem the same enthusiasm. From the moment he left, things took a different turn.

But, then when I decided to leave my post as chief executive at Burnley Football Club two years on, it seemed a good idea to resume the story. What inspired the resumption was the realisation that I had completed four more years at Burnley following a 10-year playing career there in the seventies. It was a bit like a US President having the privilege of being elected for 'Four More Years' which was a possible title for this book. The place was close to my heart, and still is. I have so many friends there. My time as a player at Turf Moor was magical. The chance to go back as chief executive was an ambition come true.

Like my first four years as a Burnley player, my second quartet also coincided with a period of triumph at the club. There was the astonishing 2008/09 season. And then there was the merry-go-round of the one season in the Premier League, the greatest league in world football. I played a part in all that. Other aspirations did not materialise – the rebuilding of the old crumbling Cricket Field Stand, but another one did, the establishment of the first Football University, of which I am now managing director, actually based within a football club.

Although this book is essentially about the four more years I had at this great club so steeped in history, it gives me a chance to take a few trips down memory lane to the days when I was a player, and the more immediate days when I was involved in stadium building.

The background to the time I spent at the club when Harry Potts was there is covered in some detail in Dave Thomas's book *Harry Potts, Margaret's Story*. Harry was one of my favourite people. Mention of Harry Potts meant I remembered the 30th anniversary of the Final of the Anglo-Scottish Cup that Burnley won. It might only have been a little medal in an obscure competition but any Cup Final win is magical.

The legendary Bob Lord comes to life in that book too. I'll mention him several times in the coming pages. Another man I respected and looked up to was the great Jimmy Adamson. Surprisingly there is little in print about him. Dave Thomas and I have tried to remedy that in this book. The opening of the Jimmy Adamson suite by Jimmy himself took place while I was chief executive. It was a proud day for me just as much as Jimmy who sadly passed away in late 2011.

I helped celebrate the great Jimmy McIlroy's Freedom of the Borough award, his MBE presented before a game on the pitch, and his 80th birthday. He had once been my old manager at Bolton. Now, here I was with him again. For more stories about Jimmy read *Jimmy Mac, The Prince of Inside Forwards,* again by Dave Thomas.

The name of Burnley director, Brendan Flood, crops up many times in this book. Every Burnley fan owes Brendan a massive thank you. For more details about his time at Burnley and the kick-start he provided you should read his book, *'Big Club, Small Town and Me'.* I'd like to think that this book very much carries on where Brendan's ends with the story of the two years following on from Wembley. It was a promotion win that brought joy and financial salvation, but also a whole raft of problems and boardroom differences of opinion.

For a richly detailed book about Owen Coyle and the promotion season and then the season in the Premiership do read another Dave Thomas book, *'Entertainment, Heroes and Villains'.* What I don't want to do in this book is cover the same ground but add to Dave's book with the behind the scenes stories. Dave for various reasons, when he did learn things that were confidential at the time, was unable to put them into print.

Read these four books and you save me the trouble of repeating things and I can concentrate on how all the events that unfolded, related to me behind the scenes.

For those people who have seen me 'perform' at a dinner as a speaker or entertaining with the ukulele, you wouldn't believe that as a younger man I would never have dared stand up even to say good morning to a school assembly, I was so nervous and unsure. But if this book does one thing it will show you how someone like me, who left school at 16, came from a very ordinary council estate, had few if any qualifications; can become reasonably successful and even wear the MBE. I even helped set up a university. I must have done something right, or been lucky, or worked hard, or decided that there comes a time when you realise that life is all about challenges and stretching yourself, rather than staying in your comfort zone.

I tell the story over and again about how in a Dale Carnegie meeting when I was about to leave football as a player, I stood up with knees trembling (well one of them was, the other was encased in plaster) to say who I was in front of 40 people. We all had to do it. It was a defining moment. I could say it was one of the moments that changed my life.

A number of things will remain vivid in the memory when I'm old and grey (not long to go). Amongst them the career I had that included some truly memorable games, playing for Jimmy Adamson, the disappointment of losing an FA Cup semi-final, the friendships that have endured, the occasional person I have never taken to, the stadiums I have been involved with, the promotion season and day at Wembley with Burnley, the 1 – 0 win over Manchester United and the establishment of the Football University at Turf Moor. Along this journey I've met some legendary people and amassed a collection of great stories. Like this one:

One night I sat in the rocking chair on the porch of my garden shed. It's just such a lovely chair in which to muse and ponder on the happy accidents that have determined my life. Two of football's greatest characters came into my head. I'd returned to Burnley just about 30-something years after old Bob Lord had sold me to Stan Ternent, then the Blackpool manager. I doubt you could find two people more irascible, and there they were one day arguing about a fee for me in Bob's boardroom. I can smile now just thinking about the confrontation.

"We want £35,000 and not a penny less," said the old warhorse and belligerent butcher.

"You can f**k off," said Stan. "I'll go to £32,500 and not a penny more."

Silence, nobody spoke, you could have cut the air with a knife. I kept quiet as I was pleased to get another chance in football. My knee ached and I knew I was on borrowed time even though I was only 30 years old.

"Tell you what. We'll toss a coin. If you lose you pay £35,000," said Lord with narrowed eyes. Boy was he fuming at being spoken to like this. His anger was nearly bursting out of the red veins in his cheeks.

As the coin flipped Stan said "Heads" and good old Queen Elizabeth didn't let him down as she landed herself face up on the boardroom table.

"Thankyou Mr Chairman," said a smiling Stan Ternent.

Lord Bob (as he once called himself at Wembley) stormed out of the boardroom £2,500 worse off. "F**k off back to f*****g Blackpool," he ranted as he left.

I was never ever to talk to Bob Lord again. I left Turf Moor and he died only a couple of years later. But, sitting rocking in the old Harry Potts chair I knew I owed him a lot. He backed Jimmy Adamson's judgement when he bought me. He alerted me to new football stadiums and stands. I don't think I let him down. Bought for £66,000, sold for £32,500; I played something like 400 games at a cost of £66,000 minus that £32,500. I was paid about £80 a week when I arrived and when I left 10 years later £450 a week plus bonuses. Value for money – make your own mind up.

After Bob Lord stormed out, Stan left too in a hurry.

"See you at Bloomfield Road at 10 o'clock on Monday morning for a Press conference," he said. Out the door he went only to pop his head back in ten seconds later.

"And make sure you score us some f*****g goals." He always was a charmer.

As I sat alone in the old boardroom with pictures of some of Burnley's all-time greats on the walls I was saddened to be leaving this great club. I'd had such a wonderful time, a magical time, I'd met some amazing characters, played in some memorable games and we'd taken on and beaten some of the best teams in the land. But now it was time to move on. The room was still and silent. There was a sense of sadness. An era of my life was over.

I limped out of the room wondering what the future would hold. I vowed never to return so that old and cherished memories would never be sullied. I switched off the light and closed the boardroom door. Believe it or not I remember thinking, "This room could do with a freshen-up." How could I possibly know that years later I would indeed return and do just that as part of the refurbishment of a Premier League Turf Moor? Life is so often stranger than fiction.

The title 'Magical' comes from the sudden realisation that it's the word that best sums up the wonderful life I have had in football. Putting things together Dave Thomas realised that it was a word that seemed to crop up in just about every chapter. I have been so lucky to have had this 'magical' time which continues right up until today.

My thanks go firstly to Malcolm McClean with whom I first started this book in 2009 and got the first few thousand words down on paper when we were flying high in the greatest league in world football.

Secondly to Clarets author Dave Thomas (this is his eleventh book) who took over the project with me, worked Malcolm's words into the narrative, and joined all the subsequent stories together. Ironically Dave and I were about to start a book way back in 2004. I had this crazy idea to take over a fish and chip shop near Turf Moor, run it for a year, transform it, get my old Burnley chums like Colin Waldron to serve, and disprove old Bob Lord's claim that he doubted that any footballer could even run a fish and chip shop. The plan was then to write a best-selling book about it. Then along came the job at Coventry so the book and chip shop were put on hold. Mind you, Burnley legend John Connelly proved Blunt Bob wrong long before I had my idea, with his classy shop in Brierfield.

Thirdly many thanks to Karl Waddicor at Vertical Editions who took the book on.

Finally, this 'magical' life would have been nothing without my marvellous wife, Sian.

I've tried not to be entirely serious. Enjoy.

Paul Fletcher MBE

# 1

# Fletch Has Some Previous

Burnley ... seven letters and just two syllables ... simple really ... that's enough for us. No need for the seven syllable Wol-ver-hamp-ton Wan-der-ers; or the Roman pretensions of an Aston Villa; or even the boys-own comic sound of Tottenham Hotspurs.

Burnley will do just fine. It's neat and compact. It says it all really. Unlike Manchester United and Port Vale, it's the name of the town we play in. It's no-nonsense down to earth stuff and I can say unashamedly, so are we. And the name of the ground, Turf Moor, is there a more iconic name for a ground in the whole of Britain? Imagine it being called the Maryland Chocolate Chip Cookie Stadium, no thanks.

This northerness may make us fair game for southern parody, but what the heck? The fact is that if Chelsea is football's Paris Hilton then we would be something more like the Bacup Premier Travel Inn. If you want to ask, "Who ate all the pies"? Then the answer is most probably "us", having once been sponsored by Holland's Pies for four years and the after match pie became a perk of the job. In a business that talks telephone numbers we still prefer just to talk.

It was thirty three years since Burnley last played in the top flight when they won at Wembley in 2009, and hard as it may be to believe, not that much had changed. Although I helped Burnley get promoted in 1973, I was also in the team that helped them out of the big-time in 1976 in the other direction. The ground; the boardroom; the demeanour of the fans; the quirky, non-corporate directors all have something of a 1976 feel about them. There's no Bingo746lottery.com Stadium for us. It's just Turf Moor – the same as it's always been. They just don't give stadiums names like that anymore (and I should know after being involved in some multi-million pound naming rights deals with stadiums like The McAlpine, The Reebok, The Ricoh) ... Turf Moor almost sounds as if it has been hewn from a hillside by men made of granite wanting to have a kick about. In that way it's very appropriate because in a world of outsourced call centres and clinically finished business parks, Burnley is still a place where hard physical work happens. Its history is cotton mills and coal mines where in the late 50s some of the Burnley team would work in lieu of national service.

It may not be a high income area but there is a real, almost Victorian work ethic about the place which has probably seeped into the club and its style of play through some form of osmosis. (Now there's a word you might not expect a footballer to use – except for Clarke Carlisle). Burnley fans, like any other fans appreciate skill and players who can excite, but as a former player it's always been my experience that a work ethic is right at the top of their list when they buy their match ticket. I can recall times when we have been cheered off the pitch even though defeated and times when victory has brought only modest ripples of appreciation. The difference has always been in the work rate. It's almost as if our fans feel that victory without a high work rate is only one step up the ladder from cheating. They loved to see sweat on the shirts when you came off the field, especially if there was some blood mixed in with it.

In 1987 Burnley were one kick away from football league extinction. On many occasions over the last 33 years we've also been a couple of quid away from financial extinction. So, the start of the 2009/10 season with Burnley in the Premiership was more than just exciting and novel. It was nothing short of a bloody miracle.

In 2008/09 we began with a new manager and could not win for the first 4 games. In our first match at Sheffield Wednesday we were two down after 10 minutes and went on to lose 4-1. We lost our second match 3-0 at home after the game had to be delayed for 47 minutes after a sky diver who was delivering the match-ball, in a claret and blue strip, missed the pitch by about 20 yards and came through the roof in the Fishwick Stand. At the end of August we were sat at the bottom of the table with egg on our faces and a hole in our roof.

Then something remarkable happened almost overnight as if the town had been visited by some kind of football Holy Spirit, or as if some psycho-analyst had cleared us of an irrational fear which had been holding us back for more than three decades. Maybe we had a fear of heights? It was a phobia that ceased to exist as the team clicked and we began an incredible ascent up the table and tasted the inconceivable highs of beating Premiership opposition in Cup games. By the 1st November we were sitting in 4th place in the Championship and we could now afford to repair the roof. Apart from losing 5 games on the trot around Christmas, the season ended in triumph. We ended the season at Wembley in a play-off final worth £60 million – the highest prize in world sport. There was a board meeting scheduled for the Wednesday after the game which, had we not won at Wembley, would have seen us staring at a situation where once again we were only a few quid from trouble and even the 'A' word had been mentioned in the boardroom.

Just before Wembley, with the manager Owen Coyle refusing point blank to take part in any discussion which involved the word 'promotion', and the rest of us not wanting to think too much about the alternative, we had to try to prepare for two scenarios which could not have been more extreme. It was a bit like hiding behind the settee when *Dr Who* comes on. You want to look because you know it could be really exciting. At the same time you don't want to look for fear of what you might see.

Still, Owen was adamant that the 'P' word was never to be mentioned in front of him. Maybe this was partly down to his numerous superstitions; maybe he didn't want to get the players' minds distracted by romantic notions. Whatever it was he was very sensitive to that pursed lip shape you have to make to sound the letter 'P' and pursing your lips was a sure way to get his office door slammed in your face. That's what happened just the week before the play-off final. "Owen," I said, "the council want to run an open top bus parade should we get p ..."

Bang. The door shut before I'd got the word out.

So we had the bizarre situation of arranging an open-top bus parade around Burnley and its environs not knowing whether or not any of the players would be there. In the end they were there as well as 30,000 Burnley fans as it finally began to sink in what we had achieved and what it meant not just to the fans, but to the whole town. Owen Coyle had delivered a miracle.

For me it was a special moment because as you may have gathered, in respect of Burnley Football Club and its promotion highs and lows, I have a bit of 'previous'. I know that I had started to take on that anonymous look of a chief executive. I could easily have been mistaken for an insurance salesman, an undertaker, a middle-ranking Civil Servant or one of those blokes who walks around the supermarket with a clipboard checking on the presentation of the end of aisle special offers. Yet it was not always like that. I was one of those lucky people who earned my living wearing the famous claret and blue shirt of Burnley FC.

I was alright as a player. I wasn't an athlete in the mould of today's elite players, but I did have one thing above all that helped me stay in the game at the top level. I was pretty good with my head, hence I was nicknamed 'The Kestrel' by the Burnley faithfuls; it was said that I 'rose like a tin of John West'.

It was this very head of mine, less grey and still flushed with the optimism of youth that played a big part in Burnley's last promotion to the top flight in '72/73. I scored the two goals against Sunderland which secured the old Second Division promotion success.

Burnley was back in the big time and I had done my bit. Under the chairmanship of Bob Lord, a larger than life local butcher, we gradually saw our best players sold off and our squad depleted. The purpose? To finance a new stand to be named after none other than the chairman himself although on the official opening day our captain Colin Waldron, live on *Match of the Day*, referred to the new stand as "The Martin Dobson Stand" as it was Dobbo who'd been sold to pay for it. Colin was fined £50 and dropped for the next match. It wasn't a good idea to mix-it with butcher Bob. When I signed for Burnley he looked me straight in the eye and said, "You're on eighty quid a week, and an extra ten if we win and if you don't score twenty goals a season you'll be on your f*****g bike back to Bolton. Have you anything to say?" And with that he simply removed his hearing aid, looked through the window and didn't turn around until he could hear my pen scratch my name on the contract.

The 1970s was also a time of real fun. The antics we got up to would fill three books. Every occasion was an opportunity for a laugh, or to set up one of your mates. Like the day we opened the new Stand that Dobbo paid for. Prime Minister Ted Heath was introduced to the Burnley team by captain Colin Waldron before the kick-off against Don Revie's Leeds United hatchet men. We weren't prepared (and neither was Teddy) for the set-up that Waldo had planned as he introduced all of us to the Prime Minister. As he walked along the line I could hear, "Prime Minister, this is our left back Albert Hungerdunger," as he introduced Keith Newton. "Hello Albert," said the PM.

"And this Prime Minister is Jimmy Slimslack," as Doug Collins shook the hand of the most powerful man in England." Jimmy (Doug) was jumping up and down in the line-up as I'd rubbed some fiery-jack on his jock strap and his balls and arse were on fire – pay-back for setting me up in mid-week. Putting fiery-jack in Dougie's underpants, by the way, was the only way to make him jump high enough to head a ball. In between Vernon Portgornie and Jerimia Nigglenoggle Colin slipped in a few "and this is John Smith" to bring some reality to the ceremony. This was classic Colin Waldron.

So I played my part in a promotion but I was also part of the start of our 33 year exile from the top flight. In a later season I limped off the field as part of a relegated, demoralised team in front of a very nice stand for its day. I know that I limped off because at that time my knee injury was so bad that I had a hot bath before every game, at half time and at the end of every game. I carried on like that for five years.

I wasn't fast when I started a game but I was always clean.

The legacy from my playing days consists of the tell-tale limp, my trophies, scrapbooks, memories and stories. For most players these things are the touchstones of their glorious past and for some all they have left to connect them to their golden age. That's where I am doubly lucky. Burnley is unusual in that an awful lot of the players I played with married local girls. They either never left the town or they came back when their playing days were over. There are ten or twelve players still in and around the town who I have remained close friends with. Secondly, I had a second career in football off the field which has seen me pulled back to the place that I came to love.

Burnley is uncomplicated, northern and properly rooted in its community. There are even two ex-managers living within walking distance of the Turf. There would have been three but sadly one of them, Jimmy Adamson, died as we put this book together.

You might be wondering why I chose this title, 'MAGICAL'. The answer is simple. My life and career has been magical; it's as simple as that. As a player I'd had the best years of my life at Burnley in the 70s. Then I left. And many years later I returned. Those extra four years were like the icing on a cake. And with so much happening while I was there it wasn't a job, it was more of a privilege.

They were exhilarating times and but for the recession and funding difficulties, they would have been even more so. It is one of my great regrets that there was no opportunity to rebuild the old Cricket Field Stand into something more modern and ground-breaking. Building stadiums had become my business and this was one reason why I was invited to become development director. But banking finances collapsed and Brendan Flood's Modus business hit trouble as a result. Had this not happened, the money and expertise would have been there to get a new stand constructed that would have been innovative and hugely lucrative for the club for years to come. That's the legacy I would love to have left.

Not that I didn't leave anything behind. Far from it. There is now in place at Turf Moor the *University & College of Football Business*. Along with several others I played an integral part in its formation and development. As Managing Director I still do. It is unique and at the moment there is nothing quite like it anywhere – a university situated in a football club teaching people how to work in the football industry, whilst they can look out of the huge windows at the pitch. I left school at 16 and now here I am playing a key role in the running of a university establishment, which was Brendan's idea. Why? Because times are changing quickly in football and to survive you need to increase non-matchday income considerably. A successful UCFB by year four has the chance of replacing the 'parachute payments'. That's how serious I believe it to be.

My industry, football, has evolved so much since its beginning in the late 1800s as a working-class sport. Players who had other jobs as well, many of them down the coalmines or in the mills, got an extra few shillings to play for their team. The mill and mine owners were often the owners of the teams and the fields that the early games were played on. When the first stadiums were built they were placed near the places of work and the town centre.

By the time I was to visit my first professional football match in 1958, football was well established all around the world. In England crowds of up to 60,000 standing spectators were not uncommon. This was certainly the case at Burnden Park, Bolton. It was just two miles away from my grandparents' house in Great Lever where I spent my early years. All of us lived in the small terraced house in Teal Street, mum, dad, me, grandma and granddad, until I was 6. Then mum and dad were given a council house on the Johnson Fold Estate. When granddad got home from work he would send me for a packet of Woodbines while my grandma filled up the tin bath in front of the fire. There he would listen to the radio and woe betide us if we made a noise and disturbed the programme. It was the kind of little house that would have made a great set for a Hovis advert on the telly today with a brass band playing outside the window.

After being squashed together in the tiny Teal Street house, the new one felt like a palace, especially with a back garden. Saturday afternoons for me in those days can only be described with one word, magical. Then, at seven years old I came of age. My grandfather agreed to take me to my first football match and life would never be the same afterwards. I don't remember who Bolton Wanderers played that day, or whether they won or lost, but I do remember not sleeping the night before because I was so excited.

My dad was a fitness fanatic and body-builder. Not a bit like me then. (Dave Thomas says I look like I've been put together in the Pixar Studios). In the summer evenings I'd be down on the Moss Bank Park playing football till it got dark. When I was older I played football for the school team in the mornings, had my lunch at grandma's (known as dinner in good old working-class Bolton), and then another game for Bolton Lads Club team in the afternoon. I reckon this was where I got my 10,000 hours of practice that Malcolm Gladwell talks about in his book 'Outliers'. Granddad was also an Arsenal fan. Sadly he never saw me play. After an afternoon game it was then home for tea. It was only 'dinner' if you were posh. Today I do call the evening meal 'dinner'. I must have moved up in the world.

In this tightly knit community of millworkers, whilst everyone made their way to their church or chapel on Sundays, likewise everyone made their way to the other religion on a Saturday. That religion was football. Burnden Park was the cathedral. Fathers and sons, grandfathers and grandsons walked together down the cobbled streets, under the old gas lamps, past the corner shops, above them row after row of chimney pots atop the terraced houses. Bit by bit the swell of the crowd got bigger. The murmur of voices increased and the noise became louder. Towards the ground the roads became narrow streets funnelling these throngs of people towards their Mecca. When the towering floodlight pylons came into view you knew you were close and the heart began to beat faster.

I remember my granddad always went for a pint of 'mild' in the Robin Hood pub. Whilst he was in there I was sent to buy a pie and a matchday programme across the street. In those days they were thin little things that cost only a few pence. I can look at one now and the images of those days with granddad come back in waves of nostalgia. This simple programme with just a few pages became his Bible for the next week or so until the next game. He would pore over it, holding it with hands that were blackened from coal dust. He was a stoker in the furnace room of a local cotton mill. It was back-breaking and he did this until he was 60 years old. He read that programme over and again, probably dreaming of being a player himself.

As granddad left the Robin Hood, we would join up along with 9 or 10 of his workmates. Together we all walked down Lever Street towards his second home, Burnden Park, the home of his beloved Bolton Wanderers Football Club. Nearer and nearer we would get, closer and closer until there was anything between 15 and 20 of us marching over the cobbles in navy blue and white scarves. Some carried huge, heavy wooden rattles. They made a deafening racket. You don't see them now. Health and Safety rules OK! I try to picture a gang of football hooligans heavily armed with rattles but I can't quite manage it.

As we walked along, the conversation was about the last game, the players, how well they were doing, Nat Lofthouse, Tommy Banks, Roy Hartle, Eddie Hopkinson, legends all. I listened avidly hanging on every word. These discussions were important. I was just seven years old but part of this group of Bolton men talking about my heroes and I was part of it. The congregation would arrive at the cathedral itself and the congregation worshipped Nat Lofthouse. The arrival at the game, fuelled with the hope of victory and the expectation of excitement was mystical. It was part of the fabric of the community.

The next 90 minutes were a release. They were a release for working men who worked long hours, from the drudgery of manual work and the worries of putting food on the table and providing coal for the fire that burned day and night in every little two-up and two-down house, where there was an outside lavatory that usually froze in winter.

The match was 90 minutes of escapism. If there was a win, which happened often in the late 50s at Burnden Park, then the next week was more agreeable, easier to bear. Monday mornings sped by quickly as the game was dissected. And in 1958 there was a real triumph when the Trotters got to the FA Cup Final – and won. How dreamlike was that for me.

That first game for me was an initiation. That day I was to see men who so far I only knew as distant names. That day I was to see Nat Lofthouse in the flesh for the first time. How could I know that several years later I would follow in his footsteps and play centre-forward for Bolton Wanderers at the cathedral, Burnden Park, and that one day he would coach me when he was manager?

And more amazing still, years after that I would return again, this time to help organise the demolition of Burnden Park and the club's relocation to a new stadium, The Reebok, six miles out of town.

But those thoughts were not in my head that day in the late 1950s. All I wanted to see was the Lion of Vienna score a goal. I can't remember if Bolton won that day. But I do know that I slept well that night, dreaming of being a footballer myself one day.

# 2

# Goodbye Comfort Zone

What do footballers do when they finish playing? The image is of the average footballer finishing with a nice fat bank account and being able to put his feet up for the next 30 years or so. The abiding picture is of the Premiership stars and the huge salaries they earn – the Gerrards and Terrys, the Rooneys, and the Lampards. The reality is different. For every Premier star there are many more who don't earn huge salaries. Beneath the tip of the iceberg lies the true picture, of honest journeymen players whose only trade is football and who face real difficulties when they stop playing. The problems they face may be monetary or emotional, or even both. Football is a hard job to leave. Fame when it ends, even if it is only local, leaves a huge void.

Even while I was playing, I dabbled with various businesses. There was a printing business, a kitchen and bathroom business and Dewhurst Removals. My dad had been a printer and in her later years so was my mum which got me interested in print and graphic design. So, even at a very early age as an apprentice at Bolton I set up a business in the back room of the stationery place where mum worked. Several times I was in there and would hear people ask did they do printing? So, with another young Bolton player, Paul Hallows, I rented a back room at Geoff Lomas's premises, bought an old Heidelberg Platen printer for £83.50 and bingo we were in business. We did letterheads and business cards on a machine that was held together by string, sellotape and elastic bands. I can't ever remember making any profit, but years later this experience stood me in good stead when I had to order thousands of pounds worth of printed material as part of the stadium business.

Dewhurst's Removals was based in Rawtenstall and this was something that was just after I finished playing. I sank £5,000 into it. My partner was hard-working and had an HGV licence. It was a firm that had been in existence since something like 1886 and the current owner wanted to sell up and retire. After a hundred years of lifting sofas I didn't blame him. By this time I was also working for 'Miniprints Photography' taking pictures of houses for estate agents so I was able to discover no end of people about to move house. Of course they all needed a removal firm, or storage. So I'd just slip them a Dewhurst's removals leaflet through the door. Part of Dewhurst's was an old Methodist chapel in the area so it was a damned good investment. Nobody got their furniture until they had paid their bill. Storage was a key component of the business and this alone was in profit. The business prospered and when we doubled our storage space by adding another floor inside the church it was even more lucrative. I even used to go out on some of the jobs with the men. Boy, were they experts at fitting large objects into small doorways and working out the order of unloading. Don't think it's a simple job of shoving things in a removal van and then sliding it all out. If you want to know how to lift a piano without putting your back out then I'm your man. The trick is simple; get someone else to do it.

Then I had another brainwave (sometimes I think my brain never sleeps). If we bought a couple of small houses we could rent these out to people who were in between moves. So, when the chance came to buy a couple of properties near the church we talked about that. My partner agreed, thought it was a great idea, but the next day went out and spent what we had in the bank on a top of the range soft-top sports car. It was the end of our partnership. Within a month I sold my half of the business to Terry Robinson, then the chairman of Bury FC. A few years later Dewhurst's went into administration. Another of my ideas had been to turn the church into apartments. We didn't do it. Sometime later someone else did and made a serious profit.

At the end of a career a footballer leaves behind a level of adrenalin and camaraderie that perhaps the average person does not experience or cannot imagine. In 2012 the 'average' football career still lasts only seven-and-a-half years. For every Frank Lampard there are 25 young players whose careers last less than 12 months. It's a short career. From a 16-year-old old who leaves school and then makes the grade, if they are lucky there are just 15 years in the game, and of those, just nine or ten at the very top. In that 15-year span the intensity of the emotions, the thrills, the goals, medals, is then gone when a career finishes. It leaves an emptiness that for some is difficult, if not impossible, to cope with. For some the answer is drinking, gambling or depression. Divorce rates increase. Some go into business and fail. A lucky few go into business and succeed. But for all of them, nothing can replace the life of a practising footballer. Although many try, only a small number become a coach or manager.

Something that Gary Neville wrote sticks in my mind: "It is impossible to replicate the feeling of walking out of the tunnel in front of tens of thousands of fans, the elation and adulation if you win a big match. It's like a drug and once it's taken away, where is the stimulant you need to wake up in the morning and test yourself."

In some ways, ironically, the lucky footballer is the one who faces an injury towards the end of his career that gives him time out of the team while he recovers, that enables him to think about what he will do when the time comes to hang up his boots. Inactivity gives time for thought and planning. It's almost a rehearsal for the real thing when it comes. It happened to me.

Others are level-headed enough to make those plans anyway. But one thing affects them all. It's thought that footballers have a gene that revolves round competition and the will to win. When a footballer finishes, if he leaves the game, that gene is unemployed and doesn't know what to do with itself. His young athletic body, which once helped this gene to help him win, is now injured beyond repair.

I guess I was lucky. I had a great career but then had the imagination and energy to make my mark in the world when I stopped playing. And I had a serious injury that meant I was laid up for a sufficient period to take stock and think just what do I do next? I never wanted to be a manager or a coach (Jimmy Adamson said there was only two things stopped me playing for England ... skill and ability) but most of the time there has remained a strong link with football. When the time came to call it a day it was also true to say I had to think hard about what skills I did have and what if anything I was actually capable of doing. The life of a footballer doesn't teach you or leave you with the qualifications to be a plumber, or an electrician, or a joiner, an engineer, a teacher or any other of 101 jobs and trades. It's also a job where for X number of years, everything has been done for you. It's a cocoon-like existence. The real world is well outside of the football world.

What I did have though was a brain, an indomitable spirit, a fund of common sense and a head full of ideas. Oh, and a couple of other useful things, I could hold a conversation and I could play the ukulele. Not a lot of footballers can do that. Failing everything else and if needs must, I could always have been a street busker outside Tesco.

I want this story to be different. I'm not going to begin by telling you all about school and how this teacher and that encouraged me to be a footballer. You can take that as read. I want this book to inspire you; not because I became a celebrity footballer (footballer yes, celebrity no), but because I earned some real success as Mr Average, Mr Ordinary, swimming about in a big pond. Let's dispel any notion that I was a brilliant footballer, a galactico, a dazzling, twinkle-toed star who could beat man after man in mazy dribbles and then casually stroke the ball home with nonchalant ease. What I had though were some limited skills, bravery, could hurl myself about and leap like a salmon. Even that though might be an exaggeration. Salmon? More like a haddock.

In 1962, the old Burnley Football Club tyrant, Bob Lord, bless him, wrote that the average footballer couldn't run a fish and chip shop. I think I managed to prove him wrong, not by running a chippy, but by showing that a footballer could go on to build stadiums, return to his old club for four years as chief executive, become an MBE, and help found a University & College of Football Business. And in doing all that I've travelled the world.

So, just how did a council estate lad who left school at 16 go on to achieve what he did? Simple: I believe that we all learn from each other, from watching, listening and copying ideas. You don't need to be a genius to work this out.

Tony Stephens, my early mentor, would constantly tell me wonderful stories about his clients like David Platt, Alan Shearer, Dwight Yorke, Michael Owen and David Beckham. These stories would be intertwined with words of wisdom. On one occasion he told me that although we might live for 70 years or more we have just three life-changing moments. These are my three, and it's thanks to these that I've achieved more than I ever dreamed:

I played outside-right for Bolton boys because as a kid I was big and fast. By the time I was 30, I was big and slow, but that's another story. But because I was big and fast as a kid, that's why Bolton Wanderers invited me to join their junior training sessions in the gym behind the old Burnden Park every Wednesday evening. I was just 15. There was nothing special about this one particular cold evening apart from the moment that changed the direction of my life and was to lead me to a new 16-year career at the top flight of British football. It would be a passport to places like Anfield, Old Trafford, an FA Cup semi-final and England Under-23 international caps. The legacy of that awakening moment lives with me still. I've travelled all over the world. I recently returned from Brazil. These are things that are direct results of a decision I made on the night in a gym behind Burnden Park.

It was chief scout George Hunt who got me the offer of an apprenticeship. He'd been watching me as a lad at Bolton Lads Club and Smithills School. At 16 I was called up for a trial for England Schoolboys at Ayresome Park, Middlesbrough where the north-west were playing the north-east. I had a good game in what was my normal position then at outside-right but on the other side was another outside-right, Dave Thomas. Maybe it was that day that he showed me what a 'real' winger should be doing, dribbling for fun with his socks rolled down. We later became team-mates and he went on to play for England. Dave tells the story of the day when he was only a lad that he was walking back home after he had been to the shop in the village. Slowly a car pulled up beside him as he walked. It was Don Revie. He wanted to see Dave and his dad and persuade him to join Leeds. Dave took him home and they sat down in the parlour. At which point Revie opened up a holdall filled with money. But Dave had already signed forms with Burnley. He and his father, both straight as a die would not give back-word.

And then, for me, something life-changing happened.

No, it wasn't Revie with a suitcase full of money. The lad's name was Dave Lewis. He too was 15 but he was only 5' 3", much, much smaller than me. But he could do something that made my mouth drop. As the ball went up into the air this kid soared up like a bird, hung in the air and headed the ball goalwards. I can still play that memory from 1965 in slow-motion. How did he do it? This slip of a lad just rose up above much taller opponents and won the ball. And then he did it again ... and again. As a winger up to now I'd never had to head a ball much. This was something I decided to remedy.

I was aware of the 'headers' of the ball in the game, people like Bolton Wanderers' own Nat Lofthouse, the Lion of Vienna. And the current centre-forward at Bolton was Wyn 'The Leap' Davies. Both of them were marvellous headers of the ball. Then I'd heard all about the great Tommy Lawton who said he could even put spin on the ball when he headed it. Their success was based on one simple asset. They knew how to jump and attack a ball in the air.

On the bus home I decided I would 'copy' Dave Lewis and teach myself to head a ball like he did. This simple decision changed my life. I was no fancy-Dan player, my feet were mostly for falling over, but eventually when I made the grade, boy could I head a ball. Day after day, month after month, I would head a ball hanging from my mother's clothes-line in the small back garden at 12 Worston Avenue, Johnson Fold Council Estate, Bolton.

A few years later Burnley paid £66,000 for me; all because I could head a ball, all because of Dave Lewis. I bought my mum a new washing line. My feet were never good enough to earn me a living as a footballer, but my head was. And I thank Dave Lewis for that. Rule one, if an idea is a good one, then copy it. And practise.

Another life-changing moment: In the film *It's a Wonderful Life* James Stewart looks across a dance floor and sees Donna Reed. As their eyes meet everyone and everything else goes out of focus. It was a magical moment caught by Frank Capra. I can relate to it. It happened to me.

Neither me nor Bolton Wanderers reserves had played well that night, in fact, I'd had a stinker. I would have been happy to go straight back home and mope about thinking what a crap game I'd had. But, full-back John Ritson suggested we go for a drink at The Beachcomber discotheque in Bank Street, Bolton. Whoever thought of naming the place The Beachcomber in a place like Bolton was either a genius or just optimistic. Bolton, still all mills, terraces and cobbled streets in the mid-60s was hardly Shangri-La. The nearest Caribbean beach was thousands of miles away. Reluctantly I agreed to go.

Although I had admired her from afar, Sian Roocroft as she was then, worked at Blain's Chemists in Market Street. But I had never spoken to her even though I'd been in there once or twice for various odds and ends. I'd always thought she looked so attractive though in her white overall amongst the bandages and cosmetics. We'd even been at school together at Smithills but our paths had never crossed. But in Blain's The Chemist she stood out so distinctly amongst the shelves of cough medicines and Fishermens' Friends. Yet still I hadn't the gumption to speak to her and if I bought anything sought out another assistant, such was my lack of confidence. Yes that's me, the bloke who now gives motivational speeches and once spoke at the Cambridge University Debating Society.

The Beachcomber was pretty much empty and quiet apart from Frank Capra who must have been lurking in a corner out of sight ready and waiting to orchestrate this second life-changing moment. As we glanced across at each other I realised I was staring, in fact gawping to use a local word, at the woman with whom I would spend the rest of my life. There was a beauty in her face and eyes, which in my opinion has increased tenfold as we have grown older together. You'll notice I said older not old. Paul McCartney wrote a song that could have been just for us.

*"Well she was just seventeen, and you know what I mean and the way she looked at me was beyond compare, how could I dance with another, when I saw her standing there?"*

My heart went boom and skipped a couple of beats. My mouth went dry. We married five years later and had two children. To date we have four grandchildren. Sian rarely watched me play football and I was grateful for that. If she'd seen my knees too soon she might not have been so keen. She is the one great joy of my life.

And decision number three: My lifelong friend Tony Stephens would often stagger me with his insights and advice. I sometimes wondered though if he was obsessed with the number three. On many occasions as I drove over the Pennines to Huddersfield from my home in Lancashire I thought about what he had said about this mystical number. I could certainly remember my third life-changing moment and when it happened. It was while I attended a Dale Carnegie course in Bolton.

It came at the end of my football career when I had that classic ex-player feeling that I was on the scrapheap, aged 30 with no idea what the future would hold. I'd read and re-read that wonderful *'How to win friends and influence people'* by Dale Carnegie and decided to enrol on a 12-week course in Bark Street, Bolton. It was week five when a moment happened that would truly change the direction of my life. It is still, once again, vivid in the memory. The course tutor, Brendan Fitzmaurice, stood in front of a big white flip-chart. He twirled a large black felt-tip marker between his fingers. He had drawn a circle and in the middle wrote two large letters – C and Z.

Next he went on to explain that every one of us has a comfort zone in which we feel most comfortable and more importantly, safe. But on occasions in life, or in business, we are required to step out of our comfort zone and we either refuse, or, we jump outside *but then get back in as soon as possible.* Yes, I can relate to that, I thought.

Brendan went on to give examples of people working in sales and things they find uncomfortable such as: cold-calling, asking for money, making a presentation to the chairman or the board, and public speaking in front of a large gathering. Yes, I thought. I can relate to all that.

He then went on to explain that every time you venture out of your comfort zone, it gets bigger, not just in the area that you have chosen, but the whole circle gets bigger and you gain more confidence in every area of your life. He then said just one sentence that would have an everlasting effect on my life from that moment on. He simply said, *"And where do life's opportunities lie, inside or outside of your comfort zone?"*

I knew that I had lived the last 16 years of my life wrapped in the cotton wool of the football industry where everything had been done for me. Now I was on my own needing to succeed in competition with others who had already had a 16-year start on me in the real outside world working in whatever industry or profession they had chosen. At this point, my football life, the goals scored, my mother's washing line in the little back garden, my worn hips, knees and most other joints you can think of, were of no use whatsoever. I was finished with the game and if I tried to cling to the comfort zone of football, I would fail. It was a stark realisation. Things were now going to get uncomfortable for me and I needed to understand that from now on, life's opportunities existed not inside the comfort zone but outside it. But in the search for opportunities, where would I begin?

I decided that as I drove home that night from the Dale Carnegie class, that as part of my discomfort, I was going to become an after-dinner speaker. Why? Because speaking in public scared the hell out of me. What a good place to start. During my football career I never had the need to extend myself. If the headmaster of the local school asked me to say a few words to a class or an assembly as I handed out the football trophies, I would politely decline and shy away, and that was in front of eight-year-olds. I would consistently say 'no' to any local amateur football club who had invited me to speak at their annual dinner. I was not going to leave my comfort zone.

As I went home that night there were conflicting thoughts. Of course I was worried about the idea of standing up in front of a room of people. But on the other hand I knew I had the tools to enable me to cope. I had a good sense of humour and could tell a joke. I had a fund of good football stories. I had minor celebrity status in the Burnley area. I had excellent Dale Carnegie training. And if at my first event I was a total flop, at least I'd have had a free meal.

How did I do? Well for the last 25 years I have been a professional after-dinner speaker and travelled around the country to football clubs, cricket clubs, golf clubs, hotels, conferences, pre-match entertainments, World Cup events, European Championships, charity functions and the Bacup Wheeltappers and Shunters Club. I've spoken in Australia, Germany, France, Iceland, India, South Africa and Ramsbottom. I've been a dinner speaker, keynote speaker and a motivational speaker. I've met with kings and queens, presidents, prime ministers, rock stars, athletes and medal winners from just about every sport you can think of. And I've worked with nearly all the top comedians on the circuit whose humour has kept me in stitches all through the years. In 2008 I spoke at the Cambridge Union following people over the years like Winston Churchill, Ronald Reagan, Nehru, Archbishop Tutu and even the Dalai Lama. I've also written a book on how to organise a profitable Sportsman's Dinner entitled *The Dinner Business* published in 1998. And there was a time when I wouldn't even speak to a bunch of eight-year-olds.

Did my comfort zone get larger every time I took on these challenges? Of course it did. As Brendan Fitzmaurice said, as he twiddled his marker pen, *"Where do life's opportunities lie, inside or outside the comfort zone?"* Make your own mind up, as I made mine. Take action as I did. Stretch yourself in the sure knowledge that as Tony Stephens would say, *"You'll never go back to the same shape."*

From a shy, gauche, 16-year-old with no qualifications worth writing about, to visiting Brazil 40 years later; from a council-house lad to four years back at Burnley Football Club as chief executive. And all because many years ago a guy with a black marker pen drew a circle on a flip chart and woke me up.

As well as all that, isn't life all about things happening by accident? Some people call it serendipity. It was a broken leg that ended my career. It was the broken leg that was still in plaster when I sat in that small room at Bark Street learning about all things Dale Carnegie. Had that leg not been broken I would still have been a player, although Stan Ternent at Blackpool might have used a different word to describe me. I was all set to join Portsmouth but had agreed to play one last game for Blackpool when Alan Ball had become manager. Fate. End of career.

It was Alan Ball who was totally destroyed, one time, by the power of the fans in the Longside at Burnley when he came up to play for Arsenal in the mid-70s. The abuse was merciless. The chants were never-ending. The volume was stunning. It was incessant. The air rained insults from start to finish. Bally ended that game unable to put one foot in front of the other, and totally unable even to make a simple five-yard pass. It was wonderful. I'm surprised after that he wanted anything to do with anybody from Burnley least of all me who pulled his leg mercilessly throughout the game.

Alan became the classic example of the great player who couldn't manage a football team for toffee. As a manager he was a nightmare – and I should know, I played for him. So often a great player will be so blessed with skill and talent that they become a legend. But when they step up into the world of management they simply lack the interpersonal skills to bring out the best in others. His training sessions consisted mainly of us having to stop and watch him do whatever he was doing at that particular moment in a practice game or a five-a-side. The whistle would blow: "Did you see what I did lads?" Play again, the whistle would blow: "Hey did you see what I did then lads?" The game would start up; the whistle would blow: "Hey did you see that lads, I got the ball, I controlled it and passed." By the fifth time we were thinking 'bugger off Alan'. And so it went on ... and on ... and on. By the tenth time we'd lost the will to live.

How I got to Blackpool in the first place was interesting enough. Manager Stan Ternent thought I could do a job. He obviously hadn't seen me play recently. Bob Lord wanted £35,000. Stan offered £30,000. I was there while they haggled. It got up to £32,500 and stalemate. They decided to toss a coin. Heads it was £35,000 and tails it was £32,500. Stan won the toss. Old Bob fumed and went puce at the idea of missing out on £2,500. By then both he and Burnley Football Club were skint and the place was a shambles behind the scenes. It was the last time Bob Lord ever spoke to me. When Stan saw me play, he didn't say much either even though I notched up a few goals playing alongside his mate Ted McDougall.

I would never be too disparaging about Bob Lord though. As chairman of Burnley Football Club he took the club to great heights. By the time I left the club his abilities had faded however, and the club was hugely in debt and totally disorganised. But at the peak of his powers he had a philosophy that was to affect me deeply. He was visionary enough to realise that people needed better stadiums and conditions in which to watch the game. He built two new stands and there were plans to build a huge new third stand that would have revolutionised the club. It was never built. But what he said and thought about stadiums stuck with me so that when I became involved in stadium design and building at Huddersfield, Bolton, Coventry and Wembley, his words about quality conditions would come back to me.

When I got back home with my leg in a pot after that final football match, I could have been forgiven for thinking my world had ended and sent out for a crate of lager. But no, I watched, learned, listened and copied and left my comfort zone behind me forever.

# 3

# How to Eat Out and Make a Profit

It might seem odd that Chapter Three should be about after-dinner speaking when what you might be expecting is a football book and rousing tales of magnificently headed goals against people like Tommy Smith and Norman Hunter. But the reason is simple. It was speaking that got me out of the dreaded comfort zone and gave me the stimulant and adrenalin rush that I'd once had as a player (and heading magnificent goals). If life is about testing yourself and finding challenges, then this certainly tested me, and still does. I got a buzz from scoring goals. I get a buzz today from speaking and entertaining – sometimes in front of more than a thousand people. And I get paid. And I get a free dinner. Although mind you, I've had dinners at some places that were just an invitation to: "elp yerself lad ter pies on't bar." And at another venue dinner came in aluminium containers from the Chinese next door. Believe it or not at one event advertised as a dinner, there was nothing to eat at all.

At most public libraries there might be a few books telling you how to be a public speaker. They'll give you sound advice on this and that, how to breathe from stomach not chest, how to have a beginning, a middle and an ending ... but they don't prepare you for the real thing. You can stand in front of a mirror all you like and rehearse your jokes but it's not the same as the big moment. It's a bit like swimming. You have to jump into the water. You can't learn from a book.

How did I become an after-dinner speaker? Well there was the Dale Carnegie moment of course and as part of it there was the first occasion when we all had to stand up and say a few words at the beginning of the course. I sat in a room of about 40 people and the instructor said, "I want everybody to stand up, tell me your name, where you live, and why you are here." I was about number 35 and as it slowly got to my turn my heart was beating at about 250 to the minute. I was horrified, petrified, mortified; this was not what I'd been expecting. Had I not been in plaster up to my thigh I would have legged it out of that room before it was my turn to stand up and address 40 strangers. But, we were all in the same boat. And we all got through it. It was five weeks after that when the circle on the flip chart moment came.

Not long after the Dale Carnegie course and the decision I made to be an after-dinner speaker (as Tommy Cooper would say, "Just like that") but with no idea how to start, a good friend of mine Mike 'Number 1' King, then a part time comedian (only half his jokes were funny) whose day job was PR Officer for the Smith and Nephew group in Brierfield, phoned me to ask did I fancy helping him to judge the 'Miss Smith and Nephew Beauty Competition'.

"We've got some gorgeous talent here," he said, "and the women aren't bad either." I duly went along to give him a hand.

As the evening came to a close, the winner crowned and everyone ready to go home, Mike invited me up on stage in front of an audience of around 200 people. Without expecting to do anything other than give the crowd a wave, suddenly he says to me, "Would you like to say a few words?" He caught me cold but no way could I wriggle out of it, nor did I want to. I was glad to grab the chance to get myself out of the comfort zone so I told a few stories about my time at Burnley, had a dig at Chairman Bob Lord (it went down well), said goodnight, heard a few ripples of applause, and went home.

I thought no more of it other than to congratulate myself on having actually pulled it off without drying up or saying anything stupid. But three days later someone from the audience asked me and Mike King to speak at their Sportsman's Dinner. We both said yes. It was our first dinner date. But I wouldn't let him call me darling. Mike learned a few more jokes… and then someone in that audience liked us and asked us to their dinner and so it went on. There was no master plan on my part. It all happened by accident, but that is exactly how Mike 'Number 1' King and I got started and Mike now prides himself on having at least 12 jokes that make people laugh.

I do not remember ever asking for a fee, or being paid a fee for at least 12 months, but that didn't matter. I was learning a trade. I listened to different comedians, learned about timing and delivery, how to put down the occasional heckler or Blackburn Rovers supporter. I learned what to do when the microphone packed in, how to handle different kinds of organiser. I served an apprenticeship. It grew and grew so that today if I had the time I could accept an engagement every weekend. I work on my own, but sometimes with the magnificent Shteve Kindon. When we work together I'm the warm-up guy. Shteve is the one who batters them into side-splitting submission.

I knew I'd arrived when I was invited to speak some years ago at the PFA Annual Awards Dinner at the Grosvenor House Hotel, London. There were 1,250 dinner-suited footballers and their guests. Without doubt it is the FA Cup Final of after-dinner speaking. It was so huge that the top table had 46 people sat there. Sir Bobby Charlton was on my right. Eusebio was on my left. I was the only person I hadn't heard of. My speech was well received. I had learned the ropes. Someone asked me before I spoke if I was nervous.

"Yes," I said, "But not half as terrified as I was some years ago in Bolton when I had to stand up and tell 40 people my name and address."

The comedian can make or break an evening. I've heard some good ones and alas some that made me cringe. One of the most memorable was Roger de Courcey and 'Nookie Bear'. Many years ago I was invited to speak at the Gary Bennett Testimonial Dinner in Sunderland. The dinner was one of a number of fund-raising events and was one of the bigger ones. It needed to go well. The comedian that evening was Roger de Courcey and Nookie Bear. I'd never met him before and he was seated a few places from me on the top table. I had no opportunity to speak to him until about 9.30.

The event was held in a large sports hall type room and was packed to capacity with around 400 guests. There were Sunderland players past and present, their wives and families, many of Gary's family and friends and lots of supporters. With a mixed audience it was an evening to be clean and courteous. A Friday night at a rugby club would be quite the opposite I can assure you. When I got the chance to talk to Roger I had no knowledge of how his act would proceed or what its content would be. "But a little bear," I thought, "what can go wrong?"

As we chatted for the first time, I happened to comment that there was a mixed audience with a lot of ladies present, and Gary's family and friends were sitting directly in front of us. I was intrigued and asked, "How do you approach an audience like this Roger, do you swear at all?"

"Under no circumstances," he replied curtly and I was taken aback by the abrasiveness of the reply. "But unfortunately," he then grinned, "this bear always swears his f*****g head off and there's nothing I can do about it." I laughed loudly at his remark and went back to my seat amused and worried at the same time.

My turn came and went. It went down OK. There are always remarks and jokes to be made about the host town or team and I reminisced about playing at Roker Park with a few local quips thrown in that people could relate to. Like did they know that legend manager Bob Stokoe who always wore a trade-mark pork-pie hat, had another one underneath only smaller?

Then Roger de Courcey was introduced. After a few warm-up jokes he opened the box and brought out Nookie Bear. I will never forget the following conversation that took place.

Roger: "Good evening Nookie."

Nookie: "Good evening Roger. Where are we tonight then?"

Roger: "We're up in Sunderland Nookie, at the Gary Bennett Testimonial Dinner."

Nookie looked around and sighed: "Gary Bennett, never f*****g 'eard of 'im."

The audience, me included, nearly fell off our chairs laughing, especially the players' table and Gary's family. If Roger had said it, it would have fallen flat. Nookie said it and it brought the house down.

Nookie then swivelled his head round to weigh up the top table: "Roger, is Gary Bennett the ugly bastard sat in the middle?"

The room erupted. The next 30 minutes were electric as that little, inoffensive looking bear ripped into everyone he (or Roger) could think of. Nookie's language was appalling and wonderful, both at the same time.

I worked with them again at a function at Huddersfield Town. This time Nookie laid into the Town chairman, Geoff Headey, a prosperous local businessman who imported wicker ware. Nookie saw an opportunity. "F**k me, I've spent 13 hours in the boot of a car, squashed up in a wicker box, and the minute I'm let out who am I sat next to? I'm sat next to ... a f*****g basket maker."

The stars and legends of sport that I've met over the years have been both staggering and thrilling. But none was greater than when I met the marvellous Stanley Matthews. This was over 30 years ago but the measure of the man is that I remember it all so well even now. When the world was very young and I was still sprightly and seeking my fortune, I was commercial manager at Colne Dynamoes. This was a near legendary non-league club that whilst Burnley was on the way down, the Dynamoes were definitely on the way up and only a few miles from Turf Moor.

In this capacity I helped to organise a function at the Dunkenhalgh Hotel in Accrington and Sir Stanley Matthews was the guest-of-honour at the Colne Dynamoes annual dinner. A packed room of over 350 dinner-suited guests (and some of them were the women) had just clapped in the top table but Sir Stan was kept back till last to make a solo entry and receive the reception he deserved. Everyone sat down and viewed the remaining top table empty seat thinking, "Bugger he isn't coming." But then, compere Mike King with the timing of a true pro, proudly announced, "Ladies and gentlemen, I am now proud to welcome Sir Stanley Matthews, MBE."

An almost reverential hush descended as this incredibly fit, white-haired legend nimbly walked into the room. His twinkle-toe, patent leather shoes could be heard tip-tapping on the ballroom floor as he entered. Then, as he walked by the first table, the whole table stood up as one and began to applaud. So did the next table and the next table as he side-stepped by each one. By the time he got to the middle of the room, all 350 people were on their feet and by the time this genius had got to the top table, the roar of the crowd was totally deafening. It was astonishing. He was 65 but looked like he could have stepped onto a football pitch anywhere and done the full 90 minutes and extra-time too if necessary.

This unplanned, spontaneous welcome lasted for several minutes and for all of us there it was a wonderful moment. I don't mind admitting a few little tears dribbled down my cheeks.

At the end of the night, Sir Stan made an unusual request and quietly asked if he and his driver could sell a few coffee mugs to anyone who "might" want his autograph. "What a strange thing to do at the end of a dinner," I pondered. They were nice mugs too when they were brought in with Stan's career history printed on the sides. And not just a few of them either. There were boxloads.

Once the function had ended Stan and his companion set up shop. Stan signed autographs and his assistant sold the mugs. Dear God I have never seen money change hands so quickly. I didn't count how many empty boxes we had to dispose of when everyone had gone. But every box contained 24 mugs. Lord knows how many were sold but the queue snaked its way halfway down the hall. That crafty old fox must have made a fortune that night as well as his fee. I doubt he was paid much when he was a player, but boy he sure made up for it at the Dunkenhalgh. Life is full of surprises. Mike King was in tears that night as well; but only because he hadn't thought of an idea like that.

Many years after that, and by this time Sir Stan was in his eighties, we talked about his playing days. We started with small talk about Bolton Wanderers and then his beloved Stoke City. I asked him had he got any regrets. Without a second thought he said, "Oh yes. I retired too early." I thought he was joking since he had retired when he was in his fifties. He had won two Second Division Championship medals with a 30-year gap in-between. And then he said something that had me really thinking he was pulling my leg.

"Do you know Paul, in my day we didn't have the benefit of the medical knowledge that today's players have. I had my first cartilage out after being injured in an over-35s match." He smiled and then knocked me for six. I'm sure he was waiting for an effect before the punchline came.

"I was 71 and I was in, and had keyhole surgery, and out of hospital in no time." He paused again. "It took a while to get over it though, I got back playing, but I was never quite the same after that." He shrugged, picked up his knife and fork and carried on eating. It wasn't a joke. He was deadly serious.

I still owe George Best a bit of money. Let me explain:

It was 1980 when the proposed transfer to Portsmouth should have happened. But what happened next is an example of how fate, not us, is in charge of much of our lives. "One last match for Blackpool" was the request. But for that I might well be living in Portsmouth today… would never have gone on the Dale Carnegie Course at Bark Street… might well be busking with the ukulele somewhere near HMS Victory. I hear it's a good spot.

The collision with the goalkeeper was entirely innocent. Both leg and ankle were broken. Apart from that I felt OK. Cue the standard after-dinner football joke. "I'd also broken my nose in three places, Burnley, Leicester and Oldham."

So: over 30 years ago a committee was set up to organise various testimonial events on my behalf. One of them was a Sportsman's Dinner with guest speakers George Best and Frank Carson. It was an unnerving experience sitting at the top table in front of 300 paying guests wondering if George would turn up. Well I assume the guests paid, if any of you didn't and are reading this, it isn't too late to cough up. The daily papers had carried a few stories about George and his problems and his non-appearances at various functions.

The knot in my stomach eased and then departed as George walked through the doors of the Astoria Ballroom, Rawtenstall, *(I know what you're thinking, a ballroom in Rawtenstall, he's making that up but honestly there was one)* to the type of ovation reserved only for superstars. I'm still waiting for one. The evening was terrific and George was perfect. His speech was superb and he sipped orange juice all night. At the end of the evening he stayed a long time signing autographs and chatting about old goals and old girlfriends.

My good friend and comedian Mike Farrell tells a lovely story about a dinner at which they both spoke in Southport. Afterwards Mike and George stayed up for a drink at the bar. The time went by, the drinks went down, the room became blurred until George got up from the easy chair, walked slowly and carefully to reception and asked for a wakeup call at 6 o'clock so he could get to his flight to Belfast. The guy on reception looked at him with all due seriousness, then at the clock and then back at him again and replied: "I'm sorry sir it IS six o'clock."

George departed the Astoria and we got on with the job of counting the evening's takings and his entourage took him back to Manchester with his fee in their pocket. It therefore came as quite a shock when two weeks later a bill arrived from George's agent which was equivalent to several times what we had already paid him. It contained items such as: first class train tickets from Scotland ... hotel accommodation in Manchester for several people ... telephone calls to America ... six bottles of champagne ... air tickets to Belfast ... taxis ... and petrol.

The testimonial chairman, my good pal and ex Burnley team-mate, Colin Waldron who himself had a spell as a Manchester United player read out the invoice at the next testimonial meeting. We looked at each other and there was a short silence. Then Colin spoke: "I suggest we rip this up into pieces, throw it in the bin, and wait and see if we hear anything else from them."

We still haven't heard a thing.

Mike Farrell is one of my favourite comedians on the circuit. You won't hear a foul word or a vile, blue joke ... just gentle, wry, quality pith.

*Social worker goes to see a client on a council estate in Wythenshawe ... it's a single mum with a very large family ... the lass is struggling with the bills and feeding six hungry lads ... all the kids are in the garden ... one by one the mother calls them in for some bread and marg ... Wayne come in yer tea's ready ... Wayne come in yer tea's ready ... Wayne come in yer tea's ready ... she shouts this out six times ... social worker says good Lord they've all got the same name ... how do you know which is which ... and the mother replies ... oh that's OK ... they've all got different surnames ...*

*There's a fella in the kitchen trying to peel some spuds with an old blunt knife ... his pal goes in and says why don't you use one of them things that peels and scrapes at the same time ... fella says cos she's gone out shopping ...*

You'll have heard of Cynthia Payne. Well if you haven't let me tell you about her. Cynthia made the headlines in the 70s and 80s when she was accused of being a 'madam' and running a brothel in London. She came to national attention when the police raided her home and found a sex party in progress where elderly men dressed up in lingerie and paid with luncheon vouchers to be spanked by young women (each to his own). She served a prison sentence in Holloway and a few years later decided to stand for Parliament as a candidate for the '*Payne and Pleasure Party*'. She was unsuccessful. Later, she took to after-dinner speaking and that's where our paths crossed.

She was good too; at that time she was very busy on the after-dinner circuit, wonderfully entertaining with her stories about her time running her London house of pleasure, and was never the least bit smutty or offensive. It was in the Isle of Man that we were at the same function speaking to bankers, solicitors and estate agents, all male, all dressed in lingerie and all of them brought luncheon vouchers. Ha ha no, I made that bit up. As we finished off and concluded the evening, she gave me her business card and I thought no more about it, slipping it into my jacket pocket. It was a few weeks later when Sian stood in the kitchen holding it in her hand. She was sorting clothes for the cleaners and had cleared the pockets.

She looked aghast. The penny dropped. I remembered. My mouth dropped open. I had forgotten what Cynthia had written on the back of the card. "Thanks for your custom Paul."

Sometimes things happen in your own life and job that make the most perfect material. In the old boardroom at Leeds Road, Huddersfield, we had several beautiful old photographs of former players. One day I got a call from reception to ask if I would see an old lady who was the wife of an ex-player who had recently died. I met her in reception and her request was simple: "My husband Tommy has just died and I want a photograph of him for the front of the funeral programme. I'm told there's a good one of him in the boardroom?"

I was pleased to show her in and she shed a small tear as she saw the old colour-tinted photograph of a young man wearing his international cap. "Ooh that's a lovely photograph of Tommy in his prime, but he had lovely red hair, is it possible to take his cap off?" I knew that with digital photography this was quite easy and I promised her we would do this and she could collect it when ready.

I got it all organised and asked the club photographer to reproduce it without his cap and showing his red hair. He rang me back to me later to ask, "We want to do this right, which side was his parting?"

So, I rang the little old widow and asked, "Do you know which side Tommy had his parting?"

"Don't be silly," she replied. "You'll find that out when you take his cap off."

Towards the end of my playing days I tried my hand at a few projects and one of them provided one of the truest and funniest stories I have ever come across. In fact it involved me and new kitchens.

Kevin Collinge was a great friend who I met in the 1970s when he came into Fletcher and Hallows Printers to order some brochures. He lived with his wife Christine and two young daughters in Helmshore, a couple of miles away from my home in Rawtenstall. He soon became a good friend and a Burnley fan and as I was getting to the end of my career and I knew my knee would not last much longer, I was interested in Kevin's kitchen business. He operated this from the town centre in Blackburn. It wasn't long before we decided to go into partnership and open a second showroom in Burnley town centre. We agreed to call it 'Paul Fletcher Kitchens' until a whiz-kid advertising agent persuaded us it was far better to call it 'Discount Kitchens' because we sold quality kitchens at discount prices. Hmmm, a big mistake eventually but nevertheless we started off well and at the end of the first year we were trading profitably. I'd train in the mornings and then go into the shop in the afternoons and learn the business. I even went out sometimes to help fit a kitchen. Funny that: years later I would be ordering thousands of pounds worth of kitchen fittings for the stadiums I helped build.

Unfortunately this was around the time of Arthur Scargill's attempts to bring down the world as we knew it. It was 1978/79 and the Winter of Discontent raged between him and Mrs Thatcher. The country was close to being on its knees and fuel shortages meant that we struggled to get deliveries on time of the kitchens we had ordered. We had a full order book but not the actual fittings and units. Cancellations caused the closure of the business. I lost my £10,000 investment (thanks Arthur), but I suppose gained double that in experience.

Now then the story: We employed two of the daftest kitchen fitters on God's earth. Both were from Liverpool, both were hard workers but unfortunately, one of them Tommy Roscoe, had a slate loose and his mate David Groves wasn't that much behind. Their whole day was fun, jokes and laughter. They took nothing seriously (except the fitting) and frequently played daft pranks. Their day ended at 6pm, usually in a pub for a 'half' on their way home. But on one occasion, a prank seriously misfired.

Mrs Crawford had a treasured budgie in the kitchen and she was having a new kitchen. She was a dear little old lady in her 70s and was as sweet a person as you could wish to meet. She lived alone with her pet budgie Sammy. One day she had gone out for the day when the fitters arrived and left them to get on with the job and the instructions to leave the place locked up when they left. They worked as hard as ever and once the floor units and the cooker were in place they wanted to get the wall cupboards up before they left for the pub. Unfortunately Tommy drilled through a gas pipe and the kitchen filled up with the fumes before they found the meter, switched off the gas, and then fixed the pipe. It was quite a common occurrence and don't forget these were the days before the mania for 'Health and Safety'. Today they'd shut the street down and evacuate everybody.

It was when they were packing up at the end of the day that they noticed one small problem. Lying flat out in the bottom of the cage with its feet in the air was the small yellow budgie. They put two and two together and decided the gas must have killed it. Being the Scousers and jokers they were, they discussed all kinds of things about what to do; resuscitate it, find a defibrillator, or give it the kiss of life. What they did do, was glue it upright onto the perch, hoping that Mrs Crawford wouldn't notice, for a day or so. They then apparently laughed themselves silly on the way to the pub.

I got a phone call the next morning early from Mrs Crawford and she was very distressed. The budgie in fact had been dead all day; and the fitters hadn't noticed it. It had been dead, believe it or not, since the day before and Mrs Crawford had left it in the cage for her daughter to come and bury it in the garden. Of course when she came back and found it sitting on the perch she'd nearly had a heart attack. It took flowers and chocolate to placate her. The two fitters laughed for a week.

Without a good MC you can struggle. A bad one can almost ruin an evening. The best MC I ever worked with was the late FA referee Neil Midgley. Others can be hilarious quite unintentionally. On a cold, wet night at a Working Men's Club in Spennymoor (and it was pretty awful outside as well), the club's social secretary, with classic flat cap and gavel, made a short announcement before the evening commenced with his introductions.

"Before I introduce our guest speaker this evening I have an important announcement for all members from our committee. As you know, the committee voted to award a cash sum of £200 to the family of any member who died during the course of the year. So far this year we have had to pay out £1,200 and the committee have decided that these payments will cease at the end of this month as some members are taking advantage ..."

There's a great camaraderie on the dinner circuit. People who are starting out can always count on help and support from the old 'uns. Tommy Docherty was the one who gave me the best advice when I was just a novice at the top tables.

"Paul," he said. "Your stories are great but they last too long; you need to break them up with some 'funnies'. An audience will get bored with a long story so repeat after me, "Doo da doo da doo da doo da joke; doo da doo da doo da doo da joke ... do da do da do da do da ... collect yer wages."

I took this on board and looked at all my stories and identified spots for a gag in them. For example one of my favourite stories is the 1 – 0 win at Liverpool in 1975. It does drag on a bit if you're not careful so I looked for spaces to include a line such as: "And in goal that night was Alan Stevenson. He was so good we called him Stevo the Cat. But this wasn't because he was agile; it was because he was the only one in the team who could lick his own balls."

The beauty of a gag like that is that you can change the name to the goalkeeper of whatever club you are speaking at, be it Notts County or Arsenal. And that is guaranteed to bring the house down.

The Doc maintains he once tried to sign me when he was manager of Manchester United but has always said since, if he had done, it would have been his biggest ever mistake. Comedians and comperes are great friends and there's serious competition to come up with a new joke. They desperately need new material and will pay £10-plus for anything new. Sometimes it can be as much as £50. That's a lot of money for a quick one-liner and the problem is that once it's told it's up for grabs by any other comedian who wants to use it. It's an intellectual property that can't really be protected. Scousers are great jokers and they tell me that Walton Jail in Liverpool is a fantastic source of jokes where the inmates will sit round a table during recreation with the newspapers, making up jokes to sell to the comics.

Just like the Doc helped me, I was able to help Frank Worthington. I hadn't seen Frank since we walked off the pitch together in 1973 and Colin Waldron asked him how much he was being paid, but he called in to see me at Huddersfield when I was working there. He said he wanted advice on how to become an after-dinner speaker. He had an encyclopaedia of jokes and stories in his head but it all needed organising. The first thing I told him was what the Doc had said to me – go and find an agent, then get one of the comedians on the circuit to write you a script, it'll cost you about £500. He took my advice and ever since he's been a great entertainer and has the added bonus of being recognisable after all these years even though he's in his 60s. Frank's long greased hair, the pencil moustache, the Teddy Boy dress, the twinkle in his eyes when the ladies walk by – they're all still there. Many ex-footballers go to pot quite quickly and become unrecognisable as the slim, athletic, good-looking guys they once were.

And I should know; I'm one of them.

# 4

# All Roads Lead to Huddersfield

The happy days at Burnley Football Club were long gone and seemed like a faded memory. It was Alan Ball at Blackpool who tried to sell me to Portsmouth. He wanted to build a new team based on the position 'he' played in midfield. So, he wanted to sell some of his strikers to raise some money. The manager at Portsmouth was Frank Burrows, an ex Swindon Town centre-half who I'd always had a few battles with over the years. He said I was the best header of a ball he'd ever played against and wanted me in his team, but only for 12 months. He told me he was re-building the team, I'd be temporary, and suggested I come down to the south coast and live in rented accommodation. Then at the end of the 12 months he would let me leave without asking for a fee. That meant I would be able to ask for a higher salary at my next club back up north. It sounded a nice idea.

I'd looked at the stadium, Fratton Park, (it's still the same today, a relic of ancient times), was shown round the town, looked at good spots for busking with the uke if I needed to, and I even looked at a few rentable addresses. On my way home I phoned my wife Sian and told her to prepare for a 12 month holiday down on the Riviera.

"St Tropez?" she asked.

"No dear, I'm sorry, only Portsmouth."

On my drive home on Saturday morning I got a call from Alan Ball back in Blackpool telling me that striker Dave Bamber had injured himself in training and would "I do him a big favour" and play at Walsall the next day. Like the good old pro I was (gullible fool more like), I agreed and on my way up the M6 I diverted to a hotel in Walsall and joined the team.

I don't remember too much about the game apart from the injury I sustained. Colin Morris took a corner and I tried to get in front of the goalkeeper who was trying to punch the ball away. The weight of the two of us came crashing down on my right ankle and I remember hearing a loud crack. I thought I'd snapped a shin pad but no, it was the ankle. X-rays then revealed the leg was broken as well. Some players get through a career without an injury worth mentioning. I hadn't suffered many, but the last one had resulted in me not getting an England call-up.

The doctor in a Birmingham hospital put the leg in plaster and suggested I stay that way for the next 12 weeks. The upside was that at least I wouldn't have to help in the house and do the hoovering. This also is where I had another stroke of good fortune as the Blackpool physio, Alan Smith who 12 months later would become the England physio, looked at the X-rays and thought the injury was far more serious than had been thought. After he had made that prognosis, the following day at 9 a.m. sharp I was seeing Mr Barnes, the top specialist at Wrightington Hospital. He confirmed, and cheered me up no end, that in his opinion I had made a "real mess" of the ankle. In the operation that followed the day after that he spent three hours "putting my ankle back together again."

In a letter to Alan Smith some days later he wrote, "I have been wrong in the past but I will not be wrong with this one. This young man will never play football again."

It was a bit startling to see that but I consoled myself with the knowledge that in my career so far it was my head that was the useful bit not my ankles. I used to look in the mirror sometimes and wonder if my head had always been that shape or was it because I'd headed the ball so much.

The good fortune was that if I'd not had such good treatment, or left the leg in plaster for 12 weeks, I might never have walked again properly. So: not feeling in the best of spirits (who would be when you'd been told you'll not play again), who should pop in for a visit but little Bally. I looked in vain for the flowers, grapes and chocolates, or even a smile.

The three-hour operation had been on a Monday. Little Cheerful Charlie came on the Tuesday. He got straight to the point and squeaked, "We want you to retire next week as we've got a letter to say that you won't play again." That cheered me up no end. Then he added, "We need the compensation money."

I looked at the long, white pot on my leg and then him, and told him I DID intend to play again and that next day I'd get him another letter from Gordon Taylor at the PFA to say that I would play again. (Gordon played outside left in the Bolton team I played in so he owed me a few favours). Actually at that particular moment I was wondering if I'd ever actually walk again or appear on *Celebrity Come Dancing*, walk through the green grassy fields of the Rossendale Valley, or kick leaves and build snowmen with my children, let alone play football. But: I suggested he was being a bit bloody premature. A few angry words were exchanged and he stormed out.

"And bring me some f*****g grapes next time you come," I yelled after him down the corridor. He hadn't even signed my pot leg.

I lay in that bed and was determined that not only would I walk properly again and do the hoovering, I WOULD get fit and even play again. At that moment I thought what a film this would make, the injured sporting hero making his vow to return against all the odds. It would be a sepia moment with slow motion flashbacks of headed goals, Bob Lord, Harry Potts, Jimmy Adamson and my granddad along with the smell of the liniment and the roar of the crowd.

"I'll be back," I said out loud with a steely glint in my eye and a firm, strong jaw. And if Steven Spielberg is reading I'd like Arnold Schwarzenegger to play the Paul Fletcher role. I was determined to get fit again and once the pot was off I did exactly that with strenuous workouts (we got a bigger heavier hoover) and I was then out running on Blackpool beach every morning and afternoon for five months. I got to know the name of every donkey – and some of them played for Blackpool. And don't forget during this period I did begin to think about what to do after football whilst I was attending the Dale Carnegie course with the leg still in plaster.

A month later, six months in all after the actual break, I played for Blackpool reserves and scored a hat-trick. It was fairy-tale stuff. The following month I was back in the first-team. Alan Ball had left by then and Allan Brown had taken over. You cannot imagine how I felt running out onto the pitch for that particular game. I'd been told I'd never play again. I'd been warned I might not even walk properly again. But I was here, running, jumping, heading, and having a good game though I didn't score. How nice that would have been. If Spielberg wants to do the film we'll make it up that I scored in this game. There and then I decided that having proved a point, to me, to Alan Ball, the donkeys on the beach, and everybody else, I would indeed retire and immediately after the match made the announcement. I think there were about three people listening.

I was fit, fully mobile, had my Dale Carnegie certificate, an excellent ukulele, and was eager to find out what the next chapter of my life and career would be. I had no idea what lay ahead other than, "I will be an after-dinner speaker" and had a wife and two children to support. I'd seen guys on street corners with a cardboard placard round their neck that said, "WIFE AND KIDS TO SUPPORT NEED JOB" and went to look for a large piece of cardboard and some string just in case.

And in the true tradition that every story has a happy ending; Blackpool got what was left of their compensation money (which wasn't a lot, in fact it wasn't a lot in the first place) and for the next six months the donkeys on the beach wondered where I was.

My career as a player was like being on holiday. I loved every second of it. But I never thought of being a manager. I was just a bread and butter footballer, bread and dripping some folk said. I didn't understand tactics and strategies and the academic side of the game. But in the 70s at Burnley I did see the beginnings of commercialism. Burnley with a guy called Jack Butterfield was very switched on to new things. Despite Bob Lord's determination that there would be no such things as supporters' clubs attached to BFC, and being very set in his ways, even he realised that in order to survive Burnley had to generate extra money, so there were lotteries, dinners, a better club shop, and people beginning to use and pay for the club's facilities. No club could survive on just gate receipts and transfer fees. I wanted to stay in football in some way but didn't want to face the sack every two years. I wanted something settled. The commercial side seemed to offer that. Plus I did realise that my new resolve, after-dinner speaking once a week, was hardly likely to pay the mortgage and keep us all in new shoes. Nor did I want to be moving house on a regular basis. I'd been in the same house for 20 years and my family, the driving force in my life, were very settled. And, once sacked as a manager, the chance of getting back into the game would be about one in five.

I left the game for six years and went into marketing to get an understanding of the world of commercialism, but always with a view to coming back. I knew I'd have to start at the bottom and work my way up rather than trade on my name. Mind you there was one little old lady in Burnley who always thought I was called Cyril after the old comedian. A few of us from Burnley went to see her on her 100th birthday. "Bless you Cyril," she said. I was touched. Then there was the after-dinner occasion when I was introduced as Paul Futcher the ex Man City player. The organiser genuinely had no idea who I really was.

What I was well aware of was that I could head a ball crossed from a corner kick, could take a penalty but that was no preparation for things like balance sheets or business plans. Perhaps the name Fletcher did come in useful. I was offered the directorship of a company selling franchises. Instead, I bought the first franchise myself: a photography business of all things. Funny that: I didn't know an aperture from a denture.

By week ten of the Dale Carnegie course I'd gotten to know all the other participants pretty well. After one of the Wednesday night sessions one of the group asked me if I would join him for dinner that night. Pardon: a bloke asking me out for dinner? Was it the pink shirt I had on, the after-shave, the way I walked – couldn't have been that I had a pot on. Had I given any signals? But, after my quizzical expression registered with him he explained he wanted to discuss some business with me. I met up with him outside and to my astonishment a yellow Rolls Royce arrived and a chauffeur hopped out and opened the door for me and my new pal to get in.

Ten minutes later we were in a Bolton restaurant (yes there were restaurants in Bolton back then) and Keith Knowles-Taylor was explaining how he had made his first million in a business called 'Miniprints' in which he sold small colour photographs to estate agents. He was clearly impressed by the cut of m' jib and asked if I would join his company as marketing director to help set up photography franchises around the UK.

The offer was flattering but I had no idea of the difference between an 'F' stop and a bus stop. I hadn't a clue about even the basics of photography. But within an hour we had done a deal. I would buy the first photography franchise for Bolton and Rossendale, learn the ropes, and then become marketing director setting up these franchises all over the UK. And that's exactly what happened. Within a month I had a new Mini-Metro with 'Miniprints' all over the doors, and a brand new Nikon FM to boot. It took me a week to understand the back of the camera from the front, and then I found out that to actually take a picture it really was better if you took the lens cap off. Even learning words like 'lens cap' was a huge learning curve. The very first job I did inside a nice lady's house necessitated the attaching of a camera flash. This I began with a flourish as if I knew what I was doing. Ten fumbling minutes later the nice lady showed me how to do it. In exchange I wondered should I show her how to head a football over her washing line.

From that early incompetence I was soon shooting 25 properties a day and charging £3.50 a house which was a sum not to be sneezed at then. Employed by all the estate agents in Bolton I was coining in around £450 a week. It was only half of what I was earning as a footballer but I was at least learning how to earn an honest living outside of the only thing that I had once known how to do.

In the evening by this time I was out regularly speaking at Sportsman's Dinners all over the country. On occasions I'd be on a top table with people like Denis Law, John McGrath, Wilf McGuiness, Bobby Charlton, Neil Midgley, Mike Summerbee, Billy Beaumont, Frank Bruno, Kevin Keegan, Tommy Docherty and a host of other stars. There'd be support comedians such as Bernard Manning, Stan Boardman, Frank Carson, George Roper and my old pal Mike (No

1) King. Mike and I still make a good team and must have done 250 dinners together over the years. It was a golden era, expanding my horizons, making contacts, learning jokes (when you've heard Mike's as many times as I have you know his jokes off by heart) and that comfort zone boundary was being pushed further and further back.

Believe it or not I made the photography franchise work and after two years work, sold it on for a good profit. I became the marketing director for the parent company with their offices in Ribchester. At last I didn't have to squeeze into a mini and could take the logo off the door. Eventually having learned the ropes, selling, bargaining, negotiating, dealing, short, medium and long term planning, I felt I was ready to go back into football. And here's where luck comes into it again. On the up and up was a local team Colne Dynamoes with a chairman/owner, Graham White who might well have taken it all the way up into the Football League. He was so very close and if circumstances had been different regarding the ground, he would have done it. But, the club was denied promotion to the Football Conference because the ground was deemed not good enough. They'd won the HFS Loans League by 27 points. Graham approached Burnley Football Club with a view to ground-sharing but the board there wouldn't play ball. Politics reigned supreme. This was the first time I met director Clive Holt.

I started at the bottom again in the non-league game and was offered the commercial manager job at Colne in the HFS Loans Division. It was a fantastic experience. Mike 'No 1' King worked there as well and it was he who rang me and asked did I fancy it? To this day I don't know what he actually did. In fact I don't think anybody knew what he did. It was a move from the comfort of the Ribchester job to the uncertainty of football and learning another new job. The sales process in football was different and after 12 months of selling lottery tickets at £1 a time every Saturday morning, selling perimeter advertising at £50 a board, match sponsorship at £150 a season, shirt sponsorship at £500 a season, and sportsman's dinners at £25 a ticket, I began to understand the intricacies of the job in football.

And the material for the after-dinner speaking began to mount up, like the story of old Mr Grimshaw.

Perimeter advertising was based on a board that was 20' long and 2' high. There was VAT to add to the basic £50 of course, and one of the easy sales was to a local butcher, Albert Grimshaw of Grimshaw's Butchers, Market Street, Colne. It was an 'easy' sale although the old codger had knocked me down to £48.75 (a verisimilitude number). Old Albert gave me hell though over the next season and taught me an invaluable lesson which in fact has made my projects and organisations millions of pounds over the last 20 years.

Albert would always ring me every Sunday morning, the day after a match at about 8.30am. He also had a slight speech impediment which made it difficult for him to pronounce his 'L's. The regular Sunday morning conversation went something like this:

"Mr Fretcher, it's Albert Grimshaw here. I was at the game yesterday and I have a compraint. There's mud on my board. Now I paid £48.75 for that board and I want it kept crean all through the game so everyone can see it. Prease will you make sure this happens for the next game."

"OK Mr Grimshaw, no problems I'll make sure it gets done."

Two weeks later: "Mr Fretcher, Albert Grimshaw here. I was at yesterday's game and I have a compraint. There was a ball boy sat reaning against my board which I paid £48.75 for. You could read 'butchers' but where the rad was sitting you couldn't see 'Grimshaw's'. Prease will you make sure this doesn't happen at the next game?"

"OK Mr Grimshaw, I'll make sure he leans somewhere else next time."

Sunday, 8.30am two weeks later: "Mr Fretcher, Albert Grimshaw here from Grimshaw's Butchers; if you remember I paid you £48.75 for a perimeter board at the ground. Na then, I was up at the ground last week to rook at it to see if it was crean and I took a tape measure with me. Na then this board is supposed to be a 20' board. But it only measures 19' 6". I'm not best preased. Can I have a rebate ..."

My spoon dropped in the Cornflakes. There were several other Sunday morning calls before he became a good friend. Mind you, I never got any rebates on the meat we bought from him. He might well have been pernickety but he was right. And that was the lesson. If you sell a 20' board it has to be 20' to the last inch. There was nothing metric in Colne then by the way. I learned from that early experience, always give the customer everything that he wants, and exactly as he wants it. It has to deliver what it says on the tin. The real secret of course is to *deliver more than you promise*. Go the extra inch. Make the little gesture. Make people smile with the deal they have got.

Years later that philosophy stood me in good stead when I was leading the negotiations in Coventry to secure 'Ricoh' as the main naming sponsors for the new arena. The negotiations were long and hard, involving long lists of 'key performance indicators', with a range of executives in Japan and the UK. I was well prepared for the 'perfection' they were seeking. There was a moment too when I sat down and suddenly realised how far I had come from the guy in that hospital bed with his leg in a pot shouting expletives at Alan Ball.

Needless to say at the Ricoh I made sure that the Ricoh perimeter signs were always "crean"; that ball boys didn't "rean" against them and they were exactly the right size. No way did I want half a dozen Japanese guys in suits wandering round the ground with tape measures. I owe a lot to Albert Grimshaw.

At Colne Dynamoes the principle was that if you didn't sell, you didn't eat. But, we got to a point where we had sold everything and used up every avenue of advertising and selling. One day my colleague Mike King and I were sitting and sunning ourselves in the middle of the pitch and everything we could see was sponsored. We'd have got someone to sponsor the Town Hall if we could but the council might not have liked that. Suddenly Mike blurted out:

"Paul I've had a little epiphany."

"You'd better go and see a doctor then," I told him. "Is it painful?"

There in the corner of the ground was a tree and Mike had spotted one last opportunity to wring money from someone.

"We'll get someone to sponsor that tree," he exclaimed in his Damascus moment. I thought I had a head full of ideas but this was intriguing.

"We'll look through Yellow Pages and find the name of a Colne pub with the word 'tree' in it. There's bound to be one. Here's what we'll do." Minutes later I found one called 'the Cotton Tree.'

A couple of days passed before the landlord of the Cotton Tree came down to Holt House stadium. We'd told him we had discovered a "cotton tree" within the grounds. As soon as he saw, he burst out laughing. We'd raided the medical room (and Sian's bathroom cupboard) and taken every bit of cotton wool we could find and glued and sellotaped them to the tree and kept a straight face when he arrived. He thought it was brilliant and went ahead and sponsored the (his) tree. The local Press made a big thing of our sponsored Colne FC cotton tree, the pub got a big splash, the landlord was well pleased, and more to the point it was worth £1,000 to the club. On occasions people came to visit the tree. That was life at Colne. With Mike King I had a whale of a time thinking up every dippy thing we could. We had some daft times just trying anything to make money and survive.

Colne Dynamoes and Graham White should have made it into the Football League. What began as an old school team, several years later was as good as a full-time club with some real ex-stars playing for them. They worked their way up the pyramid but when push came to shove Burnley wouldn't let them groundshare at Turf Moor and the Football League declared their ground unfit.

After a year or so of serving this apprenticeship, Steve Kindon a wonderful friend of mine, ex Burnley player as well, put my name forward for the job of commercial manager at Huddersfield Town. I didn't really want to leave Colne and initially thought that the job would entail moving the family to Huddersfield. None of us wanted to do that. Rossendale might not get much sunshine but it was the place we loved and still is. My roots were in Lancashire and I said no.

Have you ever had a time when you've sat bolt upright in bed at 3am in the morning and you're wide awake and suddenly realised something? It happened to me two or three weeks after Huddersfield offered the job. *What am I doing saying no?* Really, what a daft thing to do to say no; this was the chance to get back into the Football League. I can't remember if I dug Sian in the ribs and shared this eureka moment, but there was no reason why we shouldn't continue to live in the Rossendale Valley and keep all our old friends and neighbours. Huddersfield was the proverbial sleeping giant.

When I got there and surveyed the commercial scene I knew there was a lot of work to do and no end of areas where I could introduce new money-making ideas. The club didn't even have a licence to open the bars other than on match-days. And, what it had right next door was something priceless, a huge, empty, derelict 51-acre plot ripe for the club to make use of and there were ideas to build a new stadium on it. Everyone thought it was a pipe-dream. There was no Jack Walker, no pots of money, and no Huddersfield Town bulging bank balance.

And so I became commercial manager and I insisted that building a new stadium was not to be part of my brief. At this point I'd learned to run a removal business, been a kitchen fitter, had a photographic business, learned the rudiments of being a football club commercial manager, had dabbled with after-dinner speaking, and was a member of the George Formby Appreciation Society. Boy I was a real renaissance man. But, If I'd thought I had to build a stadium, when I first arrived, I might well have doubled straight back to Rawtenstall.

# 5

# You Don't Know What You're Doing

I took the commercial manager's job at Huddersfield Town Football Club on one condition; I wanted nothing to do with their new stadium. I'd heard and read about it and also spoken to the previous commercial manager. He had fallen between two stools trying to do his commercial job and simultaneously be a stadium builder. All I wanted to do was concentrate on commercial issues. Maybe there might be another cotton tree somewhere, except in Huddersfield I'd have to make it a woollen tree or Gannex. Harold Wilson who was born in Huddersfield and was a Town supporter made Gannex raincoats famous. I had an old Gannex raincoat in my wardrobe; all the Burnley team got a free one in 1973 when we won promotion. Today's players get an Armani suit.

What did I actually know about Huddersfield as a town? Well it was bigger than Burnley and is one of those typical northern towns built on Victorian industry and civic pride. Its football team had a long and illustrious history but when I got there it was pretty much dying in a stadium that was just about falling apart. Following the Taylor Report and the offers of funding for new stadiums in the early 90s from bodies such as the Football Trust, the Alfred McAlpine Stadium was one of the first new, relocated stadiums to be constructed in the UK. For me it was another example of how life revolves around three things (that magic three again); fate, being in the right place at the right time, and seizing the moment. By accepting the commercial job at Huddersfield I just happened to land in a place that was about to build a trendsetting new stadium. Old Mr Grimshaw would have been proud of me.

After fighting off any involvement with "anything to do with new stadiums" it wasn't long before a new and dynamic chairman arrived. Graham Leslie took control and his first instruction to me was, "It's your job to build a new stadium for the club." There was no refusal. I had to get a new stadium built and didn't know the first thing about it. I'd left school without an 'A' level or a spirit level. It can only have been the magnetism and drive of Graham Leslie that got me involved. You could say I was kind of sucked in. But if I'd known then what I know

now; I'd have recognised straightaway that the Huddersfield project had all the components to be a great success. It had a 50 plus acre site within a stone's throw of the old stadium. It had the realistic offers of grant funding. The local authority was keen to erect a landmark building for the town. There was a groundsharing opportunity with a local rugby club. And it had the magic ingredient of three sensible groups sitting around the planning table (there's that Tony Stephens philosophy again of the 'power of three'). It had the football club, the local authority, and me the stadium expert. Except, and I shudder to think about it now, I was no stadium expert. But there I was in at the deep end.

Graham Leslie was a strong driving force. Often a club can have a dodgy chairman with a big ego, someone occupying the chair for the kudos and prestige, or it might be someone representing others involved in the background. The local authority representative might have been a lacklustre jobsworth unable to make decisions. Luckily there were none of these characters around in the early 90s at Huddersfield Town. It was just the 'stadium expert' who'd once been a kitchen fitter (sort of) before, which hadn't taught me much about how to build a stadium.

Chairman Graham Leslie was a charming salesman who quickly persuaded Council Leader John Harman to invest £2 million in the scheme. Graham had a clear vision, knew what he wanted and knew how to achieve it. He was also a lifelong supporter of The Terriers, Huddersfield Town Football Club. Eventually after the contractual period had elapsed wherein the stadium would be named the Alfred McAlpine Stadium, it took the name GALPHARM. (Graham Alexander Leslie Pharmaceuticals)

John Harman, now Sir John Harman realised that he needed to partner with the private sector to deliver a fine, iconic building for the town of Huddersfield. He also realised that by bringing the rugby club into the same stadium, this would have massive community benefits for the town and generate more income. He also saw the potential of the golf-driving range, the cinema and the stadium as a rock concert venue. All these were things that would also generate continuous revenue and keep the place continually busy. That is the cornerstone of my stadium philosophy, that they are places that should and can be in use seven days a week as opposed to just the once on a matchday.

And then there was me, the stadium expert. The unfortunate thing at the time was that I wasn't a stadium expert. My experience was running out on occasions in front of 60,000 spectators; and I had amassed some commercial experience but I had no knowledge of ticketing, seating, viewing, pitch technology, 'c' values or any other of the 101 operational and design facets of stadium building. But I did have a few pluses. I was eager to learn, had a fund of common sense, had learned some of the principles of negotiating in previous jobs, and could think on my feet. I was also an ideas man and a grafter. Suddenly I realised I relished the challenge.

Another plus was that Huddersfield was a 'known' name. They were founded in 1908 and had a golden spell in the 1920s and 1930s when they won three consecutive League Championships under Herbert Chapman. His is one of the great names in football and he went on to lay the foundations at Arsenal that they have built on so well. Much later along came Bill Shankly and a skinny kid called Denis Law. So, there was nothing anonymous about Huddersfield Town and when money-raising is involved this is a key factor.

The old Leeds Road Stadium once held a record 67,037 crowd in February, 1932 but by 1990 there was a crowd limit of just 8,000. In cold terms this was just not a viable football business. Yet, it was still known as a true 'football town', and, there were strong rugby league traditions.

When the stadium job was offered to me in the early 1990s I agreed to take it on, but I insisted on three conditions. Firstly, my small team and I would move into new project offices away from the old Leeds Road, to allow us to concentrate all efforts on the new building, not the football. Secondly I insisted that club secretary Georg Binns would move across to help me. George was in his 60s and had lived and breathed Huddersfield Town for 55 of his years. He had been secretary for 30 years and had one simple principle: *"We don't spend money lad till we 'ave it in't bank."* Finally, to help speed up the process I insisted that if George and I agreed on any decision we could proceed without board approval. This was important. I didn't want to be kept waiting for rubber-stamping of key decisions that needed speed and urgency. George was wise and cautious with the experience of years in the job. I was young, ambitious, and always ready to take risks but sometimes I knew my ideas outraced my common sense. George's prudence balanced my youthful impulsiveness. The board had to agree that if George and I agreed on something then it was a good option.

We began with a simple brief: a 25,000 all-seater stadium, a 500-seat banqueting hall, 25 executive boxes, a 40,000-capacity for rock concerts, and parking for 2,000 cars. And 'we did it', although those three little words totally mask the blood, sweat and tears that went into it.

After its opening in 1995, the Alfred McAlpine Stadium soon became known throughout the land as a blueprint for others to follow. It was exemplified by eminent stadium specialists like Simon Inglis as "one of the finest stadiums of its kind in Europe." It was also said that whilst the world of football only talked about new stadiums; Huddersfield Town went out and built one. But first, we had to persuade Kirklees Council and Huddersfield Rugby Club to be partners in the scheme.

It wasn't easy. Initially the town council were very anti any involvement with both football and rugby clubs. They were seen as having financial difficulties and decaying stadiums. Numerous proposals had been put to Kirklees Council. All had been rejected. But, on the 8th of May, 1991, Chairman Graham Leslie and I were given one last chance to present the plans for the new stadium for Kirklees Council Policy board. We prepared carefully and went into the meeting with a good concept and an ace up our sleeve.

The meeting needed some drama and a touch of theatre so all we carried with us was a plan of the site, folded down to A4. The dozen or so councillors eagerly awaited our final set of plans showing what they expected to see (and reject), a traditional football ground, a car park and a hotel. They expected to say no yet again, and then get on again with their other important business.

But, as we unveiled the plans by unfolding the paper that eventually covered the table, it revealed just one green rectangle in the middle, measuring 4" by 3". Graham Leslie spoke. "This is all we need, a football pitch. What facilities do you, Kirklees Council require for the community? Whatever they are, we will design them and then put seats on top and turn it into a stadium. And we will not proceed until we can prove to you that it is viable."

Then we pulled out our ace. "And we will invite Huddersfield Rugby League Club in as partners to ground-share." Bingo: their eyes lit up and we stayed for another two hours discussing the plans, the facilities, and the surrounding area in this new tri-partite partnership concept.

As a football club we knew little about the rugby league club apart from two things. Firstly there was bad feeling between themselves and the council because of a complicated lease situation. And secondly their old Fartown Stadium was in a poor state of repair. Although not legally required to make major repairs for the safety reasons covered by football's Taylor Report; it would not be long before the ground became so run down that it would have to be closed on safety grounds. It was also common knowledge that the club had severe financial problems.

Once the project began to gain momentum, two of the early decisions considered capacity and design. It would have been easy to settle on a small capacity ground and visit new stadiums such as Walsall's Bescot Park, Scunthorpe's Glanfield Park, or even St Johnstone's MacDairmaid Stadium. But if we had followed any of these straightforward examples then we would have ensured Huddersfield Town would never be a big club again. Success is related to income and income is related to ground capacity. A basic 8,000, 10,000 or 12,000 stadium would have relegated the club to the lower divisions forever. We had bigger plans for Huddersfield Town. We had a dream, a vision, and a mission. So we started off by visiting what was then the best stadium in the world – The Sky Dome, Toronto, Canada.

We left for Toronto on 14th February, 1992, from Manchester Airport with a feeling of real anticipation and excitement. There were four of us, myself, Graham Leslie, Rachel Heatley and (my new commercial consultant) Tony Stephens. The Dome was wonderful. Costing over £400 million it was home to the Toronto Blue Jays and was at that time the most used stadium in the world with over 200 event days per year. This architectural masterpiece was completed in 1991 and featured a sliding roof which could open or close in 20 minutes, along with a hydraulic seating system which could create purpose-made configurations for a variety of sports and activities including baseball, American Football and soccer.

The first afternoon we waited to meet the stadium's star architect Mr Rob Robbie. We were approached by a greasy haired, scruffy looking chap with a goatee beard and dressed in a sloppy old duffle coat. He looked totally out of place in the foyer of the Hilton Hotel built into the Sky Dome. His old wellies had some ragged jeans tucked into them and he dragged in a trail of slush, snow and mud from the foul weather outside. This must be some tramp on the cadge we thought and started to edge away. And then he introduced himself. He removed his old bobble hat with the words, "Hi I'm Rob Robbie. I designed this place. You guys must be from Huddersfield, England?"

We were quite taken aback, I can tell you. This was the man responsible for designing an extraordinary open-air stadium with a sliding roof. He was marvellous, a visionary and a dreamer but at the same time a 'doer'. All of us felt totally at home in his company and came home inspired. The trip had also acted as a bonding exercise for us. We would be spending a lot of time thinking and working as a team. It was crucial that we got on together. We came back impressed by the 360-bedroom hotel in one of the stands, the lounges, leisure club and gymnasium. There was a nightclub and a staggering 80 McDonald's sales points.

The hotel bedrooms overlooked the pitch area and converted to hospitality suites on event days. We were told a lovely story by Sky Dome commercial manager David Garrick about a Blue Jays home game when the TV cameras panned round the stadium during a break in play. As the camera focused on one of the hospitality suites, it was noticed that it was still in its bedroom state and there was a naked couple cavorting and doing what naked couples do. For several seconds the nation sat and watched as the scene was broadcast live to millions of viewers.

"Well, ee by gum, that wouldn't 'appen in 'uddersfield, they'd 'ave kept their socks on." I said mimicking the best and broadest Yorkshire accent I could muster.

Rachel Heatley, development director for Kirklees Council, had been portrayed to me as being really difficult in the early stages of the project. She had rejected numerous proposals but in truth was only doing her job. But from this point on she was an absolute gem. Her incredible memory and agility with figures proved invaluable to the team as she later took us through the developmental appraisal of the Leeds Road site. She was studious, academic and attractive and in many ways reminded me of an old-style headmistress. Once I came on board she became a massive asset but a few years after the opening of the McAlpine she was tragically killed in a climbing accident.

Meanwhile back at the ranch George Binns had become more seriously involved. We realised that we needed him to be full time and dedicated to this one project. Graham Leslie and myself persuaded the Huddersfield board that George should relinquish the secretary role at the club and lock himself in the office and begin to work solely on fundraising in general, but in particular with the Football Trust. The Football Trust, a support body for sport generally and adapted following the Taylor Report, had laid down guidelines for the support of Football League clubs in 1992. £2 million was available for the First Division (now Premier League), £1 million for the Second Division (now Championship) and £500thousand for the Third and Fourth Divisions (now Divisions 1 and 2).

Huddersfield Town's allowance was therefore £500thousand. George Binns made his predictions at the next board meeting of the newly formed KSDL, Kirklees Stadium Development Limited. "I think we will get £2.5 million from the Football Trust." Once the laughter had died down we realised George was serious.

"By relocating we can ask for money in one lump sum and never need to be a continuing drain on the Trust once the stadium is completed."

We then set George loose on the Foundation for Sports and the Arts. The rugby league club was by now a keen and willing partner in the venture as they realised what a lifeline the new stadium would be for them. Heavily in debt, they lived on a shoestring. We had no idea what the Foundation might offer the project; then named the Kirklees Stadium. We thought £0.5 million. George thought we might get £1 million. Again he was right.

Choosing an architect was not an easy decision. In 1991 we attended a major stadium exhibition at the NEC Birmingham and we were confronted by a hall containing 54 'stadium specialists'. All 54 had one thing in common; whatever they proclaimed none had ever designed or built a stadium before. We saw cantilever stands and sliding roofs and removable pitches and shopping centres below stands. They were all untried and unproven. We know now we selected the right futuristic design provided by the extremely talented Rod Sheard from the Lobb Architects Partnership.

Clearly it was never plain sailing for me. This was the steepest learning curve I have ever undertaken and before completion many, many things went wrong. There was a point in 1993 when I chaired the first serious 'crisis' meeting. It was a real eye-opening 'Damascus' moment for me.

It was a meeting attended by just about all the key players in the project; the architect, the structural engineer, the quantity surveyor, project managers, main contractors and even some faces I'd never seen before. There was a problem. The main contractors, Alfred McAlpine, had discovered some seriously contaminated materials as they drilled the first piles on the old ICI site. The debate was simple: who would pay for the removal? And, who would foot the bill for the resultant delays in other work? The discussion became an argument until Rod Sheard, the lead architect said to me: "You don't understand do you, the problem is that you are a naïve client."

I was somewhat taken aback. What the hell did he mean? I looked at him with a puzzled look.

"You've never built a stadium before; you don't know what you're talking about."

There was a deadly silence around the table. All eyes were focused on me. It was one of those moments when the victim squirms inside. In short, it was a bloody awful moment. Round the table were industry specialists and experts in their field, many with 30 years' experience in the building industry not just in the UK but all over Europe. Here was I, the novice, chairing this meeting of experts.

They all looked at me but in that moment I knew Rod was right.

The truth is I can't remember exactly what I said or how I blagged my way out of that one, right at that particular embarrassing moment. But one thing was for sure, although I could run rings round these guys on a football field, here, in their own territory, I was almost the upstart, the complete novice. It was a defining moment. Rod was right; I didn't really know what I was doing.

It suddenly occurred to me there would no doubt be some clause in one of the contracts that would tell me that this was MY problem, and MY cost. I realised that I was stood there with my pants round my ankles amongst these people who had for the previous six months showed me pretty presentations and diagrams, wined me and dined me, sent flowers to my wife, been all sweetness and light – until they had been awarded the contract. And now, they were hard-edged businessmen.

Driving home that night I decided that this was a situation that would never happen again. During the course of this project I would learn everything there was to know about the building of a football stadium. I would listen to these experts and specialists, be fully aware that they would treat me like a beginner with much to learn; just as I would do the same with a 15-year-old football apprentice if I was still an old pro in the game.

And I decided one thing: I would not be a naïve client for much longer.

The big stroke of luck I had during this time was receiving a letter from Tony Stephens who had just left the marketing manager's job at Wembley and was looking for consultancy work. He and I hit it off the first time we met and I persuaded the Huddersfield board that I needed his help. He stayed with me for four years and was both mentor and friend. We still speak today. My office also became a meeting place for his football 'star' clients for whom he acted as agent. An Alan Shearer deal with Newcastle United was initiated there and signed in a terraced house up the road. A few weeks later David Beckham arrived not long after he'd scored the 60-yard goal that announced his arrival on the football scene. But in the early days I was Tony's sole concern and he guided me through many situations. He gave me all the confidence I needed to blag my way through. He had the answer to every question I asked.

His mantra was: "Knowledge is knowing – or knowing where knowledge is." In other words you don't have to know everything; you just need to know where to find the answer. He believed in being prepared to take risks and stretching yourself. When I asked how I should behave when they upgraded me to chief executive at

Huddersfield Town he simply said, "Act how you believe a successful CE would act in each situation – that's what most CE's do." When we started at Huddersfield we scrambled together £4 million. Two years later we had raised £29 million, so I must have got some of Tony's instructions right.

I try to follow his teaching to this day. His answers were based on truth, honesty and integrity which I still try to practise. He literally sat on the end of my desk and watched my every move. One day I made a call to an executive box holder and promised him some Wembley tickets. Tony made me call him back and apologise. "Never promise something you're not sure you can deliver. Never let any supporter down. These are the people who own the club, not the directors." Today I teach these concepts to the students at the UCFB, University College of Football Business, at Turf Moor. I get real pleasure from passing on his wisdom to the people who one day might be running the football industry.

It was very sad to see the old Leeds Road stadium demolished. I'd played there and scored there myself. It held memories of goals, tackles and saves. It was a part of local and football history. Every Huddersfield supporter of the right age will have his or her memories. As we tore it down though, we knew that people would transfer their loyalty to the new one. How could they not, when it was built within yards of the old one. When you see something being built you develop a sense of 'ownership' and you share in the achievement. It might have been very different if the new stadium had been six miles away.

But boy, did I drop another clanger a week before we opened the new stadium. The stadium only had three completed stands and behind one goal there was just a temporary car park area. We needed some form of barrier or fencing, but nothing expensive. So, always full of bright ideas I devised a way of using smart, easily movable, cricket sightscreens. We ordered several of these things and they were assembled the Friday night before the opening game, which as you can imagine was accompanied by bells, whistles, fanfares and every other kind of grand opening trick you could think of. This was a big, big day in the history of the club. It was the sort of day when you leave nothing to chance and plan everything to the last detail. And all this would be in front of the bigwigs and dignitaries of Kirklees.

On Friday before the first match I left the stadium just as the clock struck midnight and checked to see that I hadn't lost a shoe as I ran down the stairs. The sightscreens were just being finished off under the floodlights. When I got back the next morning they looked great and screened off the car park from the pitch. Unfortunately it was only when the players ran out onto the pitch for the warm-up on this truly landmark day for club and town (and for us) it became clear what a gaff I'd made. The players were shooting in and then one of them shouted roughly in our direction.

"WE CAN'T SEE THE F*****G GOALPOSTS!"

My heart sank, my mouth dropped. The penny dropped (sometimes I'm a really quick thinker). I'd dropped an absolute clanger. I ran down to the pitch to see for myself. This time half a dozen of them balled at me.

"FLETCH, WE CAN'T SEE THE F*****G GOALPOSTS." I heard them mutter a few other choice things as well.

What a mess-up; white goalposts and a white ball against white sightscreens. If there'd been a shovel handy I'd have dug myself a nice big hole. I slunk back to my seat. No way could I blag my way out of this one. Huddersfield lost 0 -1 that day. The first match at the new 'McAlpine', and we'd lost. And guess who got the blame?

There was a game on the following Tuesday. We had the middle section of the screens painted dark blue. Huddersfield won 3 – 1 with all three goals scored at the 'blue' end. I suppose, with the benefit of hindsight, I could have blamed Tony Stephens for the defeat and given myself a pat on the back for the win.

To allow me to concentrate on the new stadium I had employed my ex-teammate and goalkeeper Alan Stevenson as commercial manager at the club. Stevo was known as the 'cat'. This was not just for his ability but because he had once been caught peeing on the goalposts (well, that was one explanation). Stevo organised a whole host of 'Celebrating the Closure' of the Leeds Road Stadium initiatives. They raised another £250,000. The human side, the nostalgia, the memories were what made one initiative in particular quite memorable.

Alan organised a series of 'last matches at Leeds Road'. It's pretty easy, for example, to get a team from one bank to play against another bank and charge a reasonable fee. All kinds of groups and teams are interested in this kind of game. During the final week before the bulldozers came in there was something like seven games a day and the last ones were under the floodlights. We provided a full set of kit for each team, a referee and linesmen, physio, doctor and a great buffet after the game.

But one day when I had come into the ground one of the lads in the commercial department asked if I could go into the home dressing room. There was a bit of a problem. I saw what it was as soon as I walked in the dressing room. Sitting there in a Huddersfield Town strip and surrounded by beefy young men in their twenties was a far older chap. When I got closer it was clear he was 80 if he was a day and none too nimble. "Oh Lord," I wondered, "how will this frail guy cope, surely he's going to have a heart attack or something?" The risk of injury was obvious.

Just as the words were going to come out, "Look I'm sorry but it's just not possible ..." one of the young lads came over already dressed in the Huddersfield kit. He took me on one side.

"Look this is my grandfather. I know what you're thinking but this is a very special day for him. I'll take full responsibility. Don't worry everything will be fine. We've got it all organised." I accepted his word and went over to say hello to old Fred Hopkins and wish him all the best, and then went and sat in the deserted stand to watch what would happen.

During the warm-up Fred was nowhere to be seen. But when the referee got all the players together to toss the coin and they then took their positions on the field, old Fred came hobbling out in his blue and white striped Terriers strip. On his feet he had the oldest pair of boots I'd ever seen but they shone with polish and dubbin. I hadn't seen boots like them since the 50s. They belonged in a museum. His white frail legs were probably seeing sunshine for the first time in 40 years. As the referee blew his whistle to start the game Fred stood in the outside right position on the near touchline. David Hopkins got the ball and slowly jogged over to the wing where his grandfather stood. Nobody else moved. Very softly David passed the ball to Fred. As Fred controlled the ball his face creased with a huge smile and he passed it back to David. Nobody else had moved an inch. Fred then turned round and walked off the pitch and down the tunnel to the rapturous applause from everyone on the pitch and the few people watching. So that was that – I thought.

As I walked by the dressing room on my way back to my office I popped in to say hello to Fred. He was sitting on one of the benches crying. I asked if he was OK.

"Am I OK? Do you know Paul I've been a Huddersfield Town fan for over 70 years and rarely miss a game. You don't know how much I've dreamed of wearing a blue and white striped shirt and kicking a ball on this pitch. I've now achieved my little dream. I can die a happy man."

Old Fred lived another year before passing away. I'm pleased I was there to see that emotional 'moment of magic'. It's the sort of thing that fills football. It's a game that has such a hold over our lives and emotions. It can inspire and deflate. It can bring happiness and despair. I don't know who cried more that afternoon, Fred in the dressing room, or me as I walked away. For one brief moment Fred experienced what I enjoyed for a whole career.

The joy of football.

Football changes. Names of stadiums change as new investors come in. The Galpharm is now The John Smith Stadium. What we created all those years ago has changed as well – but that's another story, and not for me to tell.

# 6

# The Joy of Football

Fred Hopkins' story beautifully illustrates why I love this game of football so much. I had 16 years of enjoying something that was so different to any other job. Truth is; it wasn't a job. It was pleasure. It was the love of playing, of being fit, of having friends, of not being able to wait to get to training in the morning. Of course it all comes to an end, but for all but one of my years in the game I had the time of my life.

Joy is such a small word but conveys such a huge emotion. It seems hardly adequate to describe the thoughts in your head when you come off the field having scored a hat-trick as I did once against Cardiff. The chapter title, 'The Joy of Football' is chosen deliberately because the game has given me so much happiness. Yet, strangely, two of the games I shall always remember gave me just the opposite, despite scoring 'Goal of the Decade' in one of them.

These two games in particular illustrate just what can be good and bad for a footballer, euphoria one minute, anguish the next. They were within a week of each other. It was season '73/74 with Burnley back in Division One (now the Premiership). Jimmy Adamson was manager. We played attractive, passing football and there were games when other teams despaired of getting the ball back off us. The team was a very clever mix of workers and flair players and Adamson had instilled the team ethic perfectly. On a good day, and there were many, we were a joy to watch. Even as a player, it was a joy to watch my team-mates performing their different talents. Other coaches actually brought their youth teams to watch us play and learn from us. Old Bob Lord sat in his overcoat and pork-pie hat up in the stands and beamed and purred. His wife Hilda was next to him with what Stuart Hall once memorably called an upturned flower pot on her head.

Lord had stuck by Adamson a couple of seasons earlier when fans had wanted him out. When things had gone badly with results the relationship between him and the supporters was dreadful. After an away game at Blackpool when he needed a police escort, some of the scenes and abuse hurled at him was appalling. But in '72/73 and then the following season the good times seemed to be back. Life was good.

But if there was a weakness it was our occasional inconsistency and we lost too many games to enable us to get the final place in one of the European competitions.

And then: we had an FA Cup semi-final coming up at Hillsborough.

The previous week we had been to Elland Road and beaten the mighty Leeds United 4 – 1. This was Don Revie's team at its most powerful. In their early days they had been tough, hard and often brutal. They bent the rules and showed no physical mercy. They intimidated players and referees and were disliked intensely. Punch-ups and flare-ups were frequent. And this was an era when the game was really physical. The kickings dished out were sometimes nothing short of assault. But that was the game then. Some members of the Burnley team could also dish it out on occasions but by and large it was never our style. We always tried to play football the right way, but if a battle started, we gave as much as we took.

Don Revie sometimes took the shackles off his team and their football flowed too. They could be imperious. But a leopard doesn't change its spots and beneath the new silky, smooth football they played there remained their cynical, tough, nasty edge. This particular season for them had been triumphant when we met them at Elland Road. They would win the title that season. They did not expect to lose to little old Burnley.

The meeting was already soured by the threats made by them and Revie against Burnley's Doug Collins. He was our playmaker, gifted but delicate and brittle. In the earlier game at Turf Moor they'd told him that they'd break his legs back at Leeds. So, before the game at Elland Road manager Jimmy Adamson went to the referee and informed him, within Revie's hearing, of the threats made against Dougie Collins. Revie fumed, Adamson told us.

The ploy worked. Dougie Collins was pretty much left alone; in fact he scored a beautifully delicate goal, chipping the ball over goalkeeper Harvey's head in the second half. But Adamson's ploy also backfired. It was the rest of us that were kicked black and blue and for good measure the sly little kicks even started in the tunnel as we came out. Nobody, but nobody, other than their own fans, loved Leeds United in those days. And the worst was yet to come for one Burnley player that day.

In all my time as a player this game lives in my head even today. It represented both the highest point I would ever reach as a professional footballer – and the start of the downfall of a great team. This day we were flying, although we were not looking forward to the game as we had a much bigger game the following Saturday. But the Leeds match was one of those games when a set of individuals come together as a team to produce some glorious moments which provided lifelong memories.

I'd had flu badly the previous week and I told Jimmy Adamson that I was feeling dreadful. His answer was simple. "If you don't play in this game tomorrow, you won't be playing at Hillsborough next Saturday." In other words, 'tough luck, get out there with your team-mates and stop moaning!'

I remember vividly that the Leeds United team tried to wind us up even as we walked out onto the pitch with threats of broken legs, spitting and a couple of punches were thrown. It was clear a battle was on hand as Joe Jordan removed his front teeth.

The third clear memory is my second goal. Leeds had equalised the first Burnley goal. From a Leighton James free kick the ball bounced up in the air between Norman Hunter and me. Never in my career to date had I ever tried an overhead kick, nor had I ever practised in training. But this was one of those instinctive moments when your body just reacts to the situation and strangely I still remember the sound as I connected perfectly. The Burnley fans erupted.

They erupted even more when Dougie Collins' goal went in. It is a goal that is often forgotten when fans talk about Burnley's great goals. But it was pure genius to chip a goalkeeper from actually inside the box. He was on fire that day.

Then, finally came the incident when the great "Team of the Seventies" started to crumble and Burnley FC would start the slow decline that resulted in the Orient Game of '87 when Burnley had to win to stay in the League. The moment came when Frank Casper was tackled by Norman Hunter. Probably if it happened today Norman Hunter would have been arrested for assault. It was a tackle that was made after the ball had gone. But in those days there was never the benefit of 36 cameras recording every move by every player. All was fair and within the rules – if you could get away with it – and if the referee didn't see it. It was a man's game and players intentionally hurt each other. Frank was not just a good player, he was a great player. He made me and other players around him look and play even better. Nobody realised it at the time but it was a watershed moment in the history of the club and the story of Frank Casper. Stupidly he was patched up for the Newcastle game but had to limp off. He was out for the whole of the next season and then scored a memorable winning goal in his comeback game against QPR the season after that. But his career was over at 29 when on the verge of a call up for England. A sprinkling of forlorn appearances and he knew the damage was too great and it was time to call it a day.

In 1988 I produced a little booklet for BFC with the aim of raising funds for them. They were on their beam ends and it was only in 1987 that down at the bottom of the old Fourth Division they played the last game of the season when a defeat would have seen this once proud and famous club demoted from the Football League. They won and survived by the skin of their teeth so that it was Lincoln City that lost their league place. The game was forever known as 'The Orient Game' and is part of Burnley folklore. Not much more than 25 years earlier they had been in the European Cup and exactly 25 years earlier had been FA Cup finalists. I wrote about the Leeds game and Frank's injury in this booklet that I called *BFC and Me.* It was a collection of articles by 25 players, ex-players and non-players who had all fallen under the spell of this marvellous football club. I gave Burnley Football Club 5,000 copies to sell and also a cheque for £1,200. It's fascinating to see how much they now sell for on eBay.

Frank tried desperately to get back to fitness and had a comeback game some months later. But his day was done. He was patched up for the Cup semi-final but as good as played on one leg for as long as he could before he had to hobble off. The joy of winning that Leeds game was destroyed by the injury to a fine player.

Revie was both shocked and incandescent that his team could lose. Ironically the game was filmed as part of a documentary being made about him. The papers were filled with praise for the Burnley performance. It was seen as a disastrous day for Leeds in their local papers and our goals were described as devastating. "If they can reproduce their Elland Road form I cannot see them failing to reach Wembley," reported the *Yorkshire Post.* Leeds did not distinguish themselves in the last 15 minutes, the report went on to say, which was a polite way of agreeing that by then they had lost all semblance of self-control with bookings and the dreadful Hunter tackle. The coach took us back to Burnley as victors but we felt no sense of triumph. One of our own had been crippled by a member of a side that even before the game in the tunnel, had threatened us and some had even spat at us.

Funny how I'm writing about games that deflated us in a chapter about joy. But in football the two emotions are so often separated only by just a few days or even a few inches, and sometimes you experience them in the same 90 minutes.

How we didn't beat Newcastle United at Hillsborough in the semi-final mystifies me to this day. The bare facts say that two Malcolm Macdonald goals won the game. We know we lost, but the how still irritates after all these years. There are key points in all our lives and maybe the Cup defeat was just such a point for Burnley the club, and all of us who played for Burnley in it.

The FA Cup semi-final was just one week after the Leeds game. There are turning points, moments when we can ask ourselves, "What would have happened if ..." In the life of a football club there are moments when a result has such lasting consequences that the ensuing events take a course that determines the direction that club will go in for many, many years. The Newcastle result was just such an occasion. It's my contention that the result shaped the destiny of Burnley Football Club for years to come. And the irony was that Newcastle were actually there in the first place.

When we arrived at Largs after the Leeds game the hotel was packed with journalists. It's one clear abiding memory, just how pursued we were by the hacks. We were big news after beating Leeds. We loved the old hotel, the Marine and Curlinghall, with its log and coal fires, even in the bedrooms, and the place filled with staff all of whom seemed to be little, white-haired, old ladies. But every day we were there, you'd see players trapped in a corner somewhere being interviewed. They even came on the golf courses and in a foursome we played four journalists we roped in. They must have been desperate for a scoop. Much of the talk was of Frank Casper and his injury.

In their first game in the earlier round against Nottingham Forest, Newcastle were losing at home with ten minutes to go and were down to ten men. They were on their way out. But that was until the Geordie fans took matters into their own hands and invaded the pitch. It was mayhem. Amazingly the referee got the game started again when it should have been abandoned so bad was the invasion. Malcolm Macdonald later admitted that even the Newcastle players expected to be booted out of the Cup as a punishment. Forest were coasting home. When they came back out from being 3 – 1 down, Newcastle went on to win 4 – 3 as all the terrified Forest players simply froze. It was an unbelievable finale. As a direct result of that appalling riot Newcastle won the game. The FA ordered a replay at a neutral ground. It was a draw. The second replay was again at a neutral ground and Newcastle won. The FA have made some crass decisions in their time but the decision not to award the tie to Forest was one of their worst ever, or failing that at least to have had the first replay at Forest's ground.

The arrival at Hillsborough was something else that's etched in the memory bank. It was just a sea of claret and blue. On the way there we'd stayed at the Ainley Top Hotel near Huddersfield. There, at the team talk it was confirmed that Frank would play and Ray Hankin would be substitute. Was this the right decision? Would it have made any difference if Ray had played from the start? Numerous cortisone and painkilling injections got Frank ready.

Macdonald was not only amazed to have survived the Forest tie, but also to have won the semi. He wrote about it in his book 'Supermac'. He acknowledged what a good side Burnley had. He wrote that in the first half Burnley wiped the floor with Newcastle, that they just couldn't get the ball off them. Keeper McFaul was on overtime. Burnley did everything except put the ball in the net. The second half started the same with Burnley camped round the Newcastle penalty area. And then the inevitable happened.

If Burnley had a weakness it was leaving the two centre-halves exposed. With Macdonald thinking they were on the way out of the tie, a Burnley cross was cleared to the left and Terry Hibbit picked up the ball and volleyed it forward from about five yards outside the box. The ball flew upfield. It had to land with Macdonald. He turned; the ball flew over Colin Waldron's head and Macdonald was onto it in a flash and away. Colin grabbed hold of him but the sheer strength of the man kept him up as Colin seemed to slither down his legs whilst Macdonald stayed upright. Any other referee might have blown for the foul and stopped play. But this was Gordon Hill, no ordinary referee. He reasoned that Macdonald would stay on his feet and let play continue even though Colin was hanging on to him for grim death. And so as Colin lost his grip, Macdonald recovered his balance and caught up with the ball that was rolling away. Even then he had Alan Stevenson to beat. Stevo parried the shot and as luck would have it the ball came back to Macdonald who slotted it home even though another defender tried to get back onto the goal-line to stop the shot.

The second Newcastle goal was almost a copy of the first except that this time the long ball was played out by Terry McDermott. Macdonald was onto it, ran half the length of the field and put this one through Stevo's legs.

We were down and out. There comes a point in a game when you think this is not your day. If there was one moment in the game that decided its course, it was the moment Gordon Hill did not blow his whistle and allowed play to continue even though Colin Waldron was performing a rugby tackle on Malcolm Macdonald. Speculation still continues in my head to this day. What would have happened if ... it had been another referee not Gordon Hill? He made the right decision for Newcastle United but the wrong one for Burnley. Any other referee might have stopped play, booked Waldron or even sent him off. But this one let play go on and in so doing determined the course of events that would affect Burnley for years.

There were tears in the dressing room afterwards. Jimmy Adamson spoke for us all with three words. "We are sick," he said. We were sick because we lost to a team that were not better than us. We lost because we did not get the breaks and Newcastle did. They had every bit of luck going. We hit the woodwork twice and their goalkeeper McFaul was just about man of the match. He kept them in it. For 65 minutes we were in total control and you could see in the Newcastle eyes that they thought the result was going one way only. I can still remember Jimmy saying that it was Malcolm Macdonald that was the difference. For the first goal, of course he did well but he got a lucky break when the ball came back to him from Stevenson's save. It could have ricocheted anywhere. But this was the day it bounced back to him. Football is like that. You need luck. From that moment on the Newcastle players had a spring in their step, but our legs suddenly felt 10lbs heavier. Even so, at 2 – 0 down McFaul had to make stunning saves from different Burnley players including one wonder save when he tipped over a blistering Casper shot. We could not have played any better.

It was a silent coach that took us back to Burnley and it was not until some days later when we began to talk about this chance and that chance and the game in general. On the coach journey home there was nothing for us to say. It was filled with players who felt empty and dejected. No-one was more upset than Colin Waldron who sat on the coach with a blank, drained expression, feeling bitter with himself for letting Macdonald in.

A semi-final defeat is worse than a defeat in the Final itself. At least in the Final you have played at Wembley. And back then, it was the pinnacle of every footballer's dream. What was noticeable too was the total lack of journalists now we had lost. Almost right up until kick-off we had been deluged with them like locusts. After the defeat they simply vanished; they were only interested in the winners.

Of course it was ironic that Newcastle then went to Wembley and lost 3 – 0 to Liverpool after giving one of the poorest, weakest displays by any team seen at Wembley. The opposition they provided on the day was minimal.

In contrast what a fabulous night it was when we beat Sunderland 2 – 0 at home towards the end of season '72/73; brilliant for all of us because it was the night we clinched promotion back to Division One, today the Premier League; and brilliant for me because I scored both goals. Truth is I wasn't an out and out prolific scorer but that was the season that I did end up top scorer with 15. Nights like that in front of over 20,000 people are the ones that you treasure in your memories.

It's a rare player that doesn't cling to the game and prolong a career as long as possible. I guess we're like the proverbial boxer, always thinking he can manage one more fight. Of course I wanted to carry on as long as possible despite the increasing waistline, aching bones and weary legs. As my Burnley career headed into the late 1970s, the club was not doing well at all. In fact every season seemed to be a struggle. Nevertheless, I never lost the love of Gawthorpe, the dressing room, the banter and the camaraderie.

Despite the struggles of those final mediocre seasons I can promise you I never lost the love and joy of participation in this wonderful game. The following season we didn't push for anything, the luck ran out and Burnley were indeed relegated. Luckily I had something to fall back on when I finished the game at Blackpool and the only thing Alan Ball was interested in was the insurance money.

I tell a story on the dinner circuit that illustrates the fun we had as a group of players when we were Adamson's 'Team of the Seventies'. It concerns a game at Liverpool we played when Liverpool were all-powerful and all-conquering. Before it, during the team meeting, we sat down and Jimmy Adamson gave us all our instructions. Of course the first one was, don't be afraid of Anfield; just do what you do best and just enjoy the game.

It was September 24th, season 1974/75: The day before, one by one Jimmy called our names and gave us our individual instructions. "Stevo you will be brave and commanding, catch everything that comes into the box, no hesitation ... Keith Newton you must stop everything that comes down your wing ... Ian Brennan you will defend but overlap and get some shots in ... Martin Dobson you must control the midfield, cover at the back and help out ... Frank Casper drop back and help stifle the midfield ... Paul Fletcher run around and just drive them mad, keep them occupied, come back for corners ... Dougie Collins you must defend, defend and defend the central area ... Leighton James work hard, drop back, and provide cover ... Colin Waldron I'm counting on you to head and collect everything that comes your way ... Geoff Nulty normal game please, you must run and tackle everything ... and you Peter Noble (he paused for a second) *you, Peter Noble will be the Lone Ranger.*" All of this was said in his very slow, deliberate, broad Geordie drawl. At that the room went silent and we all looked at each other. "You Peter will get up front as much as possible. You will be up there alone ... *the Lone Ranger.*"

"Right boss", we said.

I sent Peter Noble a telegram. "Good luck," it said, "From your pal Tonto."

We won 1 – 0.

# 7

# Bolton and Wembley Revisited

During the time spent developing the McAlpine Stadium at Huddersfield I was frequently visited by other CEO's and club directors looking for solutions to their own stadium problems. At that time, in no way did I have the real in-depth knowledge that I have today covering every aspect of stadium development. I was learning as I went along. Nevertheless it was a project that drew visitors, one in particular, Graham Ball a director from Bolton Wanderers. He was leading their re-location from Burnden Park to the new site six miles away at Horwich. That one factor alone stood out; the site was six miles from the old stadium. How would people transfer their feelings that distance? Would supporters who once walked to Burnden, be prepared to get a bus or in a car to support their team. But one other factor was inescapable. The old Burnden Park ground had served its time. It was crumbling. The club too was struggling. So, the directors had made the bold decision that in order to secure the club's future, a ground move and a new stadium was imperative. In September 1996 Graham asked me to help with their project and offered me the position of CEO at the new Middlebrook Stadium, as it was called then.

The Huddersfield project was almost completed. I had a framed 'Building of the Year' hanging in my office. I'd been six years in Yorkshire travelling back and forth every day over the Pennines. It could be a time-consuming journey on some days. In winter it could be a most unpleasant and dangerous drive on occasions with the car stuck in snow or sliding on ice. I was an ex Bolton lad and player. This was my home town and first club. The Bolton offer was a new challenge; the comfort zone could be stretched again. I said yes. There was a huge emotional pull to this. The little lad who had held his granddad's hand on the way to the match in the 50s was coming back as a grown man to help re-build the stadium. Life sometimes is like fiction.

As a young lad I'd been at Bolton as a player for three years, first learning my trade as a 16-year old apprentice, then breaking into the first team in 1968. As a stadium specialist, years later, the Bradford Fire disaster hit me hard. It was an appalling tragedy and the cause was identified as burning litter that had accumulated under the old stand. I immediately thought of what we used to do as a matter of course as apprentices at Burnden Park. On Monday mornings it was our job to clean up the old stadium after a Saturday match. Three of the stands at Burnden were made of concrete terraces with simple steel crush barriers every couple of metres. These we had to paint blue in the summer. As a little lad I used to sit on them during a game while my granddad held on to me. In the rear area of the main Manchester Road Stand a seated area had been constructed for the directors and any spectators who wanted to pay a little extra, something like a shilling. A narrow corridor had been constructed and provided a route to these seats. I clearly remember that this seated area was made of thick wooden boards. They might have been something like old railway sleepers. Years of traffic had worn down the edges of these timbers and there were gaps between. Paper, litter, unwanted programmes, old newspapers, cigarette packets, and cigarette ends littered the area after every match. How easy it was to sweep as much as we could through the gaps in the boards rather than collect it all and take it to the rubbish area at the back of the stand. How easy it must have been at Bradford for the apprentices to do the same.

Nat Lofthouse had lost his job as manager and was moved upstairs into a general role. Nobody could sack him altogether, it would have been unthinkable after the service he had given and loyalty he had shown. Like many great players he was never really cut out to be a manager. When things were going wrong for the team he used to ask assistant Jimmy McIlroy to go to the bank in town for him because he couldn't face people. Jimmy Meadows got his first chance in management and when he took over he had to deal with a dressing room that was filled with disquiet.

A big game against top of the table Sheffield United was imminent. Bolton were near the bottom of Division Two facing another relegation. The occasion was to be filmed for TV and shown as 'The Big Match' the next day on Sunday. Every player got a £10 bonus for appearing on TV. It was a huge match for both clubs and in the dressing room we sat and waited to see what team Jimmy would pick. After training on Friday morning some of the established players, John Byrom, Charlie Hurley and Gordon Taylor were nervous wondering if it was the end for them. The teamsheet was pinned up. There were gasps. It was time for the new broom and in came several young reserves. One name was mine at number 9, Paul Fletcher. Nat had earlier moved me to centre-forward from being a winger. He'd noted I could head a ball. I had the marks of mother's washing line all over my forehead but all the practising had paid off.

After 95 seconds it looked like a massacre was on the cards when John Tudor scored for Sheffield. But the Bolton team, average age just 20, got back into the game. Ian Seddon equalised and this young team of reserves and apprentices could easily have gone in winning at half-time. A 'goal' from me was disallowed. A draw looked likely but then in the 79th minute debutant 17-year-old Paul Jones slipped a ball through to beat the offside trap and I was onto it to slip the ball home. On the Sunday I guess a few thousand watched the game on TV. Of course I was one of them. Another was Jimmy Adamson of Burnley.

As a player at Bolton I was eventually sold to Burnley, allegedly "to save the club" I was told; they were in such a financial mess. As a reserve I couldn't stop scoring. A prodigy they called me. Before Burnley, Everton moved in as well and saw me as an understudy to Joe Royle. I was just 18. And then disaster struck when they discovered I had a heart murmur at the medical. The transfer to Everton never happened and for 12 months I hardly played. All I could do was watch and be tested. All this was kept quiet at Bolton. It was Nat Lofthouse who got me playing again and got me over what was really a mental block more than anything else and people saying that I must rest and take it easy. I was actually knocked for six, confidence in myself shattered. In truth when I got back playing, the murmur never had any effect. If it's still there it's very quiet and keeps itself to itself. Jimmy Adamson came in and Doc Iven at Turf Moor pronounced me fit and well. He saw the condition as insignificant and saw no problem. He once gave a potential new player a medical by having him run up and down the stairs. He turned out to be a crock, but boy could he run up the stairs.

1996 and here I was back once more, not quite to "to save the club", but at least to play a part in securing its future. Much of the planning had been done and the contractor appointments made. The project had in fact just about been started already at a brown-field site that I think had once belonged to British Rail.

The new £35 million stadium the Bolton people had planned was part of a £200 million, 200 acre development. They had started the planning back in 1991 and following a public enquiry the job got the final go-ahead and work commenced in July 1996. The club had worked in partnership with Bolton Metropolitan Council and developers Emerson's to achieve a retail park and sports/leisure complex. It all included:

28,000 all-seater stadium ... car parks ... sports and exhibition hall ... cinema ... Asda ... bowling alley ... petrol station ... sports chain shops

... McDonalds drive through ... business park ... restaurants and bars ... sports academy ... 125 bedroom hotel integrated into the stadium ... residential area ... light industrial area ... the Hitachi area. This was a massive project.

By the time I took up the post the project was being run by the Bolton chairman and a fellow director assisted by secretary Des McBain. Des had once been Blackpool FC secretary when former Burnley manager Harry Potts was manager there and Harry had once been my boss. It's funny how things work out. There were painful memories of a Blackpool Burnley FA Cup game when Blackpool under Harry had won. Des was tactful enough not to mention it. It was an awful game and an awful day. It's one of the games I remember, for all the wrong reasons, although I didn't actually play.

On first visiting the site I was met by a something quite strange. All I could see was a newly seeded but green football pitch surrounded by acres of mud and building paraphernalia. Around this little oasis of green was an 8' high sturdy fence topped with spikes. They had decided to lay the pitch down and then build around it. The idea was that the playing surface would be perfect when the stadium was opened. My mouth dropped open. It really was a most impractical idea with huge implications for the building work and costs. It meant building from the outside, rather than the inside. It was a bit like building a new house by putting the carpets down first. The area where the pitch will be, in a new stadium, is always a hive of activity for numerous cranes and construction vehicles especially when it is time to put the roof on and build up the concrete terraces where the seating will go.

The design was well established and agreed between chairman, directors, architects and builders. It was too late for me to make suggestions to the original plan. There were features at that stage I didn't like. There was no seating in the corners. This would reduce the atmosphere. The glass frontage of the corporate areas separated fans into distinct areas and reduced the atmosphere. It was very much a futuristic design as anyone who has approached for the first time from the motorway will testify. From the outside it looked distinctive with an elliptical shape. It seemed to me a design led by what architects liked, rather than the real needs that a good stadium should be built around. I wasn't sure that the arched roof, rarely seen on stadiums to that point, and similar to the Huddersfield McAlpine Stadium roof, would hold in the noise as loudly and effectively as a traditional flat roof. I seemed to be the only one questioning these basic concepts. And: I had some strong reservation about the location six miles away from Burnden Park.

Nevertheless the Reebok Stadium was a fine, iconic building that looked truly dramatic as you approached so that in the background were the tree-lined hills of Rivington and Horwich. My stay was relatively short and I had no opportunity to make any major suggestions. The work I did was largely based on internal design amendments and pretty much cosmetic. The chairman and his fellow directors were very set in their ways and were not amenable to any major changes to their design. The project was clearly their baby. The major achievement I had influence over was the securing of a long-term and lucrative naming-rights deal with sports goods manufacturer Reebok UK.

Even the internal design amendments I suggested fell on deaf ears. The design of the ticket office, for example, was based very much on the old one at Burnden. Spectators would queue outside in the rain with no cover or shelter from the strong Horwich winds. It's an exposed site. The traditional design was a reinforced glass screen with a small serving hatch below and the customer shouted through what he wanted whilst the rain hammered down soaking him to the skin. But this was now 1998 when most people no longer handed cash over but used credit cards. The chance of theft was minimal especially with CCTV cameras dotted around.

The previous year I'd visited the ticket office at Glasgow Celtic. The design was similar to a warm cosy travel agent's office. There was a comfortable seating area with a coffee machine and a TV. It was so civilised. Supporters then purchased tickets, when it was their turn, seated in front of an agent. Outside the ticket office was a covered area for when there were long queues. I strongly advised the BFC stadium director to adopt these ideas, but the recommendations fell on deaf ears.

It also made great sense to have the ticket office located alongside the club shop. At busy periods staff can be interchangeable. If the two units are adjacent this encourages impulse buying from the shop when someone has bought a ticket. It is not rocket science that a winning team generates more ticket sales and certainly more shop sales. A person in a hurry will not buy his ticket and then walk round to a different part of the stadium for a browse in the shop. Again the suggestion of a change to the plans fell on deaf ears. I was told that the design was now well established.

The Reebok design also had corporate facilities in two main stands. This is common. But, when there were events taking place on non-match days, in both stands, the operational costs and utilities doubled with two sets of: reception, catering, security and so on. In today's stadium designs most corporate facilities are clustered in one stand making events more manageable and more cost-effective. The KC Stadium at Hull is an example of this with three other much simpler stands to accompany the one two-tier revenue earner.

The two commercial successes at the Reebok are the office accommodation at one end and the De Vere White's Hotel at the other. Each of these is situated in the stands behind the goals. After twelve years of operation the Reebok has certainly been a success for Bolton Wanderers. They maintained a Premiership place for 12 years, but were relegated at the end of season 2011/12. What they have not done is reach the anticipated attendances. The intention was to build a 30,000 seater venue. Approximately 28,500 are now in situ. Initially there were less than this but there was a planned facility within the design to allow them to add more seats. Their stay in the Premiership would not have happened without the financial support of owner Eddie Davies and his reported £100 million investments. The club are currently heavily in debt and relegation could be financially disastrous.

It is hard to predict what will happen now Bolton have been relegated or if Eddie Davies withdraws his support or interest. In terms of the stadium, the dreams and aims of the Bolton directors back in 1991 have paid dividends. But I sometimes wonder what would have happened if the new stadium had been built on the site of the old Burnden and had remained close to the heart of Bolton. This would be possible now by moving the pitch up one level and creating a car park below the pitch with retail shops and food retail 'wrapped' around the stadium at ground level. I have been working on this 'Stadium of the Future' concept for a number of years with Holmes Miller architects, Glasgow. The first one will be opened in 2014/15 in Ahmedabad, India.

Attendances are currently falling at the Reebok and since the heady days of Sam Allardyce and a place in the Europa League, the club has struggled more and more each season. It might be a case of saying in a few years' time that the move was great, until the home defeats and relegation arrived.

One thing I did implement at the stadium was a visitors' viewing area. It was such a simple idea and gave supporters the feeling of closeness to the relocation. The move to the new site was initially far from popular with rank and file supporters. Many resented the sponsorship provided by Reebok in fact the whole thing was seen as money oriented. But it was certainly true that something had to happen to safeguard the future of Bolton Wanderers.

The visitor centre was attended by hundreds of people during construction. Dozens called by each day. This was 'their' stadium that was going up. It was important to let them see that. On the roof of the visitor centre we installed an open air seating area. There was a viewing gallery where we installed 40 tiered seats set up in just the same way that you would find them in a stadium. The seating supplier provided them as part of the deal for approximately 26,800 seats for the stadium. The touching thing was that one supporter came EVERY day. He brought his dog, lunch and flask. He had his Wanderers scarf round his neck and he would sit there for two hours every single day watching the ground being erected for his beloved team. He even sat there when the Prime Minister visited one day. The two of them had a lovely chat while the 'Trotters' supporter continued to eat his lunch. The dog slept through this momentous meeting. It didn't surprise me that the dog was called 'Nat'. It's things like this that make up the heart of football.

One thing that has changed at the Reebok is the boardroom. When Gordon Hargreaves was chairman he decided he wanted to design the best boardroom in the Football League. There was a story that he was once embarrassed by some visiting directors at the old stadium who refused to go into the boardroom because it was so shabby. So, for the new stadium he ordered a 20-seater table that was hand-made from the finest timbers and inlaid with woods from around the world. It allegedly cost thousands of pounds. There was a private bar, four large settees, a private balcony overlooking reception and the finest cut-glass tableware and crockery, plush carpeting, chandeliers, chess tables and the most splendid ornaments that money could buy.

It could hold 100 people and was quite intimidating. You felt if you sneezed you might break a vase. Nat Lofthouse used to hate it after a game when he was expected to go in and mingle. He used to ask me to go in with him so he had someone to talk to. "I hate that place and feel so uncomfortable in it," he would say to me.

When Chairman Gordon Hargreaves left, the room was re-designed into a far more relaxed and friendlier environment.

*****

At the heart of football is Wembley Stadium. I saw it for the first time on May 3rd, 1958. I was seven years old as I walked towards the 'Twin Towers' amongst what seemed like a million other Bolton Wanderers supporters as we walked up that ancient approach to the stadium. The opponents were Manchester United. I will never ever forget that first breath-taking view of Wembley as I held my father's hand tight. Surrounding me were hundreds of adults and all I could see were shoulders and cloth caps. But then the crowd parted for a moment and there were the towers. But for Malcolm Macdonald I would have played there 17 years later. The chance never came again.

Bolton beat Manchester United that day with what even then was seen as a controversial goal. It was an incredibly physical game in the 50s with challenges and tackles that today would see red cards. Back then they were the norm and just part of the game. In this one the ball was high above the United crossbar with goalkeeper Harry Gregg standing facing the goal under the bar to catch it. Nat Lofthouse came charging in unseen behind him and clattered Gregg in the back so that he and ball fell into the back of the net. The goal stood. I doubt as a seven-year-old it mattered to me. I probably never even saw it properly standing on tiptoe most of the game peering over grown-ups' shoulders. If I see it today replayed on TV, I look and think not even in the 70s when I played, and it was rough then, and I'd done that, would it have stood.

But the chance did come to re-visit the place in late 1998 when I was approached on behalf of the Football Association to become director of commercial affairs at the new £400 million Wembley Stadium. The appointment was confirmed in April 1999 when the Football Association purchased Wembley Stadium from Wembley PLC for £123 million.

So there I was then, back at Wembley, part of the team entrusted to demolish the old lady and rebuild a spanking new national treasure. Fate works in mysterious ways. At the outset of the project no-one knew just how complex it would become, what delays there would be and how costs would multiply. When I started work I learned as much as I could about the old place, the 'Venue of Legends'. I had an office just next to the West Tower. It was built as part of the great Empire Exhibition of 1923 and cost £300,000 and had a projected lifespan of 10 years. Beneath it were the foundations of 'Watkins' Folly', a monument that was to be the second Eiffel Tower. In 1892 Sir Edward Watkins got to 155 feet before difficulty with the foundations forced him into bankruptcy. An old steam engine used in erecting the steel structure broke down and was buried amongst the foundations. 30 years later Wembley Stadium, the place that I visited with my father, was built on top.

I found it hard to believe that the Football Association never owned Wembley until 1999 and every year from 1923 they would rent the venue from Wembley PLC. Regular iconic events were staged there and many of the performers were already legends or became legends. Fanny Blankers-Koen in the 1948 Olympics, Cassius Clay, as he was then, fighting Henry Cooper in 1963, and who will ever forget Bobby Moore and the 1966 World Cup win. The visits of Pope John Paul and Billy Graham in the 60s and 70s attracted a different kind of audience. Michael Jackson performed sell-out concerts. Bob Geldof became an unlikely hero with the Live-Aid Concert on 1985. Royalty were regular visitors to present trophies particularly the FA Cup. Princess Diana had the honour in 1997 when Chelsea were the winners. '*Abide with Me*' became emotionally linked with the FA Cup with Bruce Forsyth the last conductor of the community singing in a white suit. Pele labelled Wembley his 'Church of Football' but amazingly he never played there.

In my role as commercial director I was responsible for organising some of the closure events and I commissioned artist Emma Allcock to produce a watercolour of the old Wembley before the bulldozers moved in. Her strange interpretation showed a mystical looking building with the Twin Towers white and bold. I wanted to call the painting '*From My Father's Hand*' because, like many others, this was the way I first saw Wembley, holding my father's hand. The idea was rejected and it was called '*Venue of Legends*'. Emma gave me one of her working drawings which I tweaked a little so I could give it my original name. It's my own memory of a building as I remember it in 1958.

The purchase of Wembley in 1999 included the suggestion that a condition should be the inclusion of a running track so that this would allow London to bid for the Olympic Games. But, the primary aim was to make this the greatest football stadium in the world. Simultaneously it was essential to design into the plans key commercial components that would enable it to operate profitably seven days a week.

In 1999 a draft business plan had been created which provided an interesting read. Chelsea Chairman Ken Bates had been made chairman of the new Wembley project board which intended to streamline the decision making process. The fear was that the whole process would become caught up in the bureaucracy of the FA and other governing bodies. Ken was, and still is, one of football's well known characters and I remembered his time at Oldham Athletic and Wigan Athletic long before his Chelsea fame. He reportedly "bought Chelsea for £1" when they were struggling and turned it into a magnificent club and stadium before he sold it to Roman Abramovich in 2003 for many millions.

Ken was a very quietly spoken but incredibly tough character and I grew to like him very much especially at our monthly breakfast meetings at his Chelsea Village Hotel where he would tell me of his incredible football experiences. One of them was many years ago in the 60s trying to buy shares at Burnley Football Club and join the board there until Chairman Bob Lord vetoed the possibility. At that time Ken had business interests in the Lancashire area. Football had always been a first love but as a youngster a minor foot deformity prevented any chance of playing seriously. We would meet at 8am on the last Thursday of each month. His office was festooned with photographs and pictures of himself in different situations, locations and at different events. This wasn't vanity, just a pride in his achievements. He took me through all the difficulties he'd had re-building Stamford Bridge and the problems with the wealthy local residents.

Ken resigned from the new Wembley board in 2001 on account of the lack of progress and support. He allegedly suggested that the best way forward would be to shoot the Minister of Sport, Kate Hoey. Ken sent a letter to FA chief executive Adam Crozier which made his anger clear at the lack of support he was getting from other members of the Wembley National Stadium Ltd board and Kate Hoey.

Although my role as director of commercial affairs was concentrated on the numerous commercial activities within the stadium building, it wasn't long before I became involved in the design of these facilities. The passage of time gives me the chance now to look back with real pleasure at what I did. If I take my grandchildren to a game down there it's a real thrill to think, *"Hey I did that ... this bit was me ..."*

Early involvement required market research to assess the demand for corporate facilities at all kinds of levels – local, regional, national and international, within the seating decks. There was liaison with architects, Sports Lottery and UK Athletics bodies to design this multi-purpose stadium fit to stage football and initially athletics, and good enough upon which to base future bids for European Athletics Championships, and Olympic Games bids. There were designs and sales and marketing of corporate packages, executive boxes, event day packages, a 200 bedroom hotel, office accommodation, themed restaurants, a museum, tour and visitor attractions, a health and leisure club, conference and banqueting facilities. There were brewery and catering agreements and long-term staging agreements between the three key event owners, the Football Association, the Football League and the Rugby Football League. On top of all this I headed a team of lawyers, private investigators, police and senior stewards all tasked with eliminating black market ticketing associated with major events.

The job was fascinating, demanding, frustrating and things got angry several times as the project began to run over the original timetable and budget. There were long delays over various issues all now documented fully in other publications. The whole saga dragged on for nearly eight years until the opening in 2007. Litigation and compensation claims between the warring parties went on for years after that.

Watkins' Folly caused the main contractor Multiplex real problems. The removal of the old foundations to this edifice needed explosives to level the site. Watkins' 'monument' was causing problems 100 years later. There was much debate about retaining the old 'Twin Towers' but unfortunately they were not built in stone, which would have enabled bit by bit removal and relocation, but in poured concrete. The huge arch, designed by Lord Norman Foster to be an iconic 'signature', is impressive but has never given Wembley an affectionate nickname along the lines of the 'Twin Towers'.

It was as if the whole thing was dogged with problems. There were legal disputes between WNSL and Multiplex. In December 2003 the constructors of the arch, Cleveland Bridge, warned Multiplex about rising costs and there was a delay of almost a year due to design changes that Multiplex rejected. Cleveland Bridge withdrew from the project and were replaced by Hollandia who had to start all over again. In 2004 there was a fatal accident and breaches of Health and Safety Law. In 2006 a steel rafter in the roof fell by a foot and a half forcing 3,000 workers to be evacuated. Also in 2006 sewers beneath the stadium buckled and blocked due to ground movement. There were arguments about was it faulty workmanship or was it deliberate sabotage.

Early designs featured a running track round the pitch. This was a requirement of UK Athletics as part of the £123 million National Lottery funding. In the early months every effort was made to include a track in the design. Moveable stands were one idea. A platform running track built over the pitch and first 20 rows of seats, was another. Everything that was suggested was either too complex or too costly. The inclusion of a running track would have had significant implications had it been included in the final design. The total build/footprint area would have increased. Building costs would have risen dramatically. And, the football experience would have been compromised with seats many yards away from the action as we see with the new Olympic stadium. At the end of the day this was a football stadium and Ken Bates shared that view. Much to the dissatisfaction of UK Athletics the running track plans were dropped and in my view this decision above all others made this stadium into the terrific place it is today. You cannot mix football and athletics within a single stadium without football losing its immediacy and closeness.

Wembley is thus preserved as Pele's *'Church of Football'*. Since its opening I have attended several Cup Finals and International matches. In 2009 I watched my beloved Burnley beat Sheffield United 1 – 0 in the Championship play-off final in a riveting game. Try to picture watching a game like that with a running track in between yourself and the action.

One of the happiest memories of this time I had at Wembley was one of Alan Stevenson's ideas, *'Games on the Pitch'*. I recall we sold the matches for about £28,000 each which may sound a lot but it worked out at about £1,000 a player and of course you got some special treatment and cucumber sandwiches with the crusts cut off. My great friend Colin Waldron booked the last match ever at Wembley Stadium for his friends and family and got himself sent off in a friendly football match against a team of over-50s. Colin holds the distinction of being the last man ever to be sent off beneath the Twin Towers of Wembley, which just shows that old habits die hard. Alan's initiative for these matches revolved round the FA Cup. He had a replica Cup made and after each game it was presented to the winning team at the top of the famous 39 steps. The 'ace' that Alan pulled out though was to book a 'look-a-like' Queen Elizabeth to present the trophy. She cost £250 a day for the ten days that the games took place and was worth every penny. She probably saw more football at Wembley during those ten days than all the previous monarchs put together. And, she was even there to see the 'assassin' Colin Waldron sent off. Alan, incidentally, had a spell at West Bromwich as commercial manager and pulled off one of the most imaginative sponsorship deals I have ever seen. Ron Atkinson, all bling and champagne, was manager at the time so Alan fixed up a deal with Moet & Chandon.

I left the Wembley project because life is different down in London. You can't get away from that and I was a classic example of the northern man in an alien environment. It was a tough place to work for a Lancashire lad with a wife and growing family back home 220 miles away. I got fed up of sun dried tomatoes and espresso coffee and all the bickering and disagreements. I gave up trying to find a good chip shop. I could picture old Bob Lord down there at a meeting of the Football League Committee. Allegedly he was so fed up of the 'posh' dinners in the hotel; he brought a bag of fish and chips in. Lord knows where he got them from. A waiter joined in the spirit of the thing and brought him a bottle of brown ale.

As costs escalated, the Wembley Business Plan, for which I had responsibility, along with control of the commercial incomes, was often adjusted without my agreement. There seemed to be a distinct lack of the teamwork ethic that I had enjoyed at Huddersfield. Politics seemed to rear its ugly head at every turn. Individuals guarded their positions jealously. Frankly, I seemed to spend more and more time just watching my back. Meetings became an obstacle course and less and less harmonious.

The leadership was fascinating. It's something that has always interested me. I came across an article that suggested that there are basically three types of leaders, be they chairmen, chief execs or managing directors or whatever. The 'erotic' type leads through dedication and teaching has no desire for personal gain yet they can influence millions by trying to improve their lives. People like Mother Theresa or Ghandi.

Secondly there is the 'obsessive' leader who believes in teamwork, sharing, praise, agreement, generally through cooperation, consensus and friendliness. Me I hope.

Then there is the 'narcissistic' type, the ones who don't give a damn for the feelings of others, can be utterly insensitive, ruthless and rude. Decisions are theirs and theirs alone. They often lack any empathy; are cold and unemotional. They certainly have clear visions and are determined, but this is at the expense of others. They might appear to listen, but actually don't. This seemed to be describing the leadership ethos of a couple of people I had to work with at Wembley. The article suggested two ways to deal with a narcissistic leader: one: change your views to match theirs ... or two: resign and move on. I certainly wasn't going to change my Dale Carnegie principles that had brought me great success so far. So I went for option two and resigned.

Ironically, based on success, the narcissistic leaders come out on top, but in succeeding they pay a large personal price. They drive a job through, make things happen; but they bully and coerce. People are pressured and intimidated. Bob Lord the all-powerful Burnley chairman anyone? Robert Maxwell, and taken to its extreme – Hitler.

So, it was a time for reflection and evaluation (big words for a kid who, till he was seven, used a tin bath in front of the fire). The vision for the new Wembley was 'theirs' not mine and it was clear that 'they' saw me as too docile for the harsh London environment, or meetings that were all too often confrontational and aggressive. That was and never will be my style. Was I prepared to change my ways and become a 'hard bastard' treading on people and their feelings? Did I want to participate in a project that was all about 'battles' and winning? No I was not.

The evening came when I sat and wrote out my resignation. I arranged to see Ken Bates for one last meeting. I apologised for letting him down. It was interesting that later on, he too decided he'd had enough.

It was a massive decision. I was on a huge salary with all the trimmings (as many sun dried tomatoes and cappuccinos as I could manage). I flew down to London at 6.30am every Monday morning and returned at 6.30pm every Friday evening. What sort of life was that? All five directors had the same salary package, a five-year contract, and a two-year bonus payment at the end of that. If I'd stuck this job out, I'd have been set up for life.

There are two ways to look at this. Either I was soft for jacking the job in and not staying the course. Or I was bloody brave to relinquish a post that was paying me a fortune and had a jackpot at the end of it. But at the end of the day, I valued my family, my sanity and also my pride. My whole approach to life is based on cooperation and teamwork. It's what I'd been taught by Jimmy Adamson years before and brought me real success. Wembley was the opposite it seemed to me.

I had no idea what I was going to do next. Within a week an Australian company called Bastion offered me the UK managing director's job for a bigger salary than Wembley were paying. I took on the role, established them in the UK and after two years I was looking to get back in stadiums when the phone rang. It was Doug Ellis; yes 'Deadly Doug' himself. He wanted to build the National Stadium in Birmingham. He thought the new Wembley would all end up in tears and implode. So: what about building at a new location next to the NEC in Birmingham. I had a quick think. Was Doug 'erotic', 'obsessive', or 'narcissistic'? Bloody hell he was narcissistic. "No thanks Doug, goodbye," was the gist of the conversation. He then offered me the finance director's job at Aston Villa. Bloody hell, I'd rather be a goalkeeper than work in the doldrums of finance. I went down to chat to him about it at his home in Aston. Halfway through our chat he fell asleep (my conversation was electrifying even then). His lovely wife brought me a cup of tea and said, "Don't worry, he does that when I'm talking to him, he'll come around soon." And 15 minutes later he woke and resumed our chat as if nothing had happened. I appreciated the offer but we both agreed the finance role wouldn't have suited me.

So I drove home.

Ah, the bliss of being back in Rawtenstall, the clean fresh air of the north, the endless grey skies, the rain and drizzle, the rich vowels and consonants of the locals, the homeliness of the abattoir and the tram sheds. I drank it all in. And: no more leaving Sian and the family for the week. And above all else – the chip shop at the end of the street.

Could life get any better than this?

# 8

# Sent to Coventry

I have attachments to four football clubs, Bolton Wanderers where I began my career, Huddersfield, Coventry and of course Burnley where I had the most wonderful 10 years, and then returned in 2007 for another four as chief executive. But if one club gives me cause to ask just what is going on, what has happened, and how will it all end, it is Coventry City.

25 years ago in 1987 Coventry won the FA Cup. Until 2001 they were in the Premiership but with debts of nearly £60 million. Eleven years after that, in 2012, they don't own their stadium and they have been relegated to Division One. Theirs is a sorry story of how everything can go wrong following a decision to relocate to a new stadium. That, plus a procession of managers and poor seasons, has made their recent history a painful experience for their supporters. On the field they have had to use kids when good pros were needed (but have been in short supply), backroom staff and management has been pared to the minimum. This is a club that has not lived within its means for more than a decade. It provides a manual almost on how not to proceed with a new stadium.

The Ricoh Area *appears* to be a good looking, successful and efficient building. Driving by and viewing it from the motorway some way away, it looks impressive especially lit up at night, and you could be forgiven for thinking it is a great success story. But that would belie the reality. I have often thought that if Coventry City Football Club and their supporters, at the outset, had been able to see the future and know the outcome of their move from Highfield Road and their relocation/ambitions way back in 1996, would they have elected to stay at their original home? I suspect the answer would be a resounding yes. As it is now, their club is in imminent danger of massive problems unless a large investor pops up.

The site was previously home to the Foleshill Gasworks. Today, the Arena Park Shopping Centre contains one of the largest Tesco hypermarkets. The stadium is named after its sponsor the Japanese Ricoh Company that paid £10 million for the naming rights. It was not allowed to use that name during the 2012 Olympics when sponsored names were forbidden. It was officially opened in February 2007 although it had already been open for a year before that.

The decision to relocate from the old Highfield Road was made in 1997 by the then chairman, Bryan Richardson. It was anticipated that the new home for the football club would be ready for the 2000/01 season. It was felt that what was needed was a modern and up to date stadium with better road links and car parking areas. Permission for the ground's construction was given in the spring of 1999. The revised August 2001 completion date was then over-run by almost four years. The final gas holder was not demolished until September 2002.

The original design was for a state-of-the-art stadium with a retractable roof, and a pitch that would slide out to reveal a hard floor for concerts and exhibitions. But when Coventry were relegated in 2001 and the bid to host the 2006 World Cup Finals ended in failure, the plans were downsized and simplified to reflect the new economic restraints. During construction the stadium was often referred to as the Jaguar Arena or Arena Coventry. In August 2004 it was announced that the stadium would indeed be called the Jaguar Arena in a £7 million deal. But when Jaguar hit problems and closures, the deal was cancelled.

The whole story makes a sorry, complicated and delicate saga. It encompasses over-ambition, naivety, greed and ruthlessness. The original aim that dates back to 1997 was *"to relocate from Highfield Road into a brand new stadium with the intention of maintaining Premier League status and competing in the Champions League."*

The outcome is what you see today. There is little revenue for the club other than matchday ticket sales. There is no income for the club from: food and drink, car parking, room rentals, office rentals, conference and banqueting, exhibitions, rock concerts, international football or rugby matches, casino income, fitness club or anything else that happens at the arena. And: the club pays a crippling £1 million-plus per annum in rent. The possibility of ever competing in the Champions League I would suggest has gone forever. The possibility of even returning to the Premiership is extremely remote.

The Ricoh Arena is currently owned jointly by Coventry City Council and the Higgs Charitable Trust. The football club is merely a tenant in what was intended at the outset to be *'their'* stadium. The extensive income streams that should have been theirs now go into the coffers of the council and the Trust. Funds that should have enabled Coventry to mount a serious bid to return to the Premier League are now denied to them. There are many lessons to be learned from the Coventry experience and any football club considering a partnership with their local council should draw up and totally understand a document that states what the outcomes will be before the project commences. This will prevent the council from overpowering its weaker and more vulnerable partner which I feel is what happened at Coventry.

My experience in this sorry process began as I was driving up the M6 motorway after a meeting with former Aston Villa Chairman Doug Ellis. I'd left the Wembley project when it was not just hitting the rocks, but was about to sink into a morass of delays and arguments. I had spent a couple of years with Bastion and then Doug Ellis was doing his best to get the new national stadium located in the centre of the country next to the NEC in Birmingham. The car radio was on as I drove home and I was stunned by the news that two aircraft had crashed into the New York Twin Towers. It was September 11th, 2001.

My carphone rang. It was Geoffrey Robinson MP, director and investor in Coventry City FC. He had often attracted adverse publicity but I found him to be a real gem. Within a few weeks I was installed as the chief executive of Arena 2000 Ltd, the joint venture company set up to oversee the construction of the new stadium. On arrival at the offices in the city I was introduced to a team of three people; the finance director, an architect and my PA. I remember the welcome I received was about as warm as the chilly November morning. It took me no more than an hour to decide that two of the three didn't have any idea what they were doing. Only the PA seemed to offer a genuinely warm welcome.

It became clear that for the last three years they had been making little progress. Within three months I had come to understand every aspect of the project. I parted company with the finance director and the architect and a new team took their place. Prior to that there was a first meeting when I was taken by Geoffrey Robinson to the council offices to meet various people involved in the partnership. There was the inevitable senior development officer in charge. His task was to oversee the project on behalf of the council. Geoffrey was asked to leave the room and then there began what I can only describe as an interrogation. The questions came hard and fast. If they'd shone spotlights in my face I wouldn't have been surprised. I wondered if there were a couple of 'heavies' lurking in the shadows. The questions came at me like a machine gun ... *who are you ... who appointed you ... what experience have you got ... have you met the Coventry City chairman ... have you dealt with him outside of football ... what is your job description ... how long do you intend to be here ... what is your inside leg measurement ...*

I was starting to realise that being sent to Coventry had another meaning. The hostility was obvious. It was quite clear that there was no love lost between the football club and Coventry City Council. It was a relationship that I felt never changed during all the six years that I worked at Coventry. It was a far cry from the comfortable cooperation and trust that existed at Huddersfield.

At the outset Coventry City FC had the ideal scenario and the opportunity to build a stadium without involving the city council. From that might have come the platform to establish the club in the Premier League. But, during this journey the plot was lost, ambitions grew, plans went wrong as they deviated from the original sensible ambitions. Initially, they had located a 72 acre site near the M6 motorway which would have cost around £20 million to buy and de-contaminate. Before any work began they agreed to sell half of the site, around 35 acres, to Tesco for around £62.5 million. This left a profit of £40 million-plus with which to build the new stadium. And then it all went wrong.

They became star-struck. They began to think of an all-singing, all-dancing 60,000 capacity stadium with a sliding roof and retractable pitch, costing well over £100 million. At this same time it was not certain that the new Wembley Stadium would go ahead so the dreamers at Coventry FC began to see the possibility of their location being ideal for a new national stadium. Time and money was spent on studies and as costs got higher and higher the club approached Coventry City Council for extra funding with the view that this could become not just a football stadium for the club, but a community project for the whole city. And that's where the whole thing went wrong. If only the football club had not deviated from its original simple ideals.

By the time I arrived in Coventry the deal had been struck and in simple terms it was going to be a joint venture between the football club and Coventry City Council with both parties owning 50% of the equity. The football club did not have the money to complete the purchase of the land (half of the land then being sold to Tesco to fund the stadium) so it was agreed that Coventry Council would buy the land, then conclude the deal with Tesco, all as part of their joint venture agreement.

All well and good so far then, until the city council next informed the football club that they were unable to share with them the profit on the land sale to Tesco because of "State Aid" rules. In its simplest terms state aid is where public money is used to support private businesses and in certain circumstances is illegal. Having gained the money from the land sale to Tesco the council then argued that to give any of that profit to the football club would be illegal.

Instead they offered Coventry City FC a 50% share in the company that would operate the Ricoh Arena, but they, Coventry City Council, would own all the equity in the property. It took 12 months and around £1 million in lawyers' fees to get all this to a conclusion.

As compensation the council offered the football club 50% of the operating profit from the Ricoh Arena and the business plan forecasts were looking very favourable. In addition they would receive all the football related income streams. Alas, as the project evolved Coventry City FC were relegated from the Premier League and encountered massive financial problems. Administration looked likely, but to combat this, they sold their 50% shareholding in the Ricoh Arena to the Higgs Charitable Trust for a reported (*Coventry Evening Telegraph*) £6 million. As the Higgs Trust had already invested around £2 million in the football club, the price paid for the 50% shareholding was only around £4 million. At that time the Ricoh Arena had been valued at around £37 million. The football club's 50% share of this (£18.5 million) was thereby sold for a paltry £4 million.

In the meantime there was I beavering away in the background making the whole thing look very attractive as the stadium design took shape, with additional revenue streams that were not there on the early plans, but were introduced and negotiated by me: the hotel, health and fitness club, office accommodation and the casino. However, all these income streams would be denied to the football club when they sold their shares in the Arena. They also waved goodbye to the income from catering, car parking, concerts, international matches; all of them sold away as they sold off their shares. All they were left with were sales of matchday tickets and perimeter advertising. Out of these they had, and still have to pay a rent of over £1 million a year.

In selling their shares to the Higgs Trust, the football club not unreasonably felt these shares would be held in 'safe-keeping' until times improved. Alan Higgs had been a lifelong fan of the club whilst he was alive and his son Derek told me that he had left his fortune to the 'people of Coventry.' Sir Derek Higgs, was an even bigger fan and served the club well for many years as both a director of the football club and as a director of Arena Coventry.

So: there you have it. Once upon a time a football club might have sat on a £40 million windfall with the simple job of building themselves a new stadium. It, along with new sponsorships that always find new stadiums attractive, could have established Coventry in the Premiership. All the revenue streams would have been theirs and the fans would have been happy ever after. But then they became embroiled with the local council which ultimately squeezed the club out of its own stadium by waving a large red flag called "State Aid."

It is the city council and the Higgs Trust that now harvests the money from matchday car parking and catering plus all the other non-football spin-offs that come from the stadium. The football club is effectively in a strait-jacket.

I did once wonder exactly what the city council's attitude to the football club actually was. In 2007 on the 20th anniversary of the club's FA Cup victory along with other Coventry fans I asked the city council if they would consider awarding the team with the 'Freedom of the City'. The request was met with a firm "no". They did manage to stretch to a few sandwiches at a function in the Town Hall for 30 minutes or so before a home game. In total contrast to that, during my first year back in Burnley as chief executive, I took a call from the Burnley Council chief executive requesting permission to award ex player Jimmy McIlroy the Freedom of the Town, in recognition for what he had done for Burnley over the years. Burnley Football Club unanimously agreed. It made me wonder even more if Coventry City Council actually really valued their football club.

The opening game in the new stadium was against Queens Park Rangers. Whereas once my work dress had been shirt, shorts and football boots, now it was a pinstripe suit and on many days a bright yellow hard-hat. The nerves were fluttering; so many things could go wrong. There was a huge mixture of anxiety and excitement. The journey to get this far had been long and hard, frequently fraught with differences of opinion and huge frustrations. On the morning of this day, just as I had when we opened the Galpharm at Huddersfield, or McAlpine as it was then, a number of thoughts went through my head. This huge stadium, that had eventually cost £113 million to build, stood in front of me and at times like this you could not help but think "I did that." Of course there was no end of other people involved and deserving of credit (and others who didn't) but at that moment I could not help but say, "I've done this." It was a stunning feeling. Again I remembered Bob Lord's withering words about footballers not being able to run a fish and chip shop. "Take a look at that you old bugger," I muttered to myself but not without a degree of affection. I actually liked the old dictator. I remembered the day Edward Heath came to Burnley to open the new Brunshaw Road Stand that ran alongside what is now Harry Potts Way. Bob's philosophy was clear back then. You need quality facilities and the people will come. I know Dave Thomas once talked to Ken Bates about Bob Lord. Ken was adamant that Bob Lord was way ahead of his time in terms of visions about what football stadiums and clubs needed. But, said Ken, what Lord lacked was the financial entrepreneurial know-how and contacts to implement his visions.

What I and Coventry had achieved with this stadium, and indeed at Huddersfield and Bolton, might well have been built in Burnley 30 years earlier. There were plans for shops and a huge night-club; indeed the land was bought in readiness alongside the cricket club for commercial extensions to Turf Moor. Plans were drawn up. But that was as far as it got. It's an astonishing thought that Turf Moor could have been the site of the first community football stadium all those years ago that would have generated money seven days a week. Old Bob was much maligned in his final days at the club. But in his prime, what a football thinker he was.

Funnily enough, standing there looking at this huge edifice, I thought too of my old manager Jimmy Adamson. From him I learned about the value of teamwork. He taught me to be a team player and from that I learned in later life how to get the right team together. There'd been a damned good team at Huddersfield, and at Coventry I had recruited another. We had our ups and downs with them but to be fair to Coventry City Council, they were in the project not to save Coventry City Football Club, but to regenerate a part of the city that was going to waste. They saw a chance to create jobs and bring people and revenue into the area.

Early that morning I wandered round the stadium and realised that the achievement and satisfaction was just as great as that overhead goal at Elland Road when we demolished Leeds 4 – 1. I thought too about the comfort zone that I had once happily inhabited but now couldn't remember when last I hadn't faced some sort of challenge. I thought of granddad as well. What would he have thought now? But whilst once we walked down cobbled streets and called at a corner shop for a pie, now I walked along concourses amongst potted plants in a stadium with 32,000 seats, no stanchions, uninterrupted sightlines and big translucent panels to let light onto the pitch and into the concourses. And there was the first concert to look forward to – Bryan Adams in the Exhibition Hall.

Eventually there was a change of roles and from being Arena chief executive I became the football club's managing director working under local Coventry MP, ex-Paymaster General and by now chairman of Coventry City, Geoffrey Robinson. From that moment on I was as good as working against Coventry City Council in trying to safeguard the club's best interests. Not only that but because the football club was in such a financially difficult situation players had to be sold which then angered the supporters. They were pretty much angry anyway at the state the club was in. There had been a huge debt when I arrived and it had got better, but at a cost in quality.

The sale of Garry McSheffrey in 2006 illustrated perfectly the club's impossible circumstances. The decision to sell him to Birmingham City symbolised the way the club was heading. Here was a home-grown popular lad and the best player we had. He was someone the fans identified with, one of their own. Coventry had no money and bills to pay. £4 million was too much to ignore. The phone calls and emails flooded in. It's the CEO that gets them. There was a forum for fans that I had set up to aid better communication. A meeting was called with them specially to discuss the McSheffrey sale. I was on a hiding to nothing. By the time the meeting closed the fans knew all that there was to know. Of course the club debts were discussed, the fall in season ticket holders, the search for investors, in fact all the problems that bedevilled the club. Redundancies in the car industry locally hadn't helped and that was a key factor in the disappearing support. Ironically there was discussion of the football club's aim to buy back a 50% share in the stadium. If I'd gone into the history of the thing and how it had all gone wrong, those supporters at the meeting would have been aghast. They certainly know now alright.

It can be a funny old life as a chief executive. There was me one minute fending off angry supporters; and the next I'm handing out leaflets about Chlamydia screening at the next home game. At Burnley they handed out free condoms in club colours on two occasions. Dave Thomas tells me they're now collectors' items.

For Coventry City now, the future is insecure. The owners, SISU Capital, a London based hedge-fund, were intent on reducing costs even further. Gary Stubbs, leader of the protest group set up to oppose SISU expressed real fears that Coventry could become the next Portsmouth or Luton. Fans were open-mouthed when former Canadian director, Leonard Brody, suggested that fans could text a premium number and help pick the substitutions during games. Promises of loan signings came to nothing. The owner of SISU, Finnish-American financier Joy Seppala has as far as I know, at the time of writing, never been to a game. Her representative on the Coventry board, Onye Igwe, had reportedly given just one interview during the 2011/12 season.

John Mutton, head of Ricoh owners Coventry Council announced he would not contemplate selling any share of the ground to the football club whilst SISU were in charge. Clouding the waters even further was the change of ownership of the club from SISU to Sconsett Capital, although SISU allegedly had 100% control over Sconsett and the football club. Fans rightly asked, "Just who does own the club?" Local MP Bob Ainsworth also expressed enormous worries over what was happening at the club.

Manager Andy Thorn added, "It's been a nightmare. Everyone knows how difficult this job is. We don't have a full-time scout, no fitness coach; we are using kids on work experience to do proper jobs. Basically one is doing the job of three. I don't expect any positive news in the short term unless something changes. You don't have to be a genius to see the situation isn't great. If we come out of this, we have swum the channel with a gas stove on our backs."

Peter Ward, chairman of the Sky Blues Consultation Group said, "I could almost take going into administration, dropping into League One, then living within our means and building again with a vibrant team – if that was a definite plan. But at the moment no-one knows who is in charge; who is steering the ship or where we are going. And it bloody hurts."

Maybe it was supporter Martin Sutton who summed things up best. "We keep on asking who *they* are – but they won't tell us. Nobody knows and we're going to be left with no club the way things are going."

Add to all that the suspicions that there are people in the city who eye the stadium with a view to developing it into a sort of Midlands version of the Millennium Dome, with a proper roof and a solid floor, and have no worries about saying goodbye to the football club, or kicking it out; what is there at Coventry City Football Club but a recipe for future disaster?

I left Coventry because it was clear that we needed a dynamic new manager. We began the process with the usual long list. Soon that became the short list (every short list has Brian Flynn on it) but at interview stage it was Iain Dowie who stood out head and shoulders above the rest. Within a few weeks we had him on board and he was magnificent to work with, and a fantastic motivator. I'd promised him funds to invest in the team but began to realise the cupboard was empty and there was nothing to give him. In a situation where I felt I had let him down I made an impulse decision and resigned. I put so much work into that stadium and club but leaving is one decision I have never regretted.

Peter Ward did get his 'wish' (for want of a better word). Coventry City were indeed relegated at the end of season 2011/12. I felt terribly sad. Since the day I left there seemed a grim inevitability that this was what was in prospect. Following relegation, they face reduced season ticket sales, dwindling support and even less income. There they are, now a League One club, in such a wonderful purpose-built stadium but it is very much that stadium and its costs that lies at the heart of their problems. The stadium has been their downfall.

# 9

# Four More Years

Burnley director Brendan Flood sent me a text when he heard on Sky Sports News that I had resigned at Coventry. We had already spoken some months earlier when he had visited me at The Ricoh. Burnley had announced in the summer of 2007 that they intended to rebuild one end of the ground and Brendan wanted someone with experience to add input. At that point although I was committed to Coventry we agreed to keep in touch.

I'd been asked a few times to return to Burnley. On one occasion I'd met Chairman Barry Kilby but before we could get down to talking about a possible role at BFC I had to explain that I'd just signed a five-year contract with the FA to become commercial director at the new Wembley Stadium. But I do remember thinking to myself, "What a nice guy. He's somebody I could work with."

On another occasion, when Burnley had been searching for a new CEO, I'd been visited by directors Chris Duckworth and Clive Holt at my home about joining Burnley. It was a strange meeting as I was by then in the middle of the £114 million project at Coventry. They asked if I would consider leaving and asked how much I was being paid. I explained my basic salary (without mentioning bonuses) and Clive's reaction seemed to me to be one of pleasure and relief all rolled into one that I was 'unavailable'.

Clive is part of the furniture at Turf Moor having been there something like 25 years. To be at any club anywhere that long as a director means you are either indispensably brilliant, shove millions in year after year, or like the Black Box in an aeroplane, you somehow survive every disaster and calamity and boardroom change.

So: Clive smiled and said words to the effect that, "Well that's it then. We can't afford that, no way. That's way above our budget. Come on Chris let's go back and tell the board."

I got the feeling they had visited me because they had been instructed to sound me out. I had the feeling that they wanted to find a reason, or any reason, to tick me off the list. And they'd found one. As they left I was sort of amused and curious at the same time, wondering exactly what had they come for. Anyway they left quite sharply, job done, mission accomplished. They had made the visit.

The visible symbol of Clive's love of the club, used to be the visits that he and his dog made to Gawthorpe to see the youth games. That is to say until head of youth development, Martin Dobson, put a stop to it on the grounds that no dog should be allowed onto a football pitch area in case it did a pile of you know what. And that was a rule that applied to a director just as much as any local bloke in a flat cap and wellies bringing his whippets. Of course it ended with Martin having to confront him one day.

"Change has never been easy at Turf Moor", wrote Brendan in his book about life at Turf Moor. *Traditions are often hard fought.* I've always assumed Brendan was referring to Clive and the dog.

Not for one minute would I suggest that knowing Brendan Flood would take me back to Burnley, had any bearing on the decision to resign at Coventry. The reasons for the resignation were solid and plentiful enough anyway. But it did help knowing that I could pick up a phone and speak to Brendan about Burnley. As it turned out I didn't need to phone. The text was simple enough:

*"Paul, don't forget if you fancy a cup of coffee and coming down to Burnley give me a shout."*

I replied the next day and we arranged to meet at my house in Rawtenstall. I knew I'd get a decent cuppa coffee there. We talked about the club's plans to redevelop the ground and the things that Burnley were trying to do off the pitch. New manager Owen Coyle had arrived at the club the previous month. He'd had some stunning early results especially away from home. The place had been lifted. Brendan buzzed. He speaks quite slowly but his ambition and visions came across loud and clear. It was clear he had ambition and his business at that time 'Modus' was flying. Via that business he had already made considerable £6.75m investments in the club (£3m from personal funds and £3.75m from his business – still a record investment by any director). Being an up and at 'em kind of bloke he wasn't everyone's cup of tea in the boardroom. He had raised the bar at a club that for some years had drifted along making ends meet as best they could, very much reliant on the chairman's financial input and one or two other directors like Ray Griffiths. Some directors however were ultra-cautious and were uncomfortable with Brendan's ambition. I wasn't naïve enough to realise also that I would be seen as Brendan's man. But I also realised that to a degree we were kindred spirits. He was the type of person who would make things happen and more importantly, he wanted to win on the field and not just settle for a slap up meal in the boardroom every Saturday.

Since that day Brendan has published his book *Big Club, Small town and Me.* He was very complimentary about me suggesting I was "charismatic and well connected" and my "presence was a massive boost to the club at senior level," ending by suggesting that I was "arguably the best CEO in football." I felt just as comfortable with Brendan. He was assembling a great team at Burnley FC, which had started with Owen Coyle and his backroom staff. Every department bounced ideas off each other and there was a tremendous buzz around the place. We weren't to know that this positive formula would take the club back to the top division, the Premiership, within 18 months. Brendan had many believers. But unfortunately there were a small number of people who didn't take to him.

Brendan is a 'doer' and didn't always tell people what he'd done or was planning at the club. This can be a virtue when things need action not discussion or 'death by committee'. So prior to me joining he'd done things like supporting manager Steve Cotterill in the signing of Ade Akinbiyi without consulting the minority shareholders. And why should he have? It was his money. But he hadn't told the other directors he was approaching me with a view to signing me up. Some of them got a big surprise when it was announced even though initially it was only three days a week. Alas it would be the kind of thing that some of them would bring up when things went upside down for Brendan later. Nobody grumbles at a winner. But when the winner starts losing, moods change. And the night of the long knives had yet to come when Brendan was instrumental much later in reducing the size of the board.

So, I agreed to join in a sort of re-development position and later also agreed to take on some of the chief executive's roles. In that respect it was an unusual set-up in that the chairman and Brendan shared the operating director's role which in effect took away much of the work a chief executive would do. But essentially I was there to oversee the rebuilding of the old stand at the cricket field end of the ground. It seemed the ideal team, Brendan and me; Brendan with Modus and his financial contacts and me with my stadium knowledge. And of course there was Owen Coyle leading from the front.

How could it go wrong?

I was starting all over again at the place where I had first made a football debut on March 6th, 1971. Normally when you make a debut there's not a lot you remember about the match unless you score. In this one I didn't. They were down in the relegation zone when I joined and would stay there. If they needed a few quick wins and a few goals from me to rescue them it wouldn't happen. In this forgettable game we lost 0 – 1 at home to Southampton. But it was still a great place to be and the team spirit was still intact. How could it not be? Put two dozen footballers together and there's a fourth form humour that knows no limits. I had the usual egg in my shoe and all the other practical initiation jokes that greet a new man. Survive them and you are "one of the lads." You had to be on your toes every minute otherwise you would fall for everything. On my third day Mick Docherty and Colin Waldron suggested that I should ask Eddie Cliff how his sister was getting on with her dancing lessons. I did.

Eddie immediately broke down in tears and stormed out of the room. I was totally taken aback. The only person left in the dressing room was Frank Casper and he could see there was something wrong. "What's up Fletch?" he asked.

"I don't know, I've just asked Eddie Cliff how his sister is getting on with her dance lessons and he went out very upset."

"I'm not surprised you insensitive sod," said Frank. "His sister lost both her legs in a car crash two years ago." Then he walked out just as angrily as Eddie.

I felt terrible and wondered how I could make it up to Eddie. I sat on my own for a little while wondering how I could possibly mend things. As I opened the door to leave, the four of them were outside waiting and all of them led by Eddie himself jumped on me laughing hysterically. "Gotcha gotcha," they yelled down my ear. I learned and decided there and then that I'd give as good as I got in the next few years.

Banter and a few practical jokes liven a place up. Total seriousness has never been a trait of mine. Don't forget, I play the ukulele.

The Southampton centre-half that day was the great John McGrath. He gave me a smack and broke my nose as a welcome to the First Division. Football is the only profession other than boxing where breaking someone's nose was once quite legitimate and part of the contest between opposing defenders and centre-forwards. He became a great friend of mine in later life as we travelled the after-dinner circuit. Sadly he died in 1999 apparently carving the Christmas turkey. The turkey cooked his goose for him so to speak. In his obituary Ivan Ponting described him as a mix of Attila the Hun and Desperate Dan. As a manager he was known for his wonderful team talks. At Halifax he uttered the caustic comment that they were so hard up they couldn't even afford to feed the club cat. As a result the Shay was deluged with cat food sent in by animal lovers.

After that 0 – 1 defeat Jimmy Adamson took me to one side and said," Don't think we've brought you to the club to save us from relegation. You're here for the future and you'll play a key part in a special team I'm trying to assemble. If we get relegated this season, so be it. We'll be stronger and better next season so don't let results get you down." They were real words of wisdom to a new player who had the pressure of being the most expensive signing the club had made.

"Oh and nice nose," he added. "You met John McGrath then?"

On my first new morning at Turf Moor as the development officer, I did a quick sweep of the room to see if there was any sign of a Colin Waldron joke, or an elbow to break my nose. The room was safe. What I brought with me this time in this second spell at Burnley was a clear image and a commitment to making football stadiums pay for themselves every day of the week. What was the point of having a huge building that was empty most of the year? That was the foundation of my stadium beliefs, right since the first early days at Huddersfield. Stadiums are for more than just football. They serve the community and in a place like Burnley the location is in the heart of the town, not some distant site six miles away. The walk from Burnley town centre to Turf Moor takes just five minutes. It's a ground that is surrounded by terraced streets and corner shops. The cobbles may have gone but the pies remain.

What I also brought with me to Turf Moor was an idea. That idea was what I'd called the StadiArena. The idea for this had come when I'd had a eureka moment and like most of my ideas it had started with a big mistake. We'd just officially opened the Ricoh Arena. The football element of the stadium had worked wonderfully well and Coventry had won again at home. The next job was to officially open the 8,100 capacity indoor arena located right next door to the stadium. To do this we had the legend Bryan Adams to play to a capacity audience in the Jaguar Exhibition Hall. I knew this guy would be a safe bet to fill the place from my time at the McAlpine, Huddersfield, when he had rocked the place for four hours. I'd learned then that he was a true professional, with no attitude and just a very friendly guy.

For this opening event we had 1,500 VIP corporate guests in black ties and posh frocks, paying £175 a head dining in the large banqueting area on the football stadium third floor overlooking the pitch. Before the event Bryan had come up into the suite to unveil the large silver sign that read 'THE BRYAN ADAMS BAR' located in the main banqueting suite. Now there was a trick of the trade. If ever you want a 'name' celebrity to come up and meet your corporate guests you either fork out a fistful of money or ask them to name the bar after themselves. I've never known a celebrity yet refuse this 'honour'. Having said that, and having got to know Bryan I'm sure he would have met the guests anyway.

For the show we had bought over 1,500 extra seats for the corporate guests, so they could watch in comfort, located at the back of the hall which was also licensed to accommodate another 6,500 standing spectators. Just before he arrived on stage at 9pm the place looked great. The expectancy levels were enormous and the atmosphere, electric. Then what happened next was what happens at most rock concerts. The minute he appeared on stage there was a surge forward so that there was a 25 metre gap between the seated corporate guests and the rear of the standing crowd.

The £175 per ticket corporate guests felt totally out of it marooned at the rear of the hall. Many of them left the seats and joined the crowd. But for many their night was ruined not just because of their isolation, but they were at the rear of the hall as well, miles away from the stage and for this they had paid £175. The valuable lesson I learned was that you can't turn an exhibition hall into a rock concert venue successfully. And there was the other small point that we'd had to buy in the extra 1,500-plus seats. They weren't cheap either. Truth is the cost of those seats just about wiped out any profit on the event.

The following day I walked into the empty stadium with a cup of coffee and sat down. There's something hugely impressive about a new, immaculate, empty stadium when you can just look at and admire everything about it from the green pitch to the dozens of rows of blue seats. I sat there looking at 32,000 empty seats and thought there was I the night before having to buy in the seats needed for the concert. I started to look at the stadium roof and the section of seating behind the goals and next began to consider the possibility of having a large screen or door that would effectively turn this section of the ground into a self-contained covered arena using the 7,000 seats behind the goals. Questions flooded my head about facilities such as toilets, food concessions, ticketing, parking, heating and all the 101 things needed at a concert venue. One by one I ticked them off the mental list as being either there already or easy to install.

When I got back to my desk I started to doodle. Yes, it would take a massive screen or door to close off one end of a stadium completely. But once you achieved that you had a mini covered arena – for free. My initial thoughts evolved around concertina type doors that would be rolled across on a sort of track-rail from each side of the stadium. They would be about 28 metres high so there would be a need for specialist advice about rigidity, strength and wind tolerance. I asked a couple of friends who were structural engineers in London to work on some basic ideas and solutions. They came up with a few drawings and ideas but they seemed costly and would take half a day to screen off the goal end. Was it possible?

I persevered.

In the evenings in my Coventry flat that I shared with commercial director Ken Sharp and finance director Mal Brannigan, I continued making sketches, bouncing ideas off my two flatmates. They were both happy to become involved and eventually became directors and shareholders in the new StadiArena Ltd. After six months we had modified the concept working with architects and engineers cutting down the closing time of the doors by 50%. Yet still it took too long to find an operable system. The modifications and re-designs went on for another 12 months until it seemed that there was no solution to the basic problem: just how do you close off one end of a stadium with a system that is quick, uncomplicated and efficient?

The eureka moment came at home when I was with my wife Sian watching TV. During the commercial break an advert came on that featured a young lad standing on a grass verge outside an airport eating a bag of crisps. In the background the doors of an aircraft hangar opened to allow a Jumbo Jet to emerge. The doors opened and the doors closed smoothly and quickly. I stared at the screen. Bloody hell! Aircraft hangar doors: the answer was right in front of me on the TV.

I'm a bit like Roald Dahl. I have an office at the end of my garden where I work. That's where the similarity ends though. He was a genius. I'm a plodder. It was midnight but I took a cup of coffee over to the den ready to work into the small hours. I spent two hours googling 'aircraft hangar doors' and eventually came across a Swedish company, Megadoors who manufactured the perfect solution for a football stand that would convert one end into an arena. By 9.15 the following morning I'd tracked down Alan Clark from Megadoors who explained that the product opened and closed in eight minutes, was reasonably priced and was hurricane-proof. They'd been in business for the last 30 years and over 500 of their doors had been installed around the world. Alas he was a Lincoln City fan but then we all have our problems I suppose.

Within weeks, Robert Kennedy with help from engineer Steven Morley (who designed the Wimbledon centre court closing roof) had designed a Megadoor into a football stadium stand and we started to refer to this as a Stadium&Arena, which then quite naturally shortened to StadiArena. We had our way of providing a seven-day a week area for all the events associated with a covered arena: rock concerts, product launches, conventions, exhibitions, televising of away games, banquets, markets ... and so the list went on. I explained all this to Coventry City chairman and MP Geoffrey Robinson. He advised me immediately to patent the idea. This was something I'd never considered but immediately implemented his suggestion with David Fry an attorney who specialised in patents.

Meanwhile, back in the day job at Coventry City there were little things to do like trying to find a buyer for the club (now falling on hard times), and identify and create new income streams for the commercial department. We had little time to actually market our new StadiArena idea until we mentioned it to Patrick Cassidy of the Cassidy Group, the club shirt sponsors. Patrick saw the potential, took a 50% stake in the company and began the marketing process.

So: that's how things stood when I arrived in my new Turf Moor office. It seemed that here was a club wanting to develop a new stand, were looking to produce a seven-day a week income, sought to do something exciting and had in Brendan Flood someone who could use his business contacts and company to set up the development which included a top hotel operator. All looked fair on the good ship Claret. Brendan shared his thoughts with me and said, "We needed more use of the stadium on non matchdays and if you aim high then we might end up with a scheme half as big; but club revenues need innovation to provide us with a future growth plan. The intention for me is to secure planning permission and then encourage occupier interest. I never build speculatively and always build-to-order. There is no opposition to the StadiArena idea from me personally or from others PROVIDING it can be funded and pre let."

I shared that view too and in truth, it was probably more my enthusiasm which drew some opposition.

The *Lancashire Telegraph* had already headlined the plans for the massive new development in July of 2007. £20 MILLION TURF DREAM it announced on its bold front page. A very arty impression adorned the front page complete with lawns and trees and fans in claret shirts. It all looked very ... er ... well ... artistic. State-of-the-art it said. The plan was to take three years to implement and would be completed in 2010. A brand new £10 million, 2,500-seater stand with hospitality boxes, would replace the old Cricket Field Stand. There would be a hotel, gymnasium, business centre, multi-storey car park, and restaurant. It would involve the adjacent cricket club; they would benefit with a new pavilion. The redevelopment would then move on to the Bob Lord Stand which would receive a thorough make-over including a multi-screen cinema. There would be a new club superstore, a supporters' bar and restaurant. Further around the ground in the corner there would be new dressing rooms and various media and administrative rooms in a new block built between two of the stands. All of this would take place over six phases.

Put it all together and it was seen as a vibrant way to re-generate the Turf Moor part of town. The cash would come from club directors, bank loans, private investment and grants. The completed scheme would be called the Burnley Sports and Leisure Village. The projection was that it would generate up to £3 million a year. Positive discussions had already taken place with ward councillors and the cricket club.

In conjunction with Brendan Flood the whole plan was reviewed once I'd become familiar with it. It occurred to me immediately that there was no market for a multi-screen cinema and that overall the money was being spread too thinly. My suggestion was to concentrate on the Cricket Field Stand and replace that with the StadiArena. Of course I made suggestions; it's what I had been brought in for. I introduced Robert Kennedy from Holmes Miller Glasgow who, in my view is the country's best stadium architect. He designs football stadiums for spectators and not to win awards. In recent years he has designed the KS Stadium Hull, The Walkers Stadium Leicester, The Pride Park Stadium Derby, The Ricoh Arena Coventry and the corner stand extension at Old Trafford.

Included in the Burnley redesign would be an integrated hotel with rooms that overlooked the pitch and that doubled on matchdays as private boxes. The changeover was easily implemented as we had demonstrated at Coventry. But then in order to generate funds that would help fund the whole project we had the idea to integrate not just a hotel but also private apartments. The concept was simple but stunning. As far as I was aware there was no stadium anywhere at that time that included private residences. I had the instant feeling that they would be snapped up by customers either private or business. Quality banqueting suites and exhibition areas are always needed and if they are promoted and marketed by a good team across the wider East Lancashire area the customers would come. Then there is the market for Asian weddings where on occasions there can be over 1,000 guests and Nelson very close to Burnley has a very large Asian population.

The StadiArena was the obvious suggestion. It would regenerate the area and bring functions and events that were varied and lucrative. How could it prosper in Burnley was the question? What kind of events? What were the markets? Who would the customers be? What about transport and parking? A whole array of answers was formulated. How could a small town of approximately 80,000 people support a venture like this? The key was transport and improved rail links to the Manchester area. The direct rail link needed to be resurrected. We began the campaign to have the rail link to Manchester known as the Todmorden Curve re-instated. The go-ahead for that has now been given.

Of course the costs went up. They increased from £20 million to £30 million, but much of that extra would come back from the sale of the apartments. You speculate to accumulate but it was not all plain sailing with the board and it was never a philosophy that was widely accepted. This was a board where traditionally caution had always outweighed ambition. There was opposition and scepticism. There were raised eyebrows at the sums of money involved. But it was the same scepticism from the same people that Brendan had encountered all along as he had tried to raise the bar and increase expectations. When he had joined the board he had made it clear he wasn't just there to tread water and remain in the comfort zone and eat four-course meals washed down with red wine in the boardroom every Saturday. He was not happy with mediocrity and contentment with a mid-table place. He did rub certain people up the wrong way because of his ambition and vision. He did make decisions on his own without consulting the board on several occasions. But why shouldn't he have? He was, after all, the operational director. He needed an ally and that was where I came in, willingly.

What made it more difficult was that after his bright early start, manager Owen Coyle had hit the buffers in the second part of the season. There were mumblings in the boardroom that his appointment had been an experiment and a gamble gone wrong; how on earth could a Scot with just three years' experience of Scottish management succeed in England? There was absolutely no indication of the success that was to come not much more than a year later. I don't know what gave Brendan more pleasure, the eventual promotion at Wembley or just proving the doubters wrong that Owen Coyle was a good appointment.

At the time of the announcement of the changes to the plans, and the news of the StadiArena being made public in February of 2008, there was no sign of the disaster waiting to hit Brendan's Modus business. It really was all systems go with planning applications and a clear timeframe of building works.

Let me also clarify another point about StadiArena. I owned the patent and along with partners The Cassidy Group we sold this patented technology under a licence fee of £750,000. I had arranged with the Cassidy's that the Burnley licence, as it was my old club, would be reduced to £250,000, a 66% reduction. Any profit from that which would be my share I would invest back into the club.

There's nothing palatial about the admin area at Turf Moor. My office was in the area up above the club shop and the ticketing area. On a clear day I could see across the corridor to the manager's room and various secretarial rooms. But up there was where I did everything I could to bring these development plans to a conclusion. The first signs of trouble came when Brendan told me he would probably not be taking on the chairmanship at the end of the season as he had hoped because of business pressures. I know that it had been a lifetime's ambition for him as he'd been a Claret since boyhood. The writing was therefore on the wall for any future stand development.

Brendan had already felt the vibes of change in the finance world in the summer of 2007; markets were changing, things were slowing, bankers were beginning to worry and he had already received intimations that a huge deal he was involved with was not quite as secure as he thought. He'd had a "doubtful tap on the shoulder," as he put it, from one of the banks.

By January 2008, and this was only the first month for me back at Burnley it was becoming more and more apparent in the business world that the banks were having problems. Nevertheless at that point there was still no sign of the utter immensity of the debacles to come, so on we went, with enthusiasm and optimism, with the development plans. I suppose the rest is history and well documented. There was financial chaos; getting money from banks was now as good as finished until things took an upturn. The upturn still hasn't arrived and although Brendan still had national business interests in property investment, private equity and shopping centre mall marketing, his development business, Modus Ventures Ltd, which was a national player having developed over £1 billion of commercial property since 1990, went into administration.

All StadiArena plans were put on hold. The Cricket Field Stand still stands there in urgent need of care and attention with its patched-up roof. And the doubters that saw the project as a white elephant I imagine breathed a sigh of relief and told themselves how right they had been. But football doesn't thrive on doubters. It thrives on visionaries like Brendan Flood. If the new facilities had been built I am confident that Brendan would have attracted new investors like himself, who would have been driven by the will to win.

# 10

# Clooney Tunes

Owen Coyle was a bit like Burnley when he was appointed as manager halfway through the 2007/08 season.

He was unfashionable.

As a player, he had enjoyed a short but distinguished career in the Premiership with Bolton Wanderers, had flitted from club to club in Scotland, plying his trade, drinking Irn Bru, speaking so fast no-one knew what he was talking about, scoring goals wherever he went; rarely settling for long and then learning his trade as a manager in the quiet backwaters of St Johnstone in the Scottish League Division One.

From that point of view he was just like Burnley – an outsider. When the club had to find a replacement for Steve Cotterill in November 2007, he entered the fray quite late after a recommendation from Phil Gartside, the Bolton Wanderers chairman. Quite why Gartside should be carrying a torch for Owen Coyle was never clear at the time of the appointment. Conspiracy theories abound now amongst Burnley supporters that Gartside's ploy was to get Owen into English football so that he could see how he would fare. If he proved himself he could one day offer him the Bolton job. That was the suspicion. How ridiculous. Funnily enough not much more than two years later when he'd seen how good Owen was he offered Owen the Bolton job. Funny that – thought some Burnley fans.

Brendan told me that this is how the Owen Coyle appointment materialised: "Owen's CV was firstly emailed to me by Alan Nixon and I rang Owen one night to discuss his interest in the job. I really liked him and thought his attitude matched the culture we were trying to create at BFC. The following day I got a text from Phil Gartside who suggested that we might want to have a look at Owen Coyle. I rang Phil and said that it was strange to receive his text as I'd spoken to Owen only the night before. He was very complimentary about Owen and this helped the referencing process.

"Barry was booked to go to Scotland so I asked him to meet Owen, which he did and quite liked him so we arranged a further meeting a few days later. Owen called me straight after the Barry meeting for a further discussion and it was clear that he was a very positive manager with a winning attitude.

"On the shortlist were Paul Jewell, Peter Reid, Steve Davies (Barry's choice) and Owen Coyle.

"I met Paul Jewell on the morning that Barry met Owen and felt that he would be too challenging for us ... high wage demands and transfer fee demands. Peter Reid heard that we had gone quiet on Jewell so thought he was the favourite, but Owen was always my favourite, once we had spoken."

Owen was only halfway home when his mobile rang (hands free of course). That night he crossed the Scottish border, without any of our sheep as far as we know, as the new manager of Burnley Football Club. It was a bold appointment made by two football men with local, community and family values. Both their hearts resided deep within Turf Moor. They were bombarded with responses. *"Owen who ... what do we know about him ... where's his experience ... what does he know about English football ... why not a big name manager ... what on earth have you two done ... this will all end badly ... in tears."*

And so the mutterers muttered; and those who dwelled in the zone of 'take-no-risks' shook their heads. Barry and Brendan crossed their fingers hoping they'd found the guy to "light the touchpaper and entertain." And Brendan described him rather rashly as the new Bill Shankly.

It did end in tears of course, twice actually. Once at Wembley for good reasons, when there was that memorable day in the play-off final; and then again, when he unexpectedly walked out just seven months later. But all that was ages away. Actually no, it was only a little over two years. But what a two years they were.

*****

One of Owen's earliest jobs was to locate the club's missing blimp. The club had an airship-style blimp made up and it was tethered to one of the perimeter walls. It was rather a nice blimp and was due to make its debut before a home game against QPR. It had been bought to promote home games flying high in the sky so that people would look up and say, "Ooooh there's the blimp, there must be a game." Bob Lord had done the same thing not with a blimp but by switching on the floodlights early when there was an evening game. The idea was that just like moths, the supporters would be attracted by the lights. But now there was a more spectacular idea. This blimp was 20-foot long and helium-filled. This was no small thing.

"Where's our blimp?" someone asked one morning. We all looked at each other. "Fastened to the car park wall," someone answered.

"Oh no it isn't," came the reply. We looked at each other. How could a twenty-foot blimp vanish?

Everyone went out to the car park to look. It had gone. The ropes had been cut and filled with best quality helium the thing had clearly floated up in the heavens. There was some choice language as it became obvious that this could only have been the work of vandals. And it wasn't insured.

The last person to see it claimed it was heading east but the Met Office when contact was made said that winds from the south-east would have taken it north-west. The only solution seemed to be to ask the new manager to ring his Scottish friends to keep an eye open for it as it headed into Scotland.

"Better alert the police," someone suggested.

"And air-traffic control," someone else said. The gang looked at that person with incredulity.

"Air traffic control, don't be f*****g daft."

"OK then who'll take the blame then when it brings down a small light aircraft. Can't you see the news headlines – Burnley FC blimp responsible for air disaster ... and what if it lands on Ewood?"

Traffic control was alerted pronto-quick.

We noticed early on how easy Owen was with the media. He was comfortable in front of a camera. He was articulate and could turn on the smile and the gleaming white teeth. There's a scene in the film *The Great Race*. Tony Curtis is the smooth, stylish, sophisticated lead hero. He's dressed all in white, turns to the camera, smiles, his face fills the screen, and his teeth flash and glint just once. The first time I saw it I roared with laughter. I tried it in the mirror to see if I could do it. You half expected Owen's teeth to do the same when he smiled. He loved the comparison with George Clooney. It was fact that there was strong resemblance. The only evidence of this was the word of just one female Burnley fan. But she had said it, therefore it must be fact. He was like that. The representative sample of one was the solid indisputable evidence. His will to win and compete whether it was five-a-side, or table tennis or just a quiz was so intense that he would twist and distort things until he was the declared winner. This was never in any unpleasant way; it was just that he wore you down with his competitiveness. And boy was he fit. It must have been the Irn-Bru "the drink made from girders".

His philosophy of fairness and equal treatment was intense. Whether you were a big star or a young kid starting out in the game his treatment and attitudes were just the same. It was illustrated once when Martin Dobson called me over to the youth centre. Martin was passionate about his role with the youths. He'd once been let free by Bolton years earlier when he was only 18 and remembered only too well that young lads could often be released too early. His job was to get the production line started again at Burnley. There was a good crop of youngsters coming through and we had five apprentices. They were all good but one in particular stood out as outstanding to the point where you might have thought he could well be the next Georgie Best. All apprentices are treated the same at Burnley and they get something like £200 a week. But, Martin had received a call from a relative of the lad who stood out and Martin wanted to sound me out about the uncle suggesting the lad receive £400 a week. Our thoughts were the same. If this lad was the next Drogba what's an extra £200 a week to keep him at the club? Maybe we should give it to him.

I suggested we talk it through with the manager. We did. His reply was instant and unequivocal. "Under no circumstances, he doesn't get one penny more than the others. If he's chasing the money at 17 he'll never make it in football. I'm happy to lose him tomorrow if that's the case. I know he's a brilliant prospect but if he's chasing the money he won't make it. The best thing the lad can do is knuckle down and if he shows his worth, only then will he be a hell of a player. I'm happy to speak with his uncle but he is not getting a penny more." We stuck by the decision. Two weeks later the lad signed – for £200 a week.

Much later, in fact before the Premiership season when we did a second tour to the USA, his adherence to the principle of fairness showed itself for the umpteenth time. Again there were comments that it was a waste of money although it's not unusual for the big clubs to make over a million pounds profit from these tours when they can name their price with sponsors. If LA Galaxy hadn't pulled out of a game we too would have made a few quid. At the time we regarded these trips as ways of making contact with a source of talent that might have served us well. In the end it came to nothing but it might have done. You can't spend your life thinking I'm not doing that because it might not work, when there's just as much chance that it might. I had a philosophy of being positive and forever optimistic. Brendan was the same. Sometimes you take calculated risks and that's not quite the same as gambling recklessly.

However, we'd booked the flights and we felt that the trip would be worthwhile this time playing games along the West Coast region of the USA ending in Portland. What a massive boost for staff and players we thought. The excitement was terrific. Unfortunately somewhere, somehow, there was a mix-up with the tickets and we ended up with 30 economy class seats and just four in club class. We mulled this over but as soon as Owen came into the equation he made the decision. "I'm not travelling club class, that's unfair. We will hold a ballot so that everyone has an equal chance of a decent seat. But I'm in economy," he insisted.

One of the papers did a parody of how we travelled and compared it with Man United and their private jets and luxury buses. We went economy and hired self-drive mini buses. Owen sat in his economy seat with his economy team and plotted how to have a first-class season in the Premier League (economically).

The Andy Gray saga was a real test for club and Owen. It is reasonable to suppose in my first months there he was tapped up and before any official offer was received he was clearly made aware he could earn far more at Charlton than he could at Burnley. At Burnley he had got his career back on track and was scoring goals. It wasn't unreasonable to think he might have been grateful and shown just a little loyalty to Burnley. But the loyalty that I knew in the 70s was long gone. He'd had a stunning game at Charlton and they must have thought there and then, "Hmm he could do a job for us, let's sound him out, or at least his dad Frank." Frank Gray was then on the phone to the club as often as BT ring me at home to ask would I like to come back. Except, whereas I usually tell BT to bugger off, there wasn't quite this same option with the Grays. When a player is anxious to go and declares just before a game that his head isn't right and can't play, you do the only thing. Which Owen did; he sent him from the training ground with a flea in his ear. We got some decent money for him but we then had no centre-forward.

Supporters were stunned with the replacement from Sunderland, the legend that was Andy Cole. Wow! What a strike duo, Andrew Cole and Ade Akinbiyi. Away at QPR they were unplayable and Burnley won 4 – 1. Andrew scored a hat-trick and Ade the other. Ade was another who prospered at Burnley. There's just something about this club that players respond to. It's the Arkwrights of football, the corner shop football club that's homely and friendly and where you can get away from the glare of fame. It was a remarkable night.

Andrew filled the gap, chipped in with the odd goal, showed his class on several occasions, taught the young kids at the club a few things simply by being there, and then gave us the best entertainment we'd seen at Turf Moor since Chico and his performing dogs and then Bertie Bee rugby tackled a streaker (just google Bertie Bee tackles a streaker on YouTube).

Andrew's sideshow came in the penultimate game of the season at home to Cardiff City. The crowd was down to not much more than 10,500. Fans were thinking that this new guy Coyle was nothing special. Nothing had happened to make people believe in any kind of "new dawn." Burnley was once labelled Grumpytown by former player Tommy Hutchison (and he was a crowd favourite so he had no axe to grind). At the end of Owen's first season in charge it was living up to that label.

It was clear that the current team needed change. It was in need of additional pace and power. It had so far been a season of gifted goals and bloopers of the sort that TV companies make Christmas DVD's. The Cardiff game would provide more. Meanwhile to add atmosphere to the ground there'd been a suggestion that we should have a big drum and someone banging it through a game to raise the excitement levels, a bit like the one at Sheffield Wednesday. The media department organised a secret online ballot for the fans to send their opinions and votes. It was a resounding "no." The best response was from Dave Thomas.

"Great idea but don't f*****g put it next to me."

Out came Cardiff for the game and I wondered how on earth have this lot reached this year's Cup Final? My opinion didn't change during the game. Actually it turned out to be the game with everything and those who stayed away missed a treat. It had a sleepy first period with some bits of nice tippy-tappy passing, a few bouts of head tennis and an occasional burst-through by a Burnley forward to keep us awake – just. During the lulls we had the chance to read the programme, admire the excellent free gift booklet the club gave away, and Martin Barnes' lovely fanzine, *When the Ball Moves*. Then, just when you thought this might be a tame draw Burnley scored when Graham Alexander rifled home a crisp shot. When we fashioned a superb second goal in the second half you could have been forgiven for thinking we'd end with a nice home win. It was Andrew Cole who got the second.

Home win? You must be joking. Cardiff were gifted a tame penalty. Then they equalised from a defender's goof from which the ball was rocketed home before you could blink. Bit by bit the game was livening up now and when Clarke Carlisle scored a third as the ball ping-ponged round in the Cardiff box you thought this must now be a home win. But, next up it was a Burnley own goal to level the game. So: we'd gifted them a daft penalty, given them a goal from a blooper, and scored an own goal. Only at Burnley, you might say.

But still the entertainment wasn't over on what had turned out to be a cracking afternoon. Whether there'd been some niggling going on between them during the afternoon we don't know, but next up was a major incident between our Andrew and their Darren Purse. There was what looked to be an X certificate tackle between them with each of them looking a tad reckless, although TV later showed Cole to be entirely innocent. There was a crumpled heap on the floor from which Cole emerged pointing to his leg. He showed it to the ref and anyone else around who was interested. Purse stayed down. Cole was livid. Marching to the touchline the leg was examined by management, medical staff and forensics. Purse got up, limped, and received a red card.

So: Cole is on the touchline and Purse is walking off and disappears up the tunnel. Suddenly Andrew sees not a red card but the red mist and the next thing we see is him legging it off the field in hot pursuit of Purse. By now the game has restarted but all spectators' eyes are on Cole moving so fast he is but a blur. It isn't rocket science to suppose that he is off to lamp Purse. Suddenly half the Cardiff bench realise what Cole is intent on doing and they too all leap up and chase after Cole. Next, half the Burnley bench are on their feet and racing off the field to chase the Cardiff bench who are chasing Cole who is chasing Purse. All it needed was for Benny Hill to emerge, being chased by 15 buxom girls and the folly would be complete.

Meanwhile the game continues. Spectators watch agog the mouth of the tunnel and listen and wait for sparks to fly and the sounds of fists on chins and knees in groins. In all their years of watching football they'd never seen anything like it, we all agree. By now police and stewards have run up the tunnel. We wait for developments and all this has happened in the space of just a few seconds. There can't have been anything funnier since the Keystone Cops. As Ken Bates once said, "I haven't laughed so much since grandma got her tits caught in the mangle."

It quietened down. One by one the different groups emerged and returned to the field; all bar Cole and Purse. The game petered out. Cole was named man of the match. Owen later remarked he hadn't seen anything to beat it. Supporters were all agreed. When Cole ran off to thump Purse it was the fastest they'd seen him run all season. On radio Andrew confessed to running after Purse with one thought in mind, to deck the muppet.

"If I play two games next season I hope it is home and away to Cardiff." Season ticket sales went up immediately.

By the end of the season Kyle Lafferty had decided he wanted to end his Burnley hell. He was both a hero and a villain in the eyes of the fans, he always appeared as though he was in the shop window looking for a buyer. There had been particularly unpleasant abuse and barracking in an away game at Blackpool. He had fired his own verbal replies back at the fans and thus disobeyed the unwritten rule that no matter how bad the jibes, players don't answer back.

And so the season ended. The last game was a disaster with a 0 – 5 defeat away at Crystal Palace, hardly Real Madrid. It was a shambles of a performance. The supporters were not best pleased. The grumblers in the boardroom were now louder and convinced Owen's appointment had been a poor choice. Owen said he felt physically sick on the way home. The signs of all the economic ills that would cause the StadiArena plans to be abandoned, were gathering ominously.

Talk about the new development that I had been working on for 12 months had hit a sudden silence. Brendan looked as though he wouldn't take up his option to buy more shares and step up to chairman. This was welcomed by some on the board, but not by me as in my experience clubs need visionaries on the board, not plodders.

Brendan could sense the downturn was looming, he told me sometime later: "The economy was softening but I hadn't felt the pain until Lehman's went bust in September and the banking crisis became overwhelming. My option on Barry Kilby's shares was signed early in 2007 and was exercisable in summer 2011. I was quite happy to let Barry enjoy his status in the meantime, but most of the operational responsibility became mine. Probably the best way to describe me was as a national businessman and the other directors as local businessmen. The difference I tried to bring was teamwork, ambition and belief. And I used my contacts and relationship skills to get better quality players and management into Burnley".

Owen's first few months at the club had hardly taken the place by storm. The doom-mongers on the board were pointing their fingers and mumbling, "We told you so, we told you so, this is not working out, this could be a gamble gone wrong." Centre-forward Gray had as good as walked out. Andrew Cole didn't want to stay any longer. Starlet (in his own mind) Kyle Lafferty was also wanting away, fed up of supporters' criticisms and jibes, with his head turned by attention from Wolves and Rangers. We had a trip to America that the stick-in-the-muds said was just an extravagance. The club was haemorrhaging money every month. There had been a defeat in the third round of the FA Cup, albeit to Arsenal.

And to cap all that lot, we still had no blimp. All we had was some grainy CCTV footage, a constant source of amusement on YouTube, with pictures of a numpty setting it free with his pals' giggles in the background. Just google, "Burnley Blimp gone missing," to see it rising into the blue yonder.

With all that on our minds, four of us set out in May to firm up the America trip itinerary. It was good to get away. If we'd had the contacts we'd have contacted a film crew to make one of those road movies *Four Men in a Car*.

# 11

# Riding Along in My Automobile ...

In May of 2008 we headed west across the pond to put the finishing touches to a summer tour over there. "What a waste of money," was the reaction from some corners of the boardroom. "Just make sure it pays for itself." I used to wonder sometimes if one or two of them had ever been beyond Morecambe. There was a big bright world outside of Burnley but you had to carry on past Rawtenstall to find it.

Brendan, who was still firing on all cylinders, wanted to explore the USA and develop relationships over there. He already had one or two contacts. In terms of fixing up games two out of the three destinations were successful. Richmond was the odd one out. We met the top guy from Richmond for a key meeting in the company photocopying room. Seven of us nearly passed out in the heat. Puddles of sweat gathered on the floor. When he said Richmond's most successful ever player was Lindsay Roberts, a woman, we blinked eyebrows at each other in a kind of Morse code that said, "Let's hit the road." It sure was one helluva photocopier though. But we did arrange games against Carolinas Railhawks and Minnesota Thunder.

There were four of us undertaking this memorable trip along the interstates visiting Richmond, Carolina and Minnesota to arrange games and meet people. There was an extra trip to Washington that we tagged on and from there we could fly home. The USA is a growing source of football talent. Get in there early and maybe links could be established, we thought. Earlier in the trip Brendan had casually asked, did I have my driving licence and I didn't give it much thought. When it was time to get to Washington, instead of a taxi, a large clumsy eight-seater people carrier arrived. Brendan sorted out the paperwork; we loaded up the luggage in the back. Next thing I see is Brendan striding towards me with the car keys. Next, he folds down the large rear seats to make two recliners, one for him and one for Barry. They jumped into them and looked as smug as two proverbial Cheshire cats. Sandy Stewart quietly got into the front passenger seat and they were all set.

Except me, Joe Muggins, "Where's the driver?" I asked naively.

"He's here," Brendan replied smiling. "It's you. You're the only one who has a licence. Wake us up when we get to Washington."

You know how it is when your mouth drops open and for a moment you are stunned. Well, that was me.

We sang the iconic Chuck Berry classic several times along the way. What a shame I didn't take the ukulele; but what an opportunity to regale a captive audience with tales from the 70s, and my most memorable moments (while they were awake). One of the first was the story of my Under-23 international caps, especially the one against France. It's one I found hard to forget. And I was determined they wouldn't either. Strapped in, sitting comfortably, me driving (I swear blind they all forgot their driving licences on purpose), I began the tales ... and the miles sped by along those wide US roads.

We could have used Amtrak or Greyhound buses but a car seemed a better way to see the place. The Interstate 95 we drove along was pretty much non-stop urban and industrial sprawl, mile after mile of soulless concrete and giant trucks. Find the minor roads off it and you were in the heart of US Civil War battlefield country; in fact Richmond was the capital of the Confederacy. Fredericksburg was about halfway along the journey with the 95 skirting round it. The whole area was steeped in colonial history with pretty towns, architectural gems and picturesque old housing from the previous age of the 18th and 19th centuries. Alas we saw little of it. So I plodded on with my football tales.

"Way back sometime in 1973, I think it was; I played in one of the strangest games imaginable. I was on tour with the England Under-23s along with my Burnley room-mate and great friend Alan Stevenson who was picking up yet more international caps. The tour which lasted 10 days featured games against Turkey, Portugal, Belgium and then finally France in Lyon. At the end of this tour Alan and I had to leg it over from Lyon to Cherbourg to catch the QE2 and join the rest of the Burnley team on a three-week tour of the Caribbean along with Jimmy Adamson and Bob Lord. Bob loved his cruises alright. It was a reward for winning promotion at the end of season 1972/73.

"I hadn't played in the first couple of games because Bob Latchford of Everton had the number 9 shirt, but for the Belgium game, it was my turn. This would be my third cap and what a pantomime it turned out to be. After 15 minutes and with the score still 0 – 0 the centre-half swung out his arm and smacked me in the face while the ball was at the other end of the field. Not one official saw it and the England physio led me off with blood streaming down my face from a broken nose. In those days a broken nose, lost teeth, black eyes and even the odd spell of unconsciousness were all part and parcel of combat between centre-forwards and centre-halves. And that was in the warm-up.

"I was aware that broken noses come in two packages. One, there was a depressed fracture like from a direct blow flattening the nose inwards like boxers get; two, a side fracture, a simple break either to the right or left. Through my career I have had the distinction of four broken noses courtesy of John McGrath, Mickey Droy, Jim Thomson in a training accident, and finally the one in Belgium. All of them had been simple fractures so I had got away lightly. It's the depressed fractures that leave you with a nose like a squashed sausage roll (Google: 'Steve Bruce' to see what I mean). Despite all these calamities I had managed to keep my own looks intact.

"When I finally got back to the dressing room, the physio called the doctor. I looked at my face in the mirror. My nose was now positioned beneath my right eye. It was a clean break, but a real mess. The doctor looked concerned and I asked how long it would take to straighten it as I was desperate to get back on the field. By God we were tough as old boots back then. He looked panic-stricken and told me that it was a bad break and he could do nothing, that I would have to get back home and have it straightened by a surgeon. I was more taken aback by that than the sight of the nose and all the blood. I explained to him that I had to get it sorted as in four days there was the QE2 to catch. He suggested I cancel that and book myself into a hospital back at home.

"'Miss the cruise trip – you must be joking,' I thought.

"At half-time Alan Stevenson was first back to the dressing room to see how I was. He took one look at the nose and fell about laughing and told me I looked like "bloody Quasimodo". He asked when it would be straightened. When I said nobody would straighten it he looked puzzled and realised he was going to lose his room-mate on the Caribbean cruise. There was then a long silence whilst he was thinking. Quietly he told me to wait a couple of minutes and follow him to the toilets – AND HE WOULD STRAIGHTEN IT!

"Oh God I had two minutes to decide whether to go back to Burnley and miss the cruise, or let Dr Stephenson perform cosmetic surgery on it in the toilets. Three weeks in the sun won the day.

"In the dressing room lying around were some wooden hammers and various tools for fixing studs in the soles of our boots. On one table was a particularly large wooden mallet. Stevo picked up the mallet and a towel. I found him in a cubicle waiting for me with a large grin on his face. So, there I was sat on the loo. There he was in front of me towel wrapped around one hand; and a mallet in the other. He used the hand wrapped in the towel as a block and then smartly and cleanly whacked my nose twice with the mallet. He stood back and admired his handiwork. To my astonishment he had done a fantastic job. No, he hadn't moved it over to the left side of my face; it sat nicely now where it should be, not perfectly straight, but a great improvement. Red and swollen of course but nicely in the middle of my face above my mouth. Almost perfection.

"Whilst he ran back out with the team I sat there and recovered. A few minutes later out I went and there was the doctor who had declined to do anything. He looked astonished.

"'My fred 'Tevo did dis. All he had was a habber ad dow by doze is better,' I told him. 'You could have dud it for yourself'. He went ape-shit and rushed off to look for the official international tour administrator."

Everyone in the car thought this was the end of the story and breathed a sigh of relief. They thought this was some sort of made-up tall tale. As if anyone had ever had a broken nose mended by a wooden mallet in a toilet cubicle ... ridiculous ... but I hadn't finished.

"Now this is where the story becomes quite strange. Over the next couple of days my nose and both eyes turned black and blue. There was no way I could play in the next game. So out I went that night for a meal and a couple of bottles of wine with West Brom director Bert Millichip who was in charge of the tour. We had another few drinks and got in after midnight. Back at the hotel I slept like a baby, woke, dressed, had a huge full English breakfast and went out to enjoy the 80 degree sunshine and lay down on a grassy bank behind the stadium, with a pile of refreshments and a large bottle of lemonade, and watched a ladies football match – a prelude to the Under-23 international.

"At half-time we were drawing 1 – 1 and I was turning a nice colour of pink, Ken Furphy who was managing the team, came rushing out to find me relaxing in the sunshine. All the subs had been used except Mervyn Day the West Ham goalkeeper. There was no one to replace Bob Latchford who had come off suffering from the heat. Ken astonished me. There was no-one but me to take Bob's place. It was a friendly so I could be used as an extra sub. I looked at him horrified. There I was face swollen and blackened, filled up with two bottles of wine from the night before, a large breakfast, and several cans of coke and lemonade I'd swigged down in the sweltering heat. And would I play for England? I couldn't believe it.

"And so that was how I won my fourth and last cap for England. And still the best was yet to come. The French had gone 2 – 1 up but on 78 minutes Charlie George floated over a great cross, I soared like a tin of John West, and bulleted the header home for the equaliser. I felt f*****g marvellous, I could have run all day. I couldn't remember feeling so fit and bubbling with energy. At that point Trevor Francis felt the heat and went off.

"On comes Mervyn Day and goes in goal and, guess who; Dr Stevo, with my blood still on his hands, comes out of goal to play up front with me. I'd have been better having my wife alongside me but Alan fancied himself (honestly) as a real fancy-Dan outfield player. He was determined to lay on a second goal for me. 'Now listen Quasimodo,' he said, 'get your arse into that box and I'll send over a 'floater' that even you can't miss'. He proceeded then to do the most astonishing thing.

"He got the ball inside his own half. He went on a bewildering dribble. He went past one man. He went past another. He broke forward. He chased the ball. He was suddenly in the penalty area and he had only the goalkeeper to beat. But: instead of shooting he decided to feed me the ball so I could score. And there it all went wrong. He completely missed his kick, somehow catching one leg behind the other tripping himself up, and fell flat on his face. The French goalkeeper looked at Alan laughing on the floor like he was a dipstick. The ball trickled out for a goal-kick. And that's how I missed out on a second international goal.

"How about that then? My pre match preparation was the worst imaginable. But I scored an equaliser. The nose was fixed and we headed for Cherbourg to catch up with the QE2.

"And I swear all that is a true story," I told my passengers by now desperate for the next diner and food. "I'll tell you later about Mickey Droy and his size 12 feet."

It was a moderate drive from Richmond to Washington we were making. Put your foot down and the commuters did it in two hours. I preferred to be more leisurely and talk football. I had an audience of three, and they couldn't get away. I guess the subject of hard men must have come up and the name Tommy Smith, the legendary Liverpool player, was the first that came to mind. There were a few around at the time, Billy Bonds, Norman Hunter, Ron Harris, Johnny Giles, and our very own Colin Waldron. But Tommy Smith was a man to make grown men go weak at the knees if they saw him on the team-sheet. And he was always on the team-sheet. In a very early game when Steve Kindon was just starting in the game, he reduced Steve (a big lad don't forget), to a gibbering wreck and gave him a rude awakening to the joys of professional football. In his innocence Steve had gone up to the referee and said, "Please Mr Referee, that nasty man there says he's going to break my legs."

There'd been one game at Burnley when I'd gone hammer and tongs with Emlyn Hughes doing my best to wind him up. At one corner I'd gone in hard on what I thought was him and laid him out, except it wasn't him it was, oh God, the terrifying Tommy Smith I'd got by mistake. I was horrified when I saw what I'd done. Tommy was so hard that Vlad the Impaler and Attila the Hun paled into insignificance. You messed with him at your peril and oh God I'd whacked him. I saw him rubbing his head whilst he stared at me. "You're finished Fletch in this game as soon as I get the chance to do you," he muttered with a menacing Scouse accent, eyes narrowing. And he meant it. He turned to the ref and said, "Ref, please don't send him off."

I spent the rest of that game playing every trick I knew to keep out of his way or to make sure that the referee was nearby if Tommy and me were ever close together. We won 2 – 1 and I came off in one piece thoroughly relieved. Tommy was a one-off and a Liverpool legend and funnily enough years later I came to act for him on behalf of the PFA. My passengers didn't know that. They were about to hear all about it. I began with a bit of general talk:

"It was a very physical game in the 1970s and players of opposing sides went out to hurt each other. You didn't need shin pads as much as a suit of armour. Normally, it might just be a broken nose, a cut eye, an elbow in ribs, or a kick in the shins. All of them hurt, but they were part and parcel of the game. The worst injuries were not these. They were the self-inflicted injuries, twisted knees, sprained ankle, or pulled muscles. The worst was often a 'bad back' or a 'stiff neck'. There was never anything to see, no swelling, no blood, no bruising so the manager accused you of swinging the lead. Often, as a forward or centre-half you'd spend a lot of time heading. Next day you'd wake up with a stiff neck. If it happened on a Saturday morning you kept quiet. But it could certainly affect your performance. You'd grit your teeth and get on with it but many a time I'd like to have carried a placard around with me onto the pitch; *My back is bloody killing me, that's why I'm not playing well today.*"

"It was a time when over the top tackles were quite deliberate; you knew who the culprits were as well. But, there was just as much chance of hurting yourself if you set out to damage someone else.

"One of the worst injuries of my career was a complete accident. I was leading Burnley's front line at White Hart Lane sprinting (ha ha) in front of their centre-half Mike England (Welshman actually). As he chased me (and someone chasing me was quite unusual in those days), he tripped and as he fell he put his hands on my shoulders and we both fell to the floor. It was a clear free kick and I felt a slight click in my right knee. As the game continued it began to get quite uncomfortable. I didn't know it then but what followed would be six years of pain and frustration and ice-packs. Today, with immediate attention, replacement by the sub, diagnosis, and scanning, I'd have been back in the stand before Mike England even got his booking, and there were no fancy yellow cards then. But, the one sub was already on, we were doing quite well, and so I played on. It wouldn't happen to Balotelli, he'd be wrapped up in cotton wool before he hit the floor. At this time we were doing well in the (now Premier) league and I wanted to keep playing.

"For me though it was a moment that affected me for the rest of my career. On the train home after the victory my knee began to swell. By Monday the knee had ballooned up and I had to have the fluid removed at Burnley General Hospital. It hadn't locked, so there was the assumption that there was no torn cartilage, and by Thursday I could just about walk. By Friday I could jog which meant that with cortisone and pain killers I'd be fit for Saturday. No way would this happen today. I did this for a further six months before finally breaking down. Every Sunday morning I was expected at the hospital to have the fluid drained. How convenient it would have been to do this at home but it needed a germ-free environment (since when have hospitals been germ free?) If any infection got in it could have been truly serious – as if it wasn't serious enough as I crawled around the house.

"Surprise, surprise, what did they eventually find but a torn cartilage. And by this time I'd done so much damage they could have put me in a jar and used me as a specimen. Two days after the operation I was feeling dreadful and had a high temperature. This was not normal for a routine operation such as this. I now had an infection in the knee joint, fancy that.

"I was 25 years old and in my prime (don't laugh), several months out injured and not much progress. It was decided to send me down to Harley Street to see a specialist. Apparently they knew what they were doing down there – they said. Harry Potts came with me; Jimmy Adamson had been sacked and Harry was now back at the club. Believe it or not the consultant brought in the biggest needle I'd ever seen. I thought this is a joke; they're filming a Monty Python sketch. But no, he came over and plunged this monster needle into the knee. The room went dizzy and my eyes filled with tears. I think I screamed. This is why Harley Street rooms are soundproofed.

"He hadn't finished. Next came another contraption that looked like a bicycle pump. I was surprised. I thought these guys came in Rolls and Bentleys not on a bicycle. He attached this to the needle in my knee. By this time I was seeing stars. Next he blew it up to expand the joint to get a better X-ray view. It was at this stage I passed out.

After two hours and me back in some semblance of awareness the specialist sat with Harry and me and gave his judgement.

"I'm very sorry sir, your knee is in a very poor condition and if you continue to play, you may if you are lucky last two weeks. I'm afraid your playing career is over."

Ever flippant I replied. "OK that's Harry sorted, what about me then?"

"So there I was. I had a limp and a bloody sore knee. On the scrapheap of soccer, in the prime of my career, on the verge of an England call-up, and only six months left on the contract."

(The passengers in the car were still awake to my surprise. One of them, cheeky sod, asked what time would I get to the bit about the PFA?)

Before he was sacked Jimmy Adamson was great and kept me going. "Just see out your contract," he said, "Come down and do some light training." It kept me feeling involved even though I didn't do much training. But then, after a couple of months, one Friday morning before a game against Aston Villa away, Frank Casper picked up a last minute injury. Five other first-team players were injured. Jimmy was stuck. "Fletch will you play tomorrow, what do you have to lose?" I played. We drew 1 – 1 and I played on for another six years. But: it wasn't quite the same. I could still head the ball but after every match I needed three days to recover. The cortisone and the pain killers lasted for a long time.

At the time you don't realise (and probably don't care) about the long-term effects of cortisone and painkillers. All you think about is the next game, you are desperate to play, getting through that and keeping your place, and then the next one, then the season, and then you hope a new contract will drop through the letter-box in June. Today I still suffer as a result of all those injections. My right knee was so badly damaged over a period of 20 years; it causes me to walk with a slight limp today. In turn that has worn away my left hip as I have tried to compensate. In hindsight, if I knew then what I knew now, would I have allowed the doctor to keep pumping me with painkillers just so that I could play the next game? Yes, yes and yes again I would. The pain I've had over the years is well compensated by the pleasure and great times I had as a player.

"And now the PFA bit," I told the passengers.

"One evening after I had retired, some ten years later, I was at the hospital for a check-up and somebody asked, "Do you get any industrial injury benefit?" I didn't and it was something I had never even thought about. I was aware if you got certain types of injuries it was possible to claim certain benefits but I'd never come across industrial injury benefits. I was (and still am) in touch with my old team-mate Geoff Nulty. He too had to retire because of an injury that resulted from a tackle by Liverpool player, Jimmy Case, in an Everton versus Liverpool derby game. Geoff was an extremely intelligent and well-read guy and I asked him if he claimed industrial injury benefits? "No, he replied. "What's that?"

"At this point in time my weekly income had halved and I had the princely sum of £20,000 in the bank, largely from a testimonial year. But there was a thing called a mortgage to pay. Luxury Street was not the name of our road. Geoff, after a pay-off from Everton and a court case against Jimmy Case was far better off. I suspect today owning half of Prescot, just outside Liverpool, and he is in the millionaire bracket.

"After a couple of weeks he rang me back. He'd been looking into the situation and two things seemed significant. Firstly throughout my entire football career I had paid national insurance contributions, and secondly I had (as had Geoff) received an injury 'at work.' We both, politely, put in a claim, turned up for an assessment and then before you could say, "A cheque will do nicely thank you," we were rudely shown the door. This really riled Geoff and he was livid.

"That's it," he stormed. "They've pissed me off so we're now going to claim for every ailment and bone known to medical science over the next six months. We'll get to the bottom of this and they'll be bloody sick of us by the time we've finished." This was nothing to do with money or benefits. We had our pecker up. There was a principle at stake. The 'system' didn't seem to recognise footballers with gammy knees and hips. It was wrong. How many ex-players were being denied justifiable benefits? Over the coming weeks we put claim after claim in simply to find out how this system worked and to understand the mechanics of making successful claims. We became experts and specialists in the procedure and we started to advise a few colleagues about how to make a claim.

"Many of the people we advised had genuine knee, hip and ankle injuries at a time when there were no great riches in the game and several of them had fallen on hard times. The payment of up to £30 a week made a real difference.

"After 12 months I took a call from Gordon Taylor. He'd been at Bolton years earlier with me and he was now chief executive of the Professional Footballers' Association. He'd heard that I'd had some success with these claims and asked if I'd represent more of his ex-players who had come to the PFA for help. Some of them were desperate cases and had no idea how the system worked.

"Over the next six years I represented 76 ex-players and won 75 of the claims that went to tribunal. The only one I lost was for ex-Blackburn centre-half Dick Mulvaney who was in a terrible state when I went to see him at his home in Scotland. His problem was that he had stood in the 'wall' when Bobby Charlton took a free kick. As he turned his head the ball hit him flush on his right ear. By some fluke chance the impact 'injected' fertiliser from the grass into the ear. Over the next few years it began to eat away into his skull. When I saw him in his small cottage up in Scotland he hadn't been out of the house for five years for fear of infection and was totally housebound while his wife went out to work. If that isn't an industrial injury, I don't know what is, but the application was turned down because there were no criteria in the DHSS manual. It was only the PFA funds that helped Dick. I was pleased to help him even though he had kicked me all over the field on many occasions in the 1970s.

"Some of the others I represented were Kevin Reeves, Ian Greaves, Jim Montgomery, Nat Lofthouse my old manager, Tony Hateley, Wyn 'The leap' Davies my schoolboy idol, Roy Hartle one of the hardest ever full-backs known to man, and the most fascinating of all, Tommy Smith.

"Blimey Tommy Smith," said a voice from the back seat. "At long last, you started telling this story 40 miles ago."

"Tommy Smith then: A team of top Liverpool lawyers had represented Tommy and lost the case even though Tommy had more aching bones than all the rest of us put together. Shankly was ruthless. If you were injured at Liverpool he didn't want to know. So, players went out there when they'd no right to be even standing up. If not, they lost their place to whoever was waiting in the wings; it was as simple as that. By this time I understood how the system worked to the letter and I appealed the case with one last chance to persuade the tribunal that Tommy deserved his injury benefits. So here was the irony. This man who'd kicked us all black and blue for the last 10 years was happy to accept help in winning an industrial injury claim after he'd dished out industrial injuries to scores of us.

"I soon realised why the lawyers had lost his case. Because Tommy's knees were riddled with arthritis and totally knackered; they had claimed for 'wear and tear' which in the 80s was not accepted as an industrial injury. It was ridiculous that typists could claim for wear and tear under the guise of repetitive strain injury, but professional footballers could not claim for wear and tear in their knees.

"Before I put the appeal in, I booked Tommy in with a specialist for some X-rays to see the full extent of the damage. The surgeon was immediately alarmed when he studied the X-rays. To me the inside of his knees looked like a bag of crisps. The specialist was taken aback, "Bloody hell Tommy, what a mess. When did you have both cartilages taken out of the right knee?"

"I've never had them out," said Tommy.

"Well where the bloody hell are they?" said the utterly shocked specialist. "They don't show on the X-ray, it's just bone on bone. You've simply worn them away. I've never seen that before in 30 years of doing this job. Were you in pain? You must have been."

"Yeh I was in pain," said Tommy. "But for eight years I just had painkillers and injections. That's all I remember. If I complained to the manager he wouldn't speak to me."

"I spent the next week checking old Liverpool programmes, laborious work, and calculated the number of games that he had missed. At Liverpool he was hardly absent until his later years, and then at Swansea whenever Tommy's name was missing for a few games I argued that he must have been injured. I eventually put nine separate claims in for nine separate injuries. It took two years to win the case. He was awarded a 40% disability pension at £38 a week for life, backdated for two years, plus £4,000 cash. In addition, because of the terrible state of his knees, his wife became a full-time carer and we got him a car, plus petrol and insurance allowances. Result, you might say.

"And then, do you remember the newspaper coverage when he was 'shopped'. He accepted payment to take five penalties live on TV during a televised FA Cup match. He hobbled onto the pitch, stumbled and limped up to the ball and took the kicks. Someone reported him to the DHSS who immediately stopped his pension and benefits and reclaimed the £4,000. If he had said sorry and eaten humble pie he might have been forgiven. But he blamed it on "a bloody Everton fan" that must have had it in for him. Poor Tom – and it was two wasted years for me.

"You were going to tell us about Micky Droy," said whoever was sitting in the front seat.

"Oh yeh, Micky Droy, probably the ugliest and biggest centre-half I ever played against. We can all lean against the goalposts. He could lean against the crossbar. For fun, he once went into the ring with Joe Bugner for a bit of sparring. At a time when Colin Waldron was voted 'the most handsome centre-half in football' Micky was at the other end of the scale. He was a monster. But, I relished playing against him. He had lots of skill but because of his size he was never the most nimble or quickest of players. In fact he was Player of the Year one year at

Chelsea. By the time he'd turned round, I'd gone. Plus, big 'heavy' players are poor as a rule at jumping and timing their leaps. And that for the likes of me and any centre-half is half the job. So, against a man much bigger than you, if you jump a fraction of a second before they do you can then hold yourself up by getting your arms or elbows onto their shoulders. In one match at Turf Moor against Chelsea he'd cracked me a couple of times so at half-time I asked Alan Stevenson to land the next goal kick in the centre circle so that I could have a running jump at Mickey and smack him back for the burst nose he's given me early in the game.

"It worked a treat and as I smacked this monster on the side of his head he tumbled over like a factory chimney. But sadly for me as he tumbled over, his size 12 boot came up and kicked me in the nose. I woke up an hour later in Blackburn General. I had it put back in place later that week and it's stayed straight till this day. Funny thing, you don't see many of the current centre-forwards with broken noses? Wonder why that is?

"Big, normally means slow. Larry Lloyd was another monster. And it was Micky in the Chelsea team when we came back from being 3 – 0 down at half-time to draw 3 – 3. "I'll be happy if we don't get beat 6 – 0 today lads," said Jimmy Adamson at half-time. So with the pressure off we went out and played like Barcelona. Peter Noble hit the bar in the last 10 minutes; if it had gone in, we'd have won."

We reached Washington without mishap. From the snores still coming from the back seats I wonder to this day if they listened to one word I said. But I'd enjoyed reliving these moments even if I was the only one still listening.

# 12

# The Winds of Change and a
# Parachute Hits the Roof

Brendan Flood's book *Big Club, Small Town and Me*, tells the story of the approach of the credit crunch that was to have such far-reaching effects on the economy in general and at Burnley in particular. It eventually killed all hopes of developing and re-building the old Cricket Field Stand.

The credit crunch started in earnest in September 2008. Because it hit Brendan hard, it hit Burnley hard, not only affecting the plans to re-build the Cricket Field Stand, but also to give financial support to Owen Coyle much further down the line when we were in the Premier League. It may well have impacted on Owen's decision to leave the club. Brendan told me that he was in the process of selling a stake in his development business for £30m to RBS but they pulled out in February 2008. Their reasons later became apparent as the banks kept silent on their own issues until the autumn of 2008. Then, it became a public global crisis.

Brendan turned to the Middle East but the banking disaster was moving so quickly that the whole system was on the verge of collapse. By the beginning of the new season 2008/09 the winds of change had become what Brendan described as a tsunami. The name Lehman became synonymous with that collapse. With all that in the background, Brendan's mother was dying. How he kept going was a testament to his will and strength. The football club was both his diversion and stimulation. He drew energy from his conviction that this was a squad at the club that would certainly make the top six. He was desperate to deliver for Burnley supporters.

Nobody on the board other than Brendan ever spoke about the StadiArena with me. But I was convinced it was what the club needed and pressed on with looking at the designs with a view to reducing costs. What drove me on was the sure knowledge that new buildings and facilities create interest in a club and attract investment. Look at the Arsenal stadium or Manchester City's. There is no way that the same level of investments would have been made at those clubs in their old stadiums. For those who disparaged the concept of an arena in Burnley, especially that which I proposed as part of the new StadiArena, I can only quote Mark Crabtree, chairman of AMS Neve (one of the world's leading music technology suppliers and based in Burnley). At a meeting of Burnley bondholders he said that his research showed that the area was crying out for such a venue. Promoters he had spoken to were supportive for a site for a 3-4,000 seater covered arena near the town centre in the Weavers' Triangle area.

The first two games of the season had us with our heads in our hands though. They were disasters. Brendan's conviction that this was a top-six team took a real knock.

Boardrooms can be strange places peopled by directors who are there for a variety of reasons. Directors have come a long way since Len Shackleton in his book *Clown Prince of Soccer*, once famously entitled chapter 9 'The Average Director's Knowledge of Football', and then instructed the publisher to leave a blank page. He wrote that in 1955. For sure, since then, directors have become more knowledgeable. They come in all shapes and sizes, with attitudes to match and because they are very rarely a director of more than one club at a time, they only see one view of the football world. The Burnley boardroom did in fact contain several people who knew their football but like any other it contained a cross-section of motives and agendas. I've been fortunate to work with three sets of directors in a CEO role; and then there was the Wembley board, a totally different and almost alien world. There was a group there waiting in the wings I used to call 'the Quality Street Gang'.

What Burnley had more than any other was a group, some of whom had been long-time supporters, and Burnley was in their blood. From a young age most of them had lived locally and been hooked. Years later as successful businessmen they returned and pumped money in. Men like Barry Kilby, Brendan Flood, Mike Garlick, the late Ray Griffiths, and more recently John Banaszkiewicz. Directors like this want success. They know it helps the town and puts a smile on people's faces.

There are other directors at clubs everywhere that love to be there for the kudos and prestige. They enjoy their elevated standing in the community. They are not without money; there is usually a donation to be made in exchange for the position, but once on the board that's the end of their 'investment' (they hope). They love the match-days and all the benefits that being a director brings. On a match afternoon this director may well arrive with his wife in tow, will drive into the VIP car park, be welcomed at reception, dine in the boardroom before the match and enjoy the four course meal and the not inexpensive wines. Then he/they will slip out to the best seats in the house. Afterwards they can mingle with the high and mighty of the visiting club and enjoy the after match perks and brandy perhaps. In terms of 'progressing' the club, thinking how to raise finance and new investment, being vibrant and supportive of new ideas, they have little interest, having found a comfort zone from which they have no wish to move. Risk, new thinking and visionaries disturb them. They love the status quo.

The problem is that this type of director can cost the club a lot of money, especially if he brings a wife or partner. I calculate that such a director, at any club over a period of ten years can benefit to the tune of (at a price a 'normal' supporter might pay for this kind of afternoon) a quarter of a million pounds; not to mention the experiences of visiting places like Old Trafford, Tottenham, Chelsea and Arsenal for another complimentary afternoon in the 'prawn sandwich' seats.

The board meetings that I experienced at Burnley were usually gentlemanly and amicable. I cannot recall any raised voices or heated arguments. Yes there were the natural disagreements. If there was grumbling it took place outside of these meetings.

Sheffield Wednesday 4 Burnley 1 was a result that sent shock waves through the club. The capitulation was unexpected and gave the anti-Brendan groups food for thought. A hard fought defeat or an unlucky defeat would have been acceptable but the manner of the 4 – 1 loss was almost embarrassing. Every bit of buoyancy was shaken. I'd travelled over with thousands of optimistic fans but goalkeeper Diego Penny had a nightmare game. Monday morning came and I wasn't looking forward to going upstairs to the office area at the club and bumping into Owen. I assumed his mood would be black. How wrong could I have been? I sat in the office with my door open and heard someone singing in the corridor outside. The singing then changed to a cheery whistle. The next minute Owen bounced into my office:

"Morning Fletch, how the hell are you buddy?"

We picked up our own moods from his. The place brightened up as to anyone within earshot he simply said, "Bad game Saturday, these things happen. We've got a great team and we'll be in the play-offs. It's only a bump in the road." 30 minutes later he was out of his own office and down the road to the training ground still singing and whistling. It was the perfect example of the Owen Coyle approach and it was the same at the training ground. It was a motivational skill that was crucial to the success that was to come that season.

It left the first home game of the season to bring things back on track. That wouldn't happen either. The result was equally embarrassing but for different reasons. Brendan wanted to introduce a carnival atmosphere for this first home fixture. In others you could sense the reaction, "What a waste of money." The most expensive item was a display by parachutists who would land on the pitch. It went well until the very last one. This guy landed not on the pitch but bounced onto the Cricket Field Stand roof. In its own way it was spectacular enough but not quite what was intended. The delay to the kick-off went on and on. At least the crowd had something to watch. Eventually though as the waiting went on and on it became about as exciting as watching paint dry. Meanwhile the players sat in the cramped dressing rooms. Eventually a fire engine and ladder were summoned to bring him down. The PA system announced he was down. But he was still up there and the crowd chanted, "Oh no he isn't." This was now more of a pantomime atmosphere than carnival. The game actually started with him still up there leaving a bemused crowd wondering why it couldn't have started at 3 o'clock and on time. The delay was something like 40 minutes. Sky TV and every radio station made merciless fun of us.

And the game itself: It was another defeat this time by 3 – 0 and at home! It really was back to the drawing board. With more than one doubting director after the first two games and the money being spent, two things happened. One was unplanned. Chris Eagles was sent off in the Ipswich game (as if things couldn't get any worse). Cue more comments in the boardroom at this 'star' player now out for three games. "Just an expensive show pony," said one. The second was deliberate. Owen looked at the situation and the two results made up his mind that a more mobile target man was needed up front. Brendan held his nerve and backed him. In came Steven Thompson from Cardiff City; more money, more grumbles from some of the board. But, his arrival, plus the absence of Chris Eagles, it could be said, got the season back on track. By the end of the season those grumblers were silent and smiling and drinking their champagne in celebration. Such is football.

The Carling crusade began in a small way at Bury. The win came immediately after the debacle at Sheffield Wednesday. OK it might have been a fortunate win but it restored just a little belief. There would be no league win until September 13th but points were accumulated from then on, steadily if not spectacularly at first, and simultaneously the excitement of games in the Carling Cup well and truly revitalised the club from top to bottom.

The win perhaps that brought the national headlines was the victory

My 1958 heroes

Granddad on the right

A very smart looking me with
Gran and Granddad

Just 17 years old

Early mentors Jimmy Mac and Nat Lofthouse

Party tricks aged 18 at Bolton

The old Burnden Park

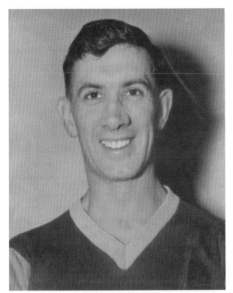

Jimmy Adamson

A Masonic Bob Lord

Margaret and Harry Potts

The running man

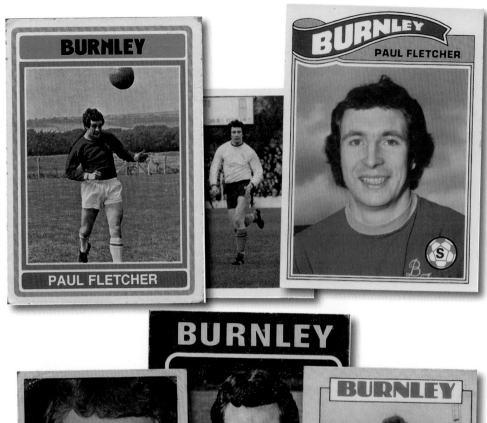

I'm only 99p on eBay!

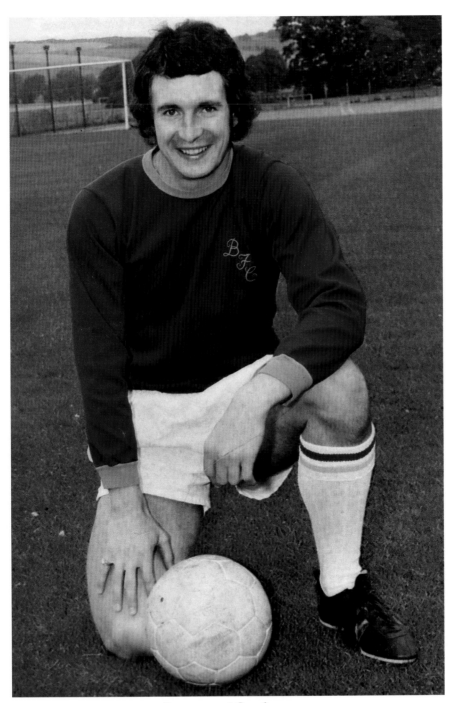

Pre-season at Gawthorpe

Heads above the rest at home to Coventry
© Howard Talbot

Action header at Highfield Road
© Howard Talbot

Celebrations after scoring
against Man City
© Howard Talbot

Last picture as a pro at Blackpool
© Howard Talbot

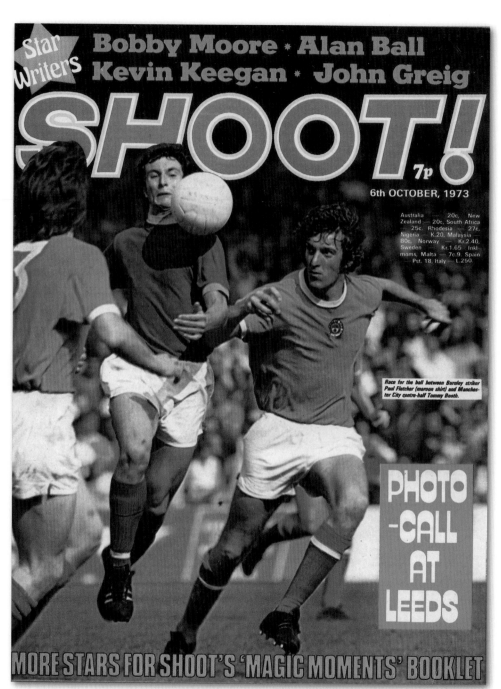

On the cover of Shoot magazine in my footballing heyday

# PAUL FLETCHER
### Testimonial Brochure

## Bolton·Burnley·Blackpool·England U23

**articles by : Brian Clough·Alan Ball rt. hon. Edward Heath·Nat Lofthouse· Norman Hunter Leighton James &**

Programme from my testimonial match showing my goal from
an overhead kick against Leeds

The award winning stadium at Huddersfield

Bolton's Reebok Stadium

The Ricoh Arena at Coventry

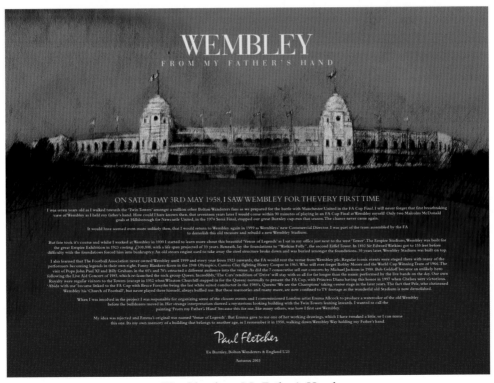

Wembley from My Father's Hand

With the trusty uke

Our number one fan with
boxed gift pen

The Wembley job

Me and Kindo after a rough night out

A heated debate at Cambridge

With the number one lookalike at the old Wembley

With Bryan Adams at Coventry

A great chairman Barry Kilby     A great visionary Brendan Flood

George Best asking me for my autograph?

My wonderful mum and dad

The annual family holiday

Stepping out with Sian and the Beatles

# 100 GREATEST CLARETS

## THE GREATEST PLAYERS FROM THE NORTH WEST
### IN CONJUNCTION WITH THE FA HERITAGE COMMITTEE

Mr Colin Waldron Esq

6th Februray 2009

Dear Mr Waldron

**In Confidence**

As you may have seen on the local TV and Media, The Football Association Heritage Committee has been contacting all 90 League Clubs and asking a random set of supporters, from all age groups, to vote for their all-time top 100 players at their Club. At Burnley Football Club this has been organised under the title **"100 Greatest Clarets"**.

Over 5,000 season ticket holders from **Burnley FC** where picked at random and contacted by email and asked to vote for their top 100 players of all time, from the many players who have represented **Burnley FC** over the last 49 years from 1960. These results are now received, collated and ready to forward to the FA Heritage Committee for a supplementary pull-out to the annual FA Heritage Year-Book which celebrates its 50 year Anniversary in 2010.

## The Awards

There are five categories of Awards to the top 100 players, all kindly sponsored by Daehbonk International Ltd:

- o **The Top 10** players at each Club will receive: *an Engraved Gold Omega Watch (value £2,586.00)*
- o The Top 11 to 20 players will receive: *an 'initialled' Harrods Leather Briefcase (valued £296.00)*
- o The Top players 21 – 35 will receive: *an Inscribed Port Decanter (value £75.00)*
- o The Top players 36 – 50 will receive: *two Burnley FC season tickets for 2009/10 season*
- o Those players voted 51 – 100 will get a: *limited edition Club Scarf.*

SPONSORED BY

official club sponsor
**HOLLAND'S**

**DAEH**BONK
*INTERNATIONAL*

official kit supplier
**errea**

M/S VERONICA SIMPSON (CO-ORDINATOR)
TOP 100 CLARETS CO-ORDINATOR (FA HERITAGE)

My greatest ever spoof

at Chelsea. The ticket sales for this Carling Cup game were astonishing with over 6,000 Burnley fans filling the away end. No-one in their right mind could possibly have expected a Burnley win (albeit on penalties) but that's what happened at a time when Chelsea were invincible at home. Every Burnley player was outstanding but the remarkable thing was the Burnley crowd. Dave Thomas sitting in the Chelsea West Stand, said the sight and sound of them was just totally astonishing. It was a result that made people sit up and take notice. Owen's name hit the headlines. A result like this raises a club profile around the globe. Brendan was ecstatic. Members of the board who were sceptics now enjoyed the glory. Light years and millions of pounds separated the two clubs but the boys from the north where the stereotype image was still of cloth caps, cobbled streets and mill chimneys had knocked out the sophisticates from the land of chardonnay, sun-dried tomatoes and filter coffee at pavement cafes. Ade Akinbiyi scored the normal time equaliser, his last for the club, and became a legend for that. The memories of a glorious night will remain for years to come. Football does this; gives you goose bumps that still return years later whenever anyone says "were you there?"

Spectacular league wins did come, at Coventry and Sheffield United. The points mounted. Confidence was high. The board enjoyed the situation.

Next up in the Carling was Arsenal and a 2 – 0 win. Arsenal were the next Carling victims on a horrible Lancashire night. Boardroom celebrations went on into the small hours. Chairman Barry Kilby celebrated his tenth year as chairman during the same month as the Arsenal win. No-one deserved the celebrations more than he did. The Press filled the back pages with miles and miles of print. Smiles filled the place for days afterwards. A real team, in every sense of the word, was emerging on and off the field. Euphoria does this and even the grumblers were silenced. The last time the board had stayed up that long after a game was way back in the mid-80s. It was very early in season 1983/84 and the board knew already that the appointment of John Bond was a mistake. They had just lost a home game to Crewe. They decided not to sack him. Had they dismissed him that night and stumped up the compensation the subsequent story of the club would have been altered.

And then came the run of defeats. The blip began on Boxing Day with a home defeat. It consisted of five league defeats in a row and more concerned faces. Comments about a failing league season returned. Not until January 31st would there be a league win and even that was unconvincing with two very late goals both scored by Steven

Thompson. But the relief was palpable when it came.

It was during this period that there was the glorious 'defeat' at home to Spurs in the Carling semi-final. Tears were shed that night in the dressing room. The first leg had been lost 4 – 1 and no-one gave Burnley a prayer in the return leg except, I have learned since, the Spurs fans genuinely feared that their brittle team would collapse if Burnley got the first goal. Burnley duly did and went 3 – 0 up backed by a crowd so passionate that the stand roofs nearly came off. It was a truly extraordinary night. But Spurs scored two thoroughly undeserved breakaway goals in the very last minutes of extra time. Every single Burnley person in that crowd was totally heartbroken. And meanwhile the league defeats continued. At that point, especially after an abject defeat at Watford 3 – 0, few if any people would have dared imagine that promotion would be won at Wembley in May. It seemed a ridiculous thought.

And then came that fluky, lucky, fortunate, late, late win at home to Charlton in the Championship. Who cared how Burnley won that day. When you lose in the last minutes of extra time you feel devastation. When you win in the very last minutes of a game there is euphoria. After five league defeats it was the tonic needed. It kick-started the remainder of the season. The final surge to the top six began.

Belief grew though after one result in particular. It was Blackpool 0 Burnley 1 on the filthiest and windiest night you could imagine where even the spray from the sea helped soak the players along with the driving rain. For an almost minute by minute account of the games and behind-the-scenes events leading up to the play-off final, read *Entertainment, heroes and Villains*, by Dave Thomas. In brief without the financial input from four directors, the club was almost at a point where it could barely pay the wages and Brendan was in a financial straitjacket.

At a board meeting earlier in January, Brendan had outlined the projected needs and reckoned that if each director would loan the club £100,000 each, this would see the club through. The full cooperation of everybody was needed but only four (and one of these was the chairman) were willing to help find the total money needed. It was clear that the board of ten was too big. It was shortly after that discussions took place to review the size of this unwieldy group. Barry Kilby, Brendan and Ray Griffiths met for lunch to discuss how they should act. Ray Griffiths described each board member in a couple of sentences, memorably describing one of them as "an after darker, no bugger knows what he does." Another one he summed up as "a bloody spiv". Eventually the board was indeed reduced in size to facilitate quicker decision making. When decisions were needed in between board meetings the chairman would ring them all to get their views. It took time. It was tabled at a meeting that the board should indeed be streamlined and that to qualify a director would need a certain number of shares. Those who did not meet the qualification or did not want to buy the shares needed would be offered an 'associate directorship' for the next three years. Five elected to accept the latter.

The Reading play-off games were nail-biters until two world class goals at Reading from Martin Paterson and Steve Thompson won the game and sent the travelling fans wild.

Wembley was reality. For fans it was a dream; for us at the club it was the nightmare of selling our ticket allocation fairly and efficiently, if we could. Believe it or not I was away on holiday and missed the chaos. At the end of the day the ticket office staff worked miracles. In just five days they shifted 36,000 tickets with a computer ticketing system that was so old even Bob Lord might have been able to operate it. But there were problems; of course there were. Some supporters queued for hours for their tickets. Some queued for hours and then were turned away. Some queued by sitting in the Bob Lord Stand until it was their turn. People couldn't get through on the phones. Online systems crashed. Ticketzone was problematic. But by some miracle the tickets were sold and the staff worked wonders. Then having survived the stress of ordering by phone or online, next there was the nerve-wracking wait for them to arrive by post, some of them very late. It was far from easy. If there was stress on the customer side of the ticket office windows, there was even more on the staff side. It was all hands to the pumps. Sonya Kilby, the chairman's wife, served coffees to the waiting queues.

The market traders set up stalls outside the club, one of them in fact directly opposite the club shop. I got a bit of stick for going out with a megaphone and exhorting people not to buy from this stall and to use the club shop. Not until I saw some video footage kindly posted on the internet by a local paper did I realise how close I was to meeting my maker. I'd stepped out into the road and a lorry missed me by inches. Some fans said they hadn't laughed so much since they saw local MP Kitty Usher's expenses claim. It was the time of the *Daily Telegraph's* exposure of the scandal of MPs' claims. The one I liked best was that submitted by Sir Peter Viggers who claimed £1,645 for a floating duck island in his garden pond. We should have asked Kitty Usher to claim for the six showers we had fitted in the dressing rooms. We discovered a new name for ticket touts – attendance facilitators.

Burnley was bedecked with flags, bunting and decorations flying from scores of buildings and houses. Cars drove round with flags and scarves draped from the windows. It looked and sounded like a Burnley Mardi Gras. The Town Hall was bathed in claret and blue light. Wembley fever hit the town. It was astonishing. The place was transformed, not just with colour but with the buzz of rejuvenation and pride. Nothing had happened like this for ten years and Stan Ternent's promotion season, except this was even more gigantic. This time the whole nation was watching little Burnley and I suspect willing it to win, unless you came from Sheffield.

The newspaper features began. Burnley had never before seen publicity like this. This was the richest game in the world coming up. There were features on Brendan Flood, Burnley's money man according to the *Mirror,* and the bright red Robbie Blake underpants he wore into the Chelsea boardroom after the Carling win down there. He was wondering this time whether to wear them at Wembley in the Royal Box. Barry Kilby was featured in the *Times* and then again in the *Mail* in a piece that contained one of the great lines:

*"Kevin McCabe plays up Sheffield United's expansion plans in India, China, Australia and Hungary. Kilby says Burnley's reach extends to Todmorden, Rawtenstall, and at a push, Skipton."*

The money flowed into the club coffers, but alas no faster than it sped out. The financial corner would only be turned if there was a win at Wembley. Brendan was really feeling the pinch. We had conservative directors who might have invested but chose not to. The club's cash flow was tight but it shouldn't have been just Brendan's responsibility to fund the club. His problems had forced the other directors to consider putting their hands in their pockets and he had significantly committed himself to help to give the club a chance of promotion. So those who did help on the final cash call deserved a good day on May 25th.

A staggering 50% of all play-off takings went to the Football League. That left the clubs to share the remaining 50%. And on top of that, that damned marker trader opposite the club shop had skimmed off another 0.00001%.

I'd had the awful emptiness of a losing semi-final back in 1974. I knew what it was like to feel the most intense disappointment imaginable. The players had already felt the desolation after the last-minute Tottenham defeat. There were still many Burnley fans that had been at Wembley in 1962 for the Cup Final that was lost. There had been many disappointments over the years for Burnley fans and coming up was a game so huge in its consequences that to lose was unthinkable. And yet to have got as far as this was also to a degree unexpected. Simply reaching the play-offs was an achievement for a club with a budget the size of Burnley's. It was similar to the Carling Cup game away at Chelsea when fans had gone in their thousands for the experience and good night out. There was an element of that regarding the Wembley game. To be a finalist gave pride enough. To win would be amazing. Every person in the town desperately wanted to win. You could say the financial future of the club was hanging on it. But not a person was certain of the result. If there was surety it was only bravado.

So many fans told me that sleep was difficult the night before. They'd wondered if the result would hinge on one piece of luck, a referee's decision, the bounce of the ball, one split second bit of magic by one inspired player. Would Alexander with another penalty decide the game? Or Robbie Blake score with a 25-yard free kick; or Martin Paterson with another screamer from 35 yards? Would Clarke Carlisle head home another bullet? Would Sheffield United be too strong, too physical and too muscular?

They told me that as early as 5am with the bright early sun rising over Turf Moor the scenes outside the ground were astounding. There were lines of coaches, street traders (bless them this time as the club shop had sold out), milling crowds and the smell of bacon sandwiches from the pub just across the road from the stadium. All the way down the motorways the cavalcades of cars and coaches made their way calling at overcrowded service stations along the route. There were hundreds of cars, vans, minibuses, limos and coaches approaching London and Wembley, the surrounding areas shabby and neglected. Some tipsy Burnley fans would soon be holding up the 'two-finger' gesture to those 'big soft Londoners' not knowing they were nowhere near London but still in Knutsford. In London, meeting them were the ranks of red and white Sheffield fans. Peace reigned.

Would it be seventh time lucky for Graham Alexander and third time lucky for Robbie Blake? Surely the football gods would this time see them rewarded after so many previous disappointments in play-off finals. I think I'd have been devastated for Graham in particular had we lost at Wembley. He was a model professional and would eventually reach 1000 games not only because he was an outstanding player but also because he had stayed injury free. He had that split second instinct for the pass. He knew where everyone was around him. All that plus his deadly penalty taking skills made him a fantastic asset. Eventually Eddie Howe would find him the proverbial 'pain in the arse' when he wasn't in the team. But to Graham's credit that was only because he wanted to play every single game and felt he always merited a place.

Surely, the Gods would see the symmetry in a Burnley win just about 50 years after the great triumph of winning the Division One title in 1959/60 with the team of Jimmy Adamson, Jimmy McIlroy, John Connelly, Brian Miller et al. Several of them were there to watch the jackpot game.

The four directors who had put money in when the chips were down were Barry Kilby, Mike Garlick, John Sullivan and Ray Griffiths. At 3 o'clock Mike Dean blew his whistle. The jackpot game was on.

# 13

# Kilby, Flood, Wembley, Reaching the Promised Land

Kilby and Flood – it's got a bit of a ring to it hasn't it? No, it's not the title of a new US detective series. Nor is it some sombre funeral director's parlour down a Burnley back street. It's actually something rather unique. It's the off-field combination of two guys who have steered the Burnley ship along through all kinds of waters, eventually reaching Wembley and then the Premier League, and then trying to steer it back again after it kind of went off course when Captain Coyle jumped ship in January of 2010. After the Wembley triumph of 2009 it took several days if not weeks for the whole scenario to sink in as the club achieved the dream, and then faced up to the practical problems of joining the elite.

Not a person could deny that this achievement, and where the club is now, is a testament to two men, Barry Kilby who joined the club in 1998 when things were at such a low ebb, and Brendan Flood who joined much later in 2006.

If Barry has been the cautious one, and rightly so when club income was so limited and it was his own money that was propping up the place, then it was the arrival of the go-ahead Brendan Flood that kick-started a slightly more risk-taking approach. The two complemented each other, a sort of Toshack and Keegan, or Clough and Taylor. They are two very different people but have always cooperated, agreed to disagree rather than argue, have fed off each other's strengths and each has compensated for the other's weaknesses. It has always been a case of two heads being better than one so that their dual role as operational directors succeeded.

Both have a common trait that always binds them. They are both genuine and huge Burnley fans. They were both introduced to the Clarets by their fathers when they were young kids. If either were to be offered a directorship at Chelsea or Arsenal they would not give it a moment's thought.

Whilst Barry Kilby put his money into the club to keep it afloat, Brendan Flood put his money into the club to spring it forward. If it was Barry Kilby who laid the foundations, it was Brendan Flood who extended the house. It was Flood money that enabled the purchases of Chris Eagles and Martin Paterson at the beginning of 2008/09. It was Flood money that enabled the club to up the wages. Whilst some board members were part of a culture of longstanding caution and would certainly have preferred to stay in the Championship comfort zone as costs and ambitions increased, it was Brendan Flood's zeal and calculated gambles that projected the club upwards. Meanwhile Barry Kilby held the board together.

Brendan Flood was more than once accused of being a gambler and a risk-taker, gambling with and risking the club's future and finances. But they were calculated gambles and intelligent risks that paid off at Wembley and with the subsequent Lucky Saloon pay-off.

Barry Kilby's father was a fanatical Burnley fan. They lived midway between Burnley and Blackburn but from the day Roy Kilby took Barry to his first game when he was about nine years old, he was hooked. His first heroes were Willie Irvine and the awesome Andy Lochhead. Andy still hosts on matchdays at Turf Moor and Barry says he is still frightened of him. His early days in football followed those of England international Martin Dobson who went on to play hundreds of games for Burnley. Barry was a year below him at Clitheroe Grammar School where both of them were captain of the school football team. Both of them went to Burnley, Barry as a youth and can proudly show any visitor his name in one of the big ledgers into which the teams were listed. But, whilst Dobbo went on to play for England, Barry only got as far as Padiham FC.

Barry began his entrepreneurial journey when he spotted an opportunity for producing scratchcards. The actual printing was contracted out and he ran this early business from his bedroom. £2 bought him two shares in a company that he called Europrint. He juggled credit and customer payments, used his garage as a warehouse and his Volvo for delivering. The big chance came when he devised a way that enabled newspapers to include bingo games. He designed a way to give each card the individual number it needed by modifying a standard printing machine. It was an idea waiting to happen, he says. Nine newspapers commissioned him to produce bingo cards. One newspaper alone needed 24 million cards. Profits increased. Soon he had a staff of ten and the concept spread to Europe. In 1994 he formed a joint venture with GTech an American company, and four years later they bought an 80% stake in Europrint. By then Europrint employed 45 people and his customers were as diverse as the *Times* and the *Sun*.

He was 49 when he became chairman of Burnley FC. It was 1998.

He'd seen them almost exit the league in 1987 when they had to beat Orient in the final game of the season. He sponsored a few games in the following years. His business was thriving and when he sold part of Europrint he had some money to invest in the club at a time when they were struggling and still owed over £3 million for the two new stands. He bought shares from directors who left and on becoming chairman put the first £1 million in. Stan Ternent was manager at the time and having a fairly rough time with results but Barry stuck by him, helped buy new players, and the reward was promotion to the Championship in 2000.

Until the club won promotion to the Premiership the finances were always problematic and Barry bailed the club out on several occasions putting more of his own money in. But Barry, whilst a millionaire is not a multi-millionaire and there have always been limits to his funding. To say the club was on a knife-edge just before Wembley in 2009 is an understatement. At one time he actually owned the ground which he bought as a way of injecting money into the club. When he began to feel uncomfortable being both landlord as owner, and tenant as chairman, he sold it on but safeguarded the ground in the small print, and the club can buy it back at any time if money is available.

One of the first things Brendan Flood noticed when he entered the boardroom for the first time was the stuffed cat that has slept on the window ledge since a game against Gillingham many years ago. It cost him £500,000 for the privilege of joining the board and asking why on earth does a stuffed cat reside on the window ledge. Apparently it brings good luck to Burnley – but not always I can assure you. Like Barry, his first contact with the football club was with his father. His father Duncan took his brothers along as well and was under instructions on Saturdays to "get the kids out of the house" and the Turf seemed the logical place to take them; except Brendan at first didn't want to go. By the end of the first game he saw against Crystal Palace (and a win) he was hooked.

It wasn't that long before he realised that Burnley sold players. They had to. When Ralphie Coates went he was devastated. He was at Hillsborough to see Burnley (and me) lose to Newcastle. He was at Turf Moor in 1979 when Celtic came and there was mayhem. It was a game when I was scared too and that didn't happen often. Like Barry he was there at Turf Moor to see Burnley beat Orient and stay in the Football League. Bad as things were he bought a season ticket. One of his greatest memories is of an away game at Bristol Rovers and there was no food kiosk at the away end. He and his mates had a brainwave. As Jamie Hoyland one of the subs was warming up, they asked him to go to the other end and get them some pie and peas. Believe it or not, with their fiver in his hand Jamie trotted off and then returned with their grub five minutes later. It's hard to imagine Berbatov doing that today for the Man Utd away fans. Mind you at Man City it's the kind of thing that Balotelli probably would do.

So Brendan had earned his spurs, just like Barry, as a travelling supporter. The urge to help grew. By 2005 he had already been contacted by Barry and sounded out but didn't feel he was ready. But he did join late in 2006, after contact from the then chief executive Dave Edmundson, and handed his cheque for £500,000 to Barry Kilby at the AGM. One of the main points on the agenda that night was not so much the arrival of a new director, but why the club had changed to Holland's Pies from a local supplier. The whole thing had left a sour taste in the town. Brendan stared in disbelief as it all got rather heated. To this day Brendan remembers the pie problem as being his introduction to the politics of the football club and a board with 10 members. The club for a while used to have the fans in to test the pies at a pie-tasting afternoon. They were given score sheets to rate the pies. I'm told the local fire brigade lads used to call in and scoff the lot. Only at Burnley – such a wonderfully homely club.

Put ten people on a committee and events follow a predictable pattern. There will be splinter groups and factions. The greater the number of members then the greater is the probability of disagreement. There's them as gets things done, there's them as quietly and happily lets 'em get on with it. And there's them as moans and groans. And then there was Clive Holt who had been there since 1986, who knew the place inside out and probably where all the skeletons were buried. The full team was Ray Griffiths, John Sullivan, Clive Holt, Ray Ingleby, Mike Garlick, Barry Kilby, John Turkington, Martin Hobbs, Chris Duckworth and Brendan Flood. Only four of them would still be there in 2011, plus the cat, a life member.

At his first boardroom meeting a week after the AGM and the great pie debate, Brendan knew he had a fight on his hands when he saw and heard the number of directors whose ambitions seemed minimal and had only one thought – get the wage bill down. And this was after he had just handed the club a cheque for half a million. The stuffed cat on the window ledge looked bemused by the whole thing. To the faces round the table he announced he hadn't joined to vote for mediocrity. There was a stunned silence; and even more so when he followed up with the promise to put in another £2 million. Brendan Flood had arrived. At that meeting the comfort zone was well and truly shattered. The silence descended again until one member Chris

Duckworth announced his approval. The cat continued to snooze.

Of these early days Brendan remembers one story. He was attending a game at Barnsley and their long serving director, Barry Taylor, took him on one side. Brendan explained that he had only been at Burnley about a month. Barry advised him firstly that unless fans who wanted to talk to him had a season ticket he should tell them to "bugger off." And secondly he advised him never to put money into the club. Naturally Brendan asked why.

"Because you're better off going to Scarborough and pissing in t'sea," he answered. Brendan didn't tell him that he'd already put two and a half million in. He possibly hadn't told his wife either.

There's no question that the pathway to the Premiership began on the night that Brendan Flood became a director. That takes no credit whatsoever away from a great and committed chairman, Barry Kilby. But what the new man provided was renewed energy, real ambition and vision. The energy and ambition that Barry had started out with several years earlier had been ground down. And in me, Brendan saw a real ally.

Brendan started his working life at Barclays Bank straight from school. He spent two years working in London branches one of which appeared to be a depository for mob money and there was a policy of "no questions asked." From there it was back north to Preston and then into the Risk Management Team in Manchester. Feeling constrained and wanting to be his own boss he went solo in 1996 into the property industry. He created Modus, an investment business eventually with assets of over a £1billion and over 40 development projects. The recession, however, hit Modus hard and resulted in its collapse.

As 2011 progressed there was conjecture as to how long Barry Kilby would remain as chairman. He has dropped cryptic hints that he was ready to use his bus pass, that's if Nick Clegg doesn't abolish them. There was speculation that if an impending financial court case with the Anglo Irish Bank goes against Brendan Flood, he might no longer pass the 'fit and proper' person test that would enable him to remain as a director at Burnley FC. What a tragedy that would be.

No-one could say that Burnley, a founder member of the Football League, had not earned the Wembley victory. The players were now up there with the team of '59/60, the team of the 70s, and the promotion teams of '81/82, ten years later '91/92, and then '93/94. Then there was Stan Ternent's team of 1999/2000. But none of them had a prize as great as Wembley 2008/09. Was this the greatest of them all? Was it not one of the finest seasons ever in the club's history?

Nobody deserved their seats at Wembley more than Barry Kilby and Brendan Flood. No-one more deserved the accolades and attention that came their way. The media exploded in a frenzy of publicity and acclamation. The pundits approved. If this wasn't a football fairy tale then nothing was.

Who was responsible for getting Burnley Football Club back into the top-flight? Was it Owen Coyle? No, he was the manager who assembled the best team the board would let him buy. Was it Barry Kilby? Partly: because he had miraculously kept the club afloat during his long tenure, often with his own money. Was it a combination of all the Burnley directors? No, some of them I always felt were apprehensive and nervous about over-stretching themselves and were comfortable and satisfied with a mid-table position, or maybe even a top end of Division One position. From some there might even have been an impression that Burnley's true place was in Division One; that the club was over-achieving by even being a Championship side. And some of them did not like Brendan Flood.

Was it Brendan Flood? Yes, yes and yes again, and to my dying day I shall say that without him, his input, vision and ambition, Burnley Football Club would never have got anywhere near Wembley. But it didn't come without a big price that Brendan had to pay, and continues to pay to this day. This chapter is a good opportunity to acknowledge Brendan's massive contribution and put the record straight. He did not have it easy and it often seemed some directors were not wholly supportive.

I like Brendan Flood very much. He enticed me back to Turf Moor when there were a number of more lucrative options open to me. He was going to assemble the funding for the new Cricket Field Stand; he was investing large sums in the club like no-one had ever done before. But some of the directors seemed happy enough just to keep the club afloat, ticking over, paying the bills and not taking risks. They enjoyed the Saturday afternoons as they were.

But Brendan was different. He didn't see Saturdays as a social occasion, a pleasant diversion, a bite to eat, a bit of status in the community and a seat in the Bob Lord. Most of all he wanted success on the field. He wanted to support Owen Coyle to the hilt. Here was an incredibly ambitious manager. Brendan recognised that accidental though his arrival might have been, a product of chance rather than design, the man was special and burned with drive and desire. He was charismatic, rallied people; and his energy rubbed off on everyone around him – but not quite all of the directors, that is to say those who were happy in the comfort zone of what they had known so far. So Brendan stuck his neck out, made independent decisions, and upset other directors who saw their noses being pushed out. It did not go down well. He was claret and blue to his bones but it cut no ice with the traditionalists. But he saw the future far clearer than them and of course his confidence at that time when he first arrived came from his Modus business empire which then was still thriving.

And so Brendan sanctioned the arrival of players like Martin Paterson, Chris Eagles and Steve Thompson. They were expensive, wage levels rose, agents fees increased. What parasites many agents are, but if you don't deal with them you don't get the players you want. And without players like Paterson, Eagles and Thompson there would have been no Wembley. Brendan sanctioned a new pay deal for Wade Elliott and boy did that lad repay it. It was brave decisions like these that made promotion a reality. I sensed some directors didn't like it. There was anxiety and worry. About a month before Wembley the club was barely solvent. The pressure on Brendan was incredible.

I could sense in board meetings at that time that there was even more nervousness at the teetering financial situation and Brendan had no more money to give. The gambles were maybe coming home to roost, a lucky draw at Southampton created more trepidation. What was wrong with settling for a good season finishing creditably in the top half of the Championship? Why do we need this pressure and uncertainty? What happens if we don't get promotion? Where will the money come from? Brendan took no notice. Money was found to pay the wages. Not all directors put their hands in their pockets. Brendan and Owen focused on just one thing, and it wasn't the electricity bill or the milkman. They saw the play-offs. They saw victory. But don't think for one minute that Brendan wasn't on pins.

Chris Eagles had already been described as a 'show pony' and a waste of money. But Brendan and Owen knew he had something special, especially when he curled in a great winning goal at the Ricoh, and another great goal at Sheffield United. He did a good job for Burnley and brought in more revenue than we paid for him. He had that elusive 'star' quality and did the unexpected. When he ran at the opposition you could see the panic. Half the time his tricks didn't come off, but he was a winger, that's how it works. I know; I played.

By the time we reached Wembley I think everybody in Burnley realised it would be a tough game against Sheffield United. They weren't pretty but they were difficult and organised. We'd got through two tough play-off games against Reading but against Sheffield the general consensus was we'd done so well to reach Wembley, a win would be a bonus and the glass half-empty brigade saw our chances as less than 50/50. But this was Wembley, a one off; who got paid how much didn't matter. Form didn't matter. All that mattered was how we played on the day – nothing else. One goal, one chance, one penalty, one player, one referee's decision might decide it. The last result didn't matter – or who sat in the directors' box.

But that wouldn't be me in the directors' box. I'd been away on holiday when the tickets arrived and all the BFC directors had taken up all the VIP tickets for themselves and families. I was told there was some space in the sponsors' area. I laughed at that. I fully understood football club politics. I rang my old mate Roger Maslin, chief executive at Wembley Stadium and he invited me along as a VIP Wembley guest. I sat having lunch on the top table with Roger and Wembley Chairman David Bernstein. More than just a few people on nearby tables were probably wondering how I'd got there. One thought lingered – maybe it would be our day?

Brendan was having a hard time. His wife Eileen's mother died the day before the Final. His property business was close to administration. His brother Chris's wife was seriously ill and in fact died the day after the Final. And he knew his neck would be on the block if Burnley lost. Other necks would be on the block too, the four who had put extra money in when it was most needed just weeks earlier. One of them paced up and down during the final minutes in the concourse unable to watch. There was a lot at stake, particularly for Brendan but he took it in his stride.

Maybe it could be our day?

I parked in a little secret hideaway I knew up by Wembley Park Station. I'd parked there on several previous occasions when I wanted to get away early. We never did solve the problem of getting 90,000 people and their coaches away from the Wembley car parks quickly. It was a thrill to drive down and see the dozens of coaches filled with claret and blue, to see the lines of them parked and their passengers getting out faces beaming. I rang up another ex-Wembley colleague and asked if I could have a short tour of behind the scenes at the ground and especially the dressing rooms, for my family and my four grandchildren. Brendan and his family were able to join us and at 1 p.m. there was something like 30 of us standing on the edge of the famous Wembley pitch after the thrill of seeing the dressing rooms and the Burnley shirts hanging up looking absolutely immaculate. The names of Blake, Thompson, Elliott, Caldwell, Jensen, Alexander, Paterson, Duff, Carlisle, Eagles and all the rest did not look out of place.

Maybe it might be our day?

For the match I sat in the VIP seating area with Roger and watched the teams arrive on the pitch. I watched the fabulous win unfold, the fantastic Wade Elliott strike for the goal, the wonderful Burnley support, and as I did so the inevitable thoughts flashed through my head. How I'd been there with my dad and seen Nat Lofthouse, but on a pitch about 50 yards south of this new one. How I'd seen the England win in 1966 when I was about 15. How I should have been there myself in 1974 in a Burnley versus Liverpool Final. And would have been if the FA had booted Newcastle out of the competition as they should have done; and awarded the game to Nottingham Forest. And Forest we would have beaten in the semi-final.

I'd seen the early plans for this stadium and had some influence on its design. Some rooms and features were there because of my part in its construction and my insistence. It was eerie to walk round the completed building, a place where I had worked on the plans for two years.

But all this was history when half-time arrived; all that mattered were the next 45 minutes, and then the final 25 minutes and then the final 10 so that for the final five long minutes we were utterly drained as we willed referee Mike Dean to blow the whistle. Into added time and then at last it was over. The sight of the Burnley fans will live with me forever. Owen Coyle had done it. Brendan had done it. I looked at some of the directors who had never fully supported Brendan celebrating wildly as if it was their own victory.

I broke down in tears. Grown men do cry and there's nothing wrong with that. This was a fairy story and they don't happen too often. This was maybe a once-in-a-lifetime experience and I'd played a small part in it. I was thrilled for Brendan and Barry but especially Brendan. He'd stuck his head above the parapet. God only knows how many knives would have been stuck in his back had we lost. But now I had a chance to implement some major plans, to build a stand, to leave a legacy and to work with and support Brendan. Fair enough, the other directors were overjoyed but would they all back Brendan now?

I looked for Brendan but couldn't see him. I looked up at the TV monitor and saw him, down on the pitch with the manager and players. Nobody deserved that more than he. He'd booked a party at a top hotel for after the game. What a magical evening it was.

On the Monday morning a BBC taxi picked me up at 6am and I was booked into the studio to go on live TV with Gary Richardson, a good friend from the after-dinner circuit. We'd shared a top table together on many occasions. He said he felt that it was such a popular win and that Burnley would become everyone's second team. It started to become a catch-phrase for many others when describing the victory. It was a victory for the 'little' team and the 'little' town. The media was quick to focus on the 33 years out of the top flight and the Orient game in '87 when Burnley nearly went out of the Football League.

With the BFC senior management team I'd been working in secret to produce a plan for if we won. Nobody dared mention this to Owen. He would have exploded. But such plans had to be made. Burnley Council had organised an open-top bus tour of the town with a champagne reception at the Town Hall. Now, job done, we could tell Owen. The weather was good. The streets were filled. I've never felt so proud. So much to do, so much to plan, a list as long as your arm, my mind was already working on them, the new fixture list to wait for, new grounds to visit, new faces to meet.

The euphoria was palpable. But a question nagged away in my head. Would ALL directors now give Brendan their full support?

And then the bombshell hit. Bloody hell, Celtic wanted Owen.

# 14

# The Golden Share

We'd beaten off Celtic's approach for Owen. There was nothing official, no formal communication between clubs at the time and the words 'tapping-up' sprang to mind. That's how it works in football. We all know it. Very often by a pet journalist who has the manager's ear and acts as the go-between. Every club I've ever been at has done it. 'No tapping up' is an agreement that everyone has broken right from Chelsea down to Rochdale so there's no point whingeing about it when it happens to you. It didn't work for Celtic though and Owen Coyle again expressed his great love for Burnley and its supporters. He suggested he would be staying the course and nobody doubted him because he was the Messiah. What we didn't know was that a different offer was lurking round the corner only months away.

By now the shirt sponsors were FUN88. What a name. Not much FUN if we got hammered 6 – 0 by the likes of Liverpool and Chelsea (thankfully we didn't, hammered yes, 6 – 0 no). Supporters laughed. It was funny how it happened. Sometimes you worked damned hard to set up an investment deal like the people from New York we'd been in touch with earlier. In 2009 I took a call from Dr Steven Siegel (no not the action hero) a guy I'd already met when there was a deal lined up with Coventry City worth £30million. Coventry turned it down. He was a real New York city slicker and represented his 'investors' who wanted to know if Burnley wanted investment. I explained that the answer was yes but in my view the board would not sell more than 49% of the shares so that they would keep ownership of the club. Steve said his people were very serious and had already had an offer to buy Blackburn Rovers some 12 months earlier, turned down. He came over to meet Barry and Brendan but like so many deals, nothing materialised.

But then something sort of just landed in my lap. Sometimes out of the blue there comes a phone call from a 'mate' with a proposition. It was a call I took from the son of an old Rawtenstall neighbour who was in a bar late one night with a representative from an Asian gaming group called FUN88. Quite casually they'd had a conversation and it came about that FUN were looking to do shirt sponsorship with a

Premier club. Talk about chance! Within a month introductions were made, meetings were set up, and our commercial manager Anthony Fairclough went on to set up the best shirt deal ever for Burnley Football Club. Some things you can plan for months and they don't happen. Some things just 'happen'. It's all about contacts, a friend of a friend. There's this word serendipity that again seems very appropriate.

Being in the Premier League felt surreal, yet one day that summer Barry Kilby and I were heading down to Melton Mowbray to join the annual meeting of all 20 Premier League clubs when the three newcomers are welcomed into a business that is now worth over £1billion.

Years of printing lottery tickets and scratchcards for national newspapers had lost its excitement and Barry had sold out. "I've got everything I need, a fantastic house and a great car. So what else can I spend my money on," he wondered. "There's a football club down the road and I might be able to do some good."

He set out to help his club thinking he'd never get his money back. To his probable astonishment he did, thanks to the Premier success when the directors were able to reclaim their loans. That's an important perception. They were loans not gifts. His wife is the feisty Sonya who more than once has turned on people who have dared to criticise him, especially in the bad old days of incessant struggle when he was exhorted to "put yer 'and in yer pocket Kilby" when he took his seat in the Bob Lord Stand. His car, his pride and joy is a silver Bentley with a personalised registration plate. Why shouldn't he indulge himself?

As we glided (or should that be glid) through the Leicestershire countryside and the land of the legendary Melton Mowbray pies; at least we were arriving in style in the Bentley, having set out from homely Turf Moor and its surrounding back streets. Eventually we pulled into the grounds of the hotel; we were the Premiership minnows. It became apparent straightaway that a gap existed between us and 'them'. The Bentley soon paled into insignificance when we saw the helicopters that other directors had arrived in, one even had 'go-faster- stripes and bull-bars'. It's not often you get gazumped in a Bentley. "Welcome to the Premiership," we said to each simultaneously. For a moment I wondered if the kitty might run to our own club helicopter in claret and blue. Probably not, I decided.

The afternoon get together was a very relaxed and informal affair followed by a Wednesday night formal dinner when we all convened, two people from each club, chairman and chief executive. How on earth should we handle this, we wondered. We'd talked it through. Do we doff our caps, hide in the corner or wait till we're spoken to?

Course not, just be ourselves. Take it as it comes. Go with the flow. We've earned the right.

In the room sat some of the most important figures in football. Chairmen and chief executives from Manchester United, Chelsea, Manchester City, Liverpool, Tottenham, Everton, Bolton Wanderers, Blackburn Rovers. The room and menu was splendid and no expense was spared. For the connoisseurs, the finest wines were available but this didn't interest Barry and me. A couple of pints of Moorhouse's Pendle Witch would do us. Some of the people there were the ones who had first conceived the idea of the Premier League way back in 1992. Rick Parry, whose brainchild it was, was guest of honour. Yes, the Premier League had been a rip-roaring success; now a billion pound industry, the most successful league in the world, the best attended league in the world and a league that was broadcast to 216 countries with the multi-millions shared between the clubs represented round these tables.

From my time in football and at other clubs I knew most of the characters there, the good, the bad and the dodgy. Some were there to make money; some were there to become famous on TV, some were there to win national trophies and others were there to win European and world titles.

And a few were there because their dads had taken them to their first football matches many years before, it was in their blood, and life had never been the same for them since.

The night turned out to be simply magical. They actually present the newly promoted clubs with a Golden Share which is your ticket to the Premier League and all its riches. It entitled us to a sum of approximately £60 million over the next two years, at least seven televised games and then a sliding scale of payments depending on where the team finished at the end of the season.

That evening at 7.30 prompt at the inauguration dinner, Sir Dave Richards the Premier League chairman opened the proceedings and invited Wolverhampton Wanderers to go up and receive their Share. There was an enthusiastic round of applause. Then it was Birmingham City. There was another hearty round of applause.

"And now," announced Sir Dave Richards, "I'd like to invite the play-off winners to come up and receive their Golden Share ... congratulations to Burnley Football Club." Barry and I could not believe what happened next. The room erupted. We exchanged astonished glances as the whole room rose to their feet to give us a standing ovation. I don't mind saying I had a huge lump in my throat as I watched Barry walk up there. I pictured him for a second as a small boy holding his dad's hand, walking along Brunshaw Road to watch Burnley. What would his father have thought if he could have seen that moment and heard the acclaim? Quite honestly it was a deeply moving moment and his dad would have been so very proud of him.

It was an unforgettable moment of magic and we were astounded by the amount of goodwill in that room for Burnley. We've said it many times, we have this suspicion that we are many people's second club and that's the way it felt in that room even amongst all these movers, shakers, and mega millionaires who had arrived by helicopter. Everybody likes a fairy tale story. Everybody likes a giant killer. There was no-one in that room who hadn't heard of or seen the games against Arsenal, Fulham, Chelsea and Spurs in the Carling Cup. We had joined them on a shoestring. Compared to the debts and budgets of some of these giant clubs Burnley were the paupers. We hadn't realised that we were other clubs *other club.*

Over the next two days we got down to more business with all the clubs seated in alphabetical order around a huge circular table. It was a bit like King Arthur and the Knights of the Round Table. It took a while to sink in that we were sitting amongst all these people and that we weren't actually dreaming. We had Chelsea, one of the biggest clubs on the planet, to our right and to the left of us were arch rivals Blackburn Rovers and Bolton Wanderers. Of course we had no idea then that Phil Gartside, chairman of Bolton Wanderers, all smiles and bonhomie, would be the Darth Vader villain at Burnley in six months' time. You could forgive any Burnley fans for thinking that he was the direct cause of Burnley's relegation from the Premier League when he came calling for Owen Coyle. But it was truly ironic that he was also responsible for the even greater parachute windfall that was to come to Turf Moor.

Parachute payments were discussed at length. Phil Gartside had his suggestion accepted that parachute payments should be extended to four years. In addition the old 50% sum followed by another 50% for two years was changed. He argued that it was important that clubs had the chance to get straight back into the Premiership at the first attempt when they were relegated and for that they needed more money in the first year. Everyone agreed so that the first two payments were structured at 55% and 45%. Then, another two years were added to this. This two-year extension was a massive win for Burnley Football Club. Barry turned to me with his face all lit up and said, "Bloody hell, how much is that extra worth to BFC? My calculations are £16 million."

I'd done a few calculations myself and had got it to £16.5 million.

Yes it was real. We walked out of that meeting nearly £17 million better off with the two-years extension. It was the equivalent of 37,728,624 Holland's meat pies. Not bad for one meeting. It was wonderful and such an eye-opener to be a part of all the discussions that went on that covered refereeing, youth development, players' contracts, ticket prices and football agents. We kept pinching ourselves to make sure it was happening.

There has always been a massive rivalry between Burnley and Blackburn Rovers but at this glittering get-together Barry and I got on really well with Blackburn chairman John Williams (he left after the new owners the Venkys arrived), and chief executive Tom Finn (he would go as well). I've played in local derby games against them and I reckon it evened out at 50-50 over the years in the ones I played. Blackburn's centre-half Glen Keeley regularly gave me a good kicking at Ewood Park but I usually gave him the runaround at Turf Moor. They used to get poor crowds of not much more than 9,000 but we'd get double that at Turf Moor. No-one knew in those days that local business man and Blackburn fan Jack Walker would be the first to show the world how to buy a Premier League title when he went on his spending spree. None of us saw this coming back in the mid-70s.

Fans used to walk to games together and sit side by side without trouble in days gone by. Not so any more. Blackburn chairman John Williams and chief executive Tom Finn were genuinely excited to have us in the room and offered to "help us in any way possible, all you have to do is ring."

It was a bit like the first day at a new school and Sir Dave Richards played the part of the helpful beaming headmaster. "Don't let the big clubs dominate you," he advised. "Just say your piece and speak up. You're part of the Premier League now."

So we did just that. David Gill the Manchester United chief executive (and a real smart cookie) put the case for the big clubs and their thinly-veiled attempts to monopolise youth development throughout the country. I stood up and offered an opposing view. (Yes me, the guy who a few years earlier wouldn't have stood up in a school assembly to say good morning to the kids and whose knees shook at the Dale Carnegie session when we all introduced ourselves.) The fact is that clubs like Man Utd and Arsenal and Chelsea have such a massive pull that they could attract all the kids in the country if they wanted to. The problem is though that if they attract 100 good young lads then 95 of them will have no chance of making it. If only five of them could come to Burnley, two of them might break into the professional ranks.

Currently at a small club if a lad is good enough he might be sold on to a bigger club and the club that has developed him gets a decent payday and a healthy return on all the work they have put in. But the new proposal was that the big clubs could cherry pick all the good young talent at small clubs and pay a pittance in compensation. It isn't right. At least I argued against this two years ago and still do. David Gill (Man Utd CEO) said, "Paul, you have to accept that a young player would rather come to Manchester United than Burnley?"

"Yes" I agreed. "But isn't it better that he spends a couple of years in the Burnley first team, learns his trade, then if he's any good you can come along and buy him, the finished article".

No, he didn't accept my point and this position may result in many young players, who would have made it at Burnley or Preston or Luton or Torquay, being seduced by the big clubs far too early and never making the grade. Alas two years later the proposals have been accepted and the lower league clubs will suffer as a result.

So there we were. On day one we stood up and took on the biggest 'club' in the world, said our bit and argued that youth development was of huge significance to a club like Burnley and that the new proposals would be potentially ruinous to 'little' clubs.

After dinner everyone congregated round the bar. Barry was bushed by 11 and went off to bed. In truth it had all been a draining experience. It really was like the first day at school when you join a new class. I was as tired as Barry, ready to join him (not in the same bed) but forced myself to stay up. There was a chance to do a bit of fraternising and networking with all these top dogs. Here was a chance to get to know them a little better as they began to let their hair down. Whilst sitting around the bar the starchiness and formality had long since evaporated. A few scoops mellow people and lightens the mood. Personalities change. The barriers come down. Believe it or not it wasn't long before we were playing a few silly games. The chairman of Birmingham City was winning the stakes to pull a £5 note from under an upturned bottle without it falling over. The stakes got higher. It got sillier when Allan Duckworth the Bolton CEO challenged the Chelsea CEO in the £5 note game and suggested that if he won, "I win Drogba."

I did the same challenge with David Gill for the "final repayment of the Chris Eagles transfer." Alas three months later when the payment was due he forgot I'd won. Just before midnight one of my new best friends discovered I played the ukulele and it just happened to be in the boot of the car, in case I'd decided to do some busking at a motorway service station. Ten minutes later we were in full swing. If the *Sun* photographers had been there there'd have been some interesting pictures of some of the world's most powerful football figures singing and dancing to the tune of *When I'm Cleanin' Windows*, with the Burnley CEO on uke wearing a set of George Formby teeth.

Through all this I was stone cold sober. I needed to get to know these characters as I might well be negotiating with them over the next few months. Such negotiations might well be a lot easier after I'd had some of them sitting on my knee singing, *"You are my sunshine, my only sunshine ..."*

The step up in infrastructure required from a small Championship club moving to the Premier League can take you by surprise. It was especially daunting for us because until the final kick of the season we had no idea whether or not we would be in the top flight or fighting against the banks for survival.

All we knew was that it would be one or the other. Win at Wembley and the bank manager would be ecstatic. Lose and we faced real problems, even the faint possibility of the 'A' word being mentioned. And there would certainly have been criticism in the boardroom with Brendan Flood the target from the "I told you so" brigade. But, the team came through; finger nails were allowed to grow again. The advancing grey hairs were stopped in their tracks.

There were a number of immediate problems. Firstly the Premier money did not arrive overnight by courier. There was a time lag; in fact the payments were still some way off. Secondly the manpower and staffing to cope with the new administrative headaches just weren't in place. You can't just take people off the streets and slot them into a new job – even if you had the cash. The ticketing systems and computer set-ups were OK for the Championship but the demand for Wembley tickets had shown just how inadequate they were and how understaffed we were.

It would be fair to say we muddled through on a few occasions. Some problems were of our own making because of the limited infrastructure. This was a giant leap we faced. Only those behind the scenes could have been aware of the enormity of it. The midnight oil burned on many nights.

And through all this my ambition remained the same – to build a profitable new stand for my old club.

On occasions in the final weeks of 2008/09 there had been elements of comedy and farce introduced in the situation because of the manager's point-blank refusal to entertain the word promotion. And yet we had to be prepared for the eventuality especially once we qualified for the play-offs. I got the senior key people together about a month before Wembley. Six of us squeezed round the table in my office. The drinks cupboard in some Premier boardrooms was probably bigger than my room. I said, "Right, think forward four weeks and imagine that we have won promotion to the Premiership. Come back one week from now and report on all the things each of you will need to do, to be prepared for Premier League regulations and standards." I figured that it would all come so quickly that once the unmentionable 'P' word happened, we would barely have time to think. So, I needed a costed plan to present to the board which we could implement right away if the impossible became reality.

A week later we began to go through everything. One example: the TV gantry has some of the most wonderful views of the Burnley moors in the faraway of the yonder. They're stunning. People like Dave Thomas tell me (he sits over in the James Hargreaves Stand opposite these wonderful views) that if it's a dull, boring game, the views offer great consolation especially on a blue-sky day. But, no way could the gantry accommodate more than half a dozen people and Premiership games are broadcast to over 200 countries. An extension would be imperative. Then there was the directors' box. Some Prem clubs would want to bring a couple of dozen people with them. It was hopelessly inadequate. The Press room would need alterations. Suddenly we faced interest from not just Bacup and Rawtenstall but from countries around the globe that devoured information and every televised game. These were just three of the new 'needs' out of many, many more. It would be a good opportunity to give the whole stadium a facelift and celebrate the history of the club in quality pictures that explain the journey over the last 100 years.

I initially costed the upgrades at £1.5 million-plus. I knew immediately that this would produce horrified looks and gasps from the usual suspects. But it didn't seem that much in relation to what was coming. Back to the problem though – the time lag between money needed immediately, and when it would be available. It meant more bridging loans.

There was a board meeting on the Wednesday after the Wembley triumph. It was scheduled to be a 'financial review' meeting in case we lost and the future looked gloomy. The agenda was to look at the substantial deficits and this would involve hard decisions. But, with good news and a whole new scenario it was expected by people like Brendan and me that this meeting would now take on a whole new complexion of anticipation, excitement, satisfaction and positivity. My plans for dealing with all the operational issues seemed like a bargain basement deal at the £2 million cost I now envisaged. A whole raft of extras had been added to the three major needs we identified. I walked into that boardroom expecting an immediate, smiling, enthusiastic rubber-stamp. In addition, the costs of the new stand had been scaled back from the earlier £30 million to something around £15 million but that was a subject I decided to leave until the next meeting.

If I expected immediate approval I was in for a rude shock, however. Some people were in no mood for speedy rubber-stamping. A huge and heated debate ensued and my request for the costs I envisaged was refused. I was open-mouthed. A suggestion that a small token bonus should be paid to staff for helping the club achieve promotion was also rejected, even though these people had put in the same Herculean efforts as the playing staff. One board member said something like, "What have they done to deserve a bonus? They should be thinking themselves lucky they still have a job."

The objections I suspect were a direct result of Brendan's policies and ways of working. His tolerance and encouragement of risk had pushed some people out of their comfort zones to a place where they were uncomfortable. There was a battle of cultures. Some wanted the club to be a big fish in a small pond and Brendan wanted the club to be a little fish in a big pond.

If things get too comfortable and established in a boardroom you end up in mid-table. Magical things don't happen when you are happy to settle for what you have got. What's that saying? Fortune favours the brave. It's true. Whilst Barry Kilby had been solid, dependable, playing the straight bat at one end, keeping the innings ticking over; Brendan at the other had been out there doing deals, phoning his contacts, speaking to people like Fergie, bringing in a player here, a player there, backing Owen to the hilt, trying to set things up in the USA and hitting a few sixes. Then he'd tell the rest of the board about it. Some didn't like it. They felt out of the loop.

That's how I had been brought to the club. Brendan knocked on my front door one night and asked did I fancy joining the club to help them build a new stand and develop Turf Moor. Of course I said "yes" and before I knew it there I was working as a consultant in the office of the development director. But Brendan just did it. He hadn't told anyone. It was some months later that I took up the position of chief executive. They say that it's easier to ask for forgiveness than permission, but it made board meetings difficult at times. Long before I'd arrived and before Owen Coyle was in situ, it was Brendan who had organised Ade Akinbiyi to join Burnley without consulting anyone. More than one director was indignant. But then where would the club have been if Brendan had not adopted this direct one-man approach, had not invested money, not acted independently? Probably about mid-table without the Premier league experience and the windfall it brought.

Brendan's decisions have turned out to be well balanced judgements. He often challenged a board that didn't like being challenged. He'd worked hard to become a successful national operator and an investor in several business sectors. He was bold and decisive at the right moments and those decisions were all about backing Owen Coyle and then hanging on to him when Glasgow Celtic came sniffing. They most certainly offered him the job as their manager and he turned down a king's ransom to stay at Burnley where the attraction was the Premier League. A boy from Paisley chose to stay in Burnley in preference to his home town club and a European stage. I don't think he would have stayed without Brendan Flood's support. When he wanted something, Brendan saw that he got it. It made the Modus problems all the more significant. When the development business at Modus went into administration Brendan was unable to offer Owen the inducements to stay at Burnley when Bolton's Phil Gartside was the next one to come sniffing – only this time successfully.

It takes a strong man to continue to give the level of attention to Burnley that Brendan was giving, whilst simultaneously his business was being hit hard, fellow directors were criticising, and, on top of that his mother-in-law died the night before the Wembley Final. He brought a new style of operating to the club and I can understand that some people were on edge about that. But, I simply HAD to get the proposed £2 million improvements implemented at the club. Astonishingly one comment at the board meeting debate was, "We have to get back to the pre-Flood era." I think some members of that board were just desperate to get back to the days of 'prawn sandwiches' for the next few years, even if it meant relegation. I suspected they felt their noses had been put out and didn't like it.

Brendan wasn't at that critical board meeting. I didn't repeat the comment to him. Possibly the director who said it wanted it conveying to him. Where did I stand in all this? If I was seen as Brendan's man, then that was fine with me. As far as I was concerned his vision represented the future for Burnley. It was sod's law that the recession hit the economy. I was determined to see these plans for improvements implemented and determined to see them through. With the support of Barry Kilby they were eventually given the green light. I remain astonished that there were people there who questioned them.

I didn't know it then, but this anti 'change' attitude at board level was to have a massive impact on Brendan's next futuristic vision of a 'Football University'. Incredibly the revenue from this idea, (at a time when financial fair play was arriving in football and clubs had to find ways to make more profit from their stadiums), could make more money for BFC than the parachute payments. After 20 years working in the commercial side of football stadiums this was the best idea I had ever heard. I could see Brendan's vision. UCFB had the chance of keeping BFC in the Premiership next time round. Sadly, out of the five directors on the Burnley board, only one would back him. This time around, with this idea, if he wanted to take a risk he would have to do it with his own money (and the support of the one other director). This time if he wanted to proceed with his visionary idea for Burnley FC, he could gamble on his own if he wanted. So he did.

Meanwhile, I persevered and got my £2 million and Turf Moor was to get its first major facelift for 33 years. The full list was daunting:

New AstroTurf pitch and drainage at Gawthorpe ... refurbished admin offices, new PA system, refurbished youth development offices, relocated catering offices, player dressing room upgrades, kitchen extensions, new Desso pitch at Turf Moor, refurbished corporate and hospitality suites in Bob Lord Stand, collection and display of club memorabilia in new cabinets, improvements to 1882 Lounge, refurbish corporate facilities in James Hargreaves Stand, refurbish the now Jimmy Adamson Suite, upgrade ticket office, extend club shop, refurbish Chairman's Lounge, relocate score and display board, extensive re-carpeting, refurbish manager's office, new players' lounge, upgrade media facilities, extend dug-outs.

Not a lot there then?

Something I'd been doing during the last few months had been the discussions with Burnley Council and Burnley Cricket Club about the idea of relocating the cricket club to a new site at Towneley in order to facilitate the building of the new stand. We offered to pay up to £1 million for a new club house and underpin the club for the next 15 years if they would agree. We knew they would lose money from football car parking and the numbers of people who went in the club on a matchday. A new club house would have brought them more money through the better facilities for banqueting, weddings and seasonal functions. Although everything seemed lined up and a new stand seemed feasible, it never happened and it all slowly wound down. I could sense that some of the Burnley board anyway were having cold feet. I knew exactly who was leading the negativity and I knew why he was doing it. But Brendan stayed supportive and it was clear that if he could have become chairman as he hoped, the non-believers were concerned that he would encourage more national businessmen on the board, which would result in the ultimate removal of the passengers.

In July, the Premier League sent their inspector, Derek Johnson, to visit Turf Moor. The purpose was to give us advice on all the things that we had to get up to scratch. He hadn't been in my singalong group, more's the pity. We felt that the plan we put together was a good one and we were making progress. Derek had a look round the dressing rooms, the same ones that had been built 35 years earlier and hadn't changed much apart from a few coats of paint. In those long-gone days teams would arrive with one skip of kit, a dozen towels and a packet of chewing gum. Today they will come with almost a skip for every player and their own X-ray machines, ice machines and emergency equipment. You get 18 players and a dozen non-playing staff. That's an awful lot to squeeze into a room not much bigger than a broom cupboard. We were happy enough they had a chair and a peg and a block of green Sunlight soap to share. This was Burnley not the Ritz Carlton. They were visiting to play football not to have a relaxing break. Football is at the point now where it's more like Status Quo turning up than a football team.

Although Derek was not exactly impressed with the dressing rooms (my bathroom is better), he just told us to write in, plead our case, and we would get special dispensation for a year; then we would certainly have to get them up to scratch. Great, I thought, that frees up some of my £2 million to use on other items on the list. I can budget to do the dressing rooms later.

I found it strange then that Sir Dave Richards, the Premier League chairman, should make a special trip to Burnley some weeks after Derek's inspection. I've known David for many years since my early days as an after-dinner speaker when I would sit next to him on the top table at Sheffield Wednesday. It was he who rang to offer me the job of commercial director at the new Wembley Stadium. We chatted for a while and then he said, "Do you mind if we have a quick look round whilst I'm here?"

We walked around the ground for a quick tour (we normally charge £6.50) and he seemed keen to get to the dressing rooms. The stadium manager was with us at this point and dropped in what was an interesting bit of trivia. Little did we realise it would cost us money. "And strangely, the home dressing room is six inches bigger than the away dressing room." All very innocent; how could that entertaining bit of non-information have such an impact? I can only imagine that some clubs had been raising questions about our facilities because this little quip came back to hit us and things escalated quite dramatically.

At this point we were just FOUR days away from the first home game and the visit of Manchester United. Sir Dave left to go to London and as I was packing up late in the day to leave for the weekend (Stoke the opening game the next day away) I heard the soft purr and chatter of the fax machine. Incredibly, the FA still communicated by fax. I could have left it and picked it up on Monday. But some sixth sense told me to take a peek. Maybe I'd won something from *Readers Digest*. What could be so urgent as to warrant a fax at 4.45pm on a Friday afternoon?

It was from Mike Foster the secretary of the Football League. Sir Dave had obviously been in touch with him. The fax said that the league would, yes, give us 12 months dispensation to get the dressing rooms sorted on condition that we allocated the "bigger" dressing room to the away team. As I was digesting this the phone rang. It was Mike Foster. "Paul did you get my fax?" he asked. "What do you think?"

I was certainly taken aback and thinking on my feet. Frankly it was all a bit absurd. Change dressing rooms for the sake of six inches. You must be joking I was actually thinking. "Well look Mike I can't say anything now, I'll have to speak to the manager. This is his territory. I'll call you Monday because I think I know what he'll say. He'll go ape-shit. It's been the home dressing room for 35 years."

I knew what the answer would be and Owen was on the end of the line when I called him, fortunately. My prediction was pretty much spot on. He went apoplectic. So, there I was with the Premier League on the one hand saying swap dressing rooms, and the manager on the other turning puce saying on no account was he moving, these were the lucky dressing rooms. There was no point involving the chairman or Brendan. The stuffed cat that lay on the window ledge in the chairman's room was no help either. I got Doug Metcalfe the stadium manager later in the evening at 9.30 pm. We met at Turf Moor and stood in the away dressing room. They'd been brand new when I was a player and I was fond of them, they held so many memories. Now I was cursing them and Dave Richards and Mike Foster and the extra six inches. We had a tape measure and double checked each dressing room. The folklore was true. The home room was indeed six inches bigger. It amounted to roughly a square metre (yes we have gone metric in Burnley, not sure about Bacup though). It went through my mind that maybe we could somehow make the home dressing room smaller. Nope Owen would not have liked that.

We found some torches, wandered down deeper into the bowels of the old stand and discovered that the away dressing room adjoined the old boiler room. Squeezing in amongst the pipes and valves we realised that there was an extra bit of space between all this paraphernalia and the wall. With a bit of luck we could find the extra space but this meant calling in a local builder. He turned up at 10.45pm that night when I explained the problem. Who says you can never get a builder at short notice? By 11.30pm we had worked out that we could knock down a wall and rebuild if we put a girder in to take the load. The away fans sit directly overhead. I could just imagine half a dozen of them crashing through into the dressing room ceiling seeing Wayne Rooney sat on the toilet reading *The Sun* if we didn't do the job right.

I returned to Turf Moor at 10am the next morning on my way to the Stoke game. The lads had worked through the night. The wall was down, the girder in place and they were getting ready to put the new wall up. They were Burnley fans and considered it a job of honour to get it done in time for Man U on the Tuesday night. This was more than a job. This was about helping the Clarets get started in the Premier League. It looked like all would be well and ready in time, in fact by Tuesday lunchtime. But hell, then there was another fly in the ointment. Someone pointed out that there were so few showers; why not add them whilst they were working. Frantically we worked out there was room for another six showers.

Don't knock British tradesmen. These guys were superhuman and played a blinder. Late Tuesday afternoon one hour after they swept up the last bits of debris and had got the showers in as well as the new wall, a huge, shiny coach pulled up at the players' entrance carrying the Premier League champions, Sir Alex, and all their skips. Most of the skips had to stay in the corridor. Some of them were so big they had their own driver. On Tuesday afternoon I faxed Sir Dave and Mike Foster to tell them everything we had done. There was no need to switch dressing rooms. It was a huge relief. Those builders were well and truly a part of the Burnley 'family'.

Tony Livesey, a TV and radio presenter and Burnley fan, joined me at a Fans Forum the following week. We tell the fans what's happening at these meetings, and on pain of not repeating anything tell them a little of the behind the scenes stuff. We can relax a little and say things and how we see them with a bit more frankness than usual. I described the dressing room fiasco. You would have thought that Tony too would abide by this. His journalistic instincts however couldn't resist a good story. Shortly afterwards he went on live TV and told the whole tale. It was no big deal other than prompting a bit of a media scrum as the other Press guys latched onto the story of our inadequate dressing rooms. The *Sun* even wanted pictures of Wayne on the loo and the bandwagon began to roll.

There have been lots of stories over the years about how dodgy managers have sabotaged away dressing rooms either by turning the heating on full, or turning it right off, or blocking off the hot water to the showers, removing light bulbs and even painting the walls black. We would never do that but nonetheless the dressing rooms became a hot topic. The media decided that they were our deliberate secret weapon and yet we had gone to all the trouble to actually extend the away room. I can't remember any paper actually mentioning that. But, we did what Sir Dave and Mike wanted. Even the bars of Sunlight soap are now 30% bigger. And who knows maybe the Man U galacticos now have Sunlight in their own marble, gold-tapped bathrooms.

My philosophy was to "do the right thing" at all times. Sometimes you have to choose between profit and doing the right thing. Too often profit wins the day and I guess I too have sometimes fallen to that. But more often than not it's human needs that come first. Yes we have to be business-like if we are to get anywhere and compete. The season ticket mayhem that we got caught up in prior to the debut in the Premiership was a reminder. It was all hugely chaotic when we realised that we were entering into uncharted territory. For a start there weren't enough staff. On top of that some had elected to take their holidays (as people do) and were away at the most critical time. But the furore caused by promotion left us well and truly exposed. We were excited about season ticket sales. There were 7,500 plus season ticket holders and the prediction was that we might sell 12,000. In fact we sold 17,500. It was incredible. ST mania took over. It meant a sell-out for every home game and some quick thinking to get a section of what was normally the away stand, ready for home fans. That posed all kinds of logistical problems not the least of which was segregation. There was a suggestion that we should sell season tickets to Burnley supporters in the Cricket Field Stand. This might be costly and lose us money as these seats could be sold to the visiting supporters at a higher price. But, to their credit, the board approved the idea and agreed that a couple of thousand less away fans, replaced by a couple of thousand home fans making a real din, would create be far better atmosphere which would be more beneficial than the extra revenue it would create.

But whilst sell-outs sounded great there was the small problem of getting all these season tickets out. "No problem," I thought, "I can talk all this through with Elaine the ticket office manager;" except Elaine was away for two weeks. Slight problem there then; normally it was never a problem but the volume of extra work this year was horrendous. For the ST book there is a voucher at the front over which we overprint the row and seat number that the ticket relates to. Our normal practice is to order them well in advance. With Elaine away no-one immediately noticed that all these vouchers had Coca Cola Championship printed on them. So there we were, demand had more than doubled; many of the staff were on holiday and we had all these unusable vouchers. It meant they had to be re-ordered and that meant a two-week delay to get them posted out or available for collection. Elaine returned all smiles and sun-tanned to ask, "Is everything finished then, has everything gone alright?"

Things were further complicated by the 'Chairman's Pledge'. This was Barry Kilby's promise to issue a free season ticket to everyone who had bought one for the previous season. He had made this pledge during the actual previous season long before notions of promotion became reality. It was a way to encourage a few extra people to invest in a ticket and generate extra income. I suppose he/we could have argued that the pledge only applied to the next Championship season. But we didn't and Barry K. agreed to extend his gift to loyal supporters for the Premier season. So, something like 7,500 people got a free ticket to the Prem season. It was an astonishing offer, I don't think it had ever been done before and everything was in place the season before I arrived back in Burnley. The mechanics of making it happen were not quite straightforward. Fans first had to physically pay for the season ticket as usual. Without that there would have been serious cash-flow problems. Then it had to be refunded. There was no 'real' money in the bank until August and the first wodge of Premier dosh. It made a situation that had to be managed carefully. The whole thing cost the club around £2 million.

The response to the delay in repayments produced a spectrum of responses. Some said fine, no problem pay us whenever. Others wanted it immediately. Some even turned up at the club and I had them in my office refusing to leave until they received their money back. Some asked if they could use it to buy a 'share' in the club. Some simply donated it to the youth department. It was a noble gesture but was then mis-interpreted by a handful of corporate members. It was never ever intended that the offer included a complete refund to box holders and members of various matchday clubs like the 100 Club, the chairman hadn't budgeted for that. But to Barry Kilby's credit he did reflect on this and then agreed to repay the 'season ticket element' of all corporate membership packages, but not repay for the food and parking and free programmes etc. as average season ticket holders had to pay for these extras. He insisted that all Burnley fans would be treated equally and fairly.

Unfortunately one supporter caused the club real difficulties and it all became extremely unpleasant. This supporter had paid around

£1,200 for a 100 Club ticket in the Bob Lord Stand. He was offered £396 by the club, the price of a season ticket 'seat'. That was the Chairman's Pledge that was on offer. How could the club possibly refund amounts such as £1,200 to everybody who had paid that amount, or the huge sums that corporate box-holders had paid? The club honoured that pledge with everyone but the supporter believed that he was entitled to the full refund of £1,000 plus. No agreement was reached and it became a legal wrangle in the civil courts. The supporter was upset; so were we. The dispute dragged on for over 12 months and cost a lot in lawyers' fees. But Barry would tell me 'Paul it's not the money it's the principle that matters. I will be fair and treat every season ticket holder equally'. The club decided not to allow this supporter to buy any more tickets believing that his actions were damaging to the club. He in turn argued that being "banned for nothing" left him with a social stigma after many years of support. The whole thing dragged on for months and he reported the club to The Premier League, a Football Supporters organisation, The Football League and eventually to the Independent Football Ombudsman. He even had his photograph taken outside the club in a story in the *Telegraph*. The club still feels that it was entirely right in its offer of the basic £396 season ticket. It was a fantastic offer, totally unique, and wonderfully generous gift from the chairman to all his loyal season ticket holders. Has any other club ever done anything like this on promotion to the Premier League?

To draw a line under the matter and save Barry Kilby the embarrassment of attending the small claims court, the club eventually paid this particular fan the full cost of his 100 Club seat, but we felt it only right to tell him that he would no longer be able to buy more tickets to watch BFC. It is intended that this decision will be reviewed annually.

This was a real shame. I know that Barry was very upset by this issue at a time when he should have been celebrating each day.

Elaine was back from her holidays. Tickets were flying out of the door and we seemed to be getting to grips with everything. There were just a few season tickets left one Monday morning when I turned up and climbed the stairs to my office. I was on a sort of autopilot, thinking about the long list of things to do, and not really noticing anything either side of me. But just as I was about to turn into the office, I did see an elderly man, probably in his 70s, standing in the corridor outside. He was shivering and didn't look too good. He looked like he needed a doctor. Did he think I was a GP? He didn't sound too good either as he greeted me with a shaky voice.

"Are you Paul Fletcher? I'm Mr Arkwright. And I'm starting to feel very ill."

I could see that and I asked him what the problem was? "Nobody can find my season ticket. I've not slept for three nights and I've not been eating. I'm shaking with worry. I don't know who to talk to about it."

A problem like this, face to face, not an anonymous email, not a phone call, somebody right there in front of you brings you into the real world immediately. You can't fob off someone standing there who clearly sounded like he was genuinely worried and upset. I took him into the office and got him a cup of tea. Meanwhile Elaine filled me in about the ticket. Just as concerned as I was, she explained, "Paul he hasn't paid. We've had no money from him."

The solution was easy and quick enough. Maybe his cheque was missing or mislaid somewhere or lost at the GPO sorting office. "Tell him we just haven't cashed his cheque, tell him to write out a new one, and sort out the ticket today. If the old cheque turns up one day we'll just tear it up."

But there was another problem. "Paul because we've had nothing from him we've sold his regular seat." Oh God, the guy had sat in this seat for 33 years.

More quick thinking: "Elaine check who now has this seat and find me a phone number so I can contact them."

I phoned the new seat holder and explained the situation. We chatted about Colin Waldron's winning goal at Preston in 1973. I offered him an extra seat if he would let Mr Arkwright have his old seat back. He agreed. Another problem solved in the typical day of a football club CEO. Sometimes there's a choice between having your hard-hearted business head on or doing the right thing. It would have been easy to say to Mr Arkwright, "Sorry tough luck, your mistake, go home and be ill and don't sleep." But this supporter had been with us for 33 years and probably more he hadn't mentioned. He deserved to retrieve his favourite seat for the Premiership season. If I couldn't help him do it, "then what a poor do," as we say in my neck of the woods.

In the end we lost the price of the season ticket we'd given away. But at least we saved the NHS some money.

# 15

# Half a Season and Goodbye Owen

With a packed pre-season, including another trip to the USA, and then more pre-season games in the UK it was a frantic time between Wembley and the opening of the new season. If my job was to get the tickets out and the stadium ready, as well as look at every available commercial opportunity; it was Owen who prepared the team. Sometimes as an ex-player it was tempting to make suggestions. I knew what the reaction would be though. So I didn't.

Both Owen and Brendan were keen on the second trip to the USA although as ever, the usual people on the board grumbled that we couldn't afford it and wouldn't a trip to Ireland or Austria have been better and cost less? But Owen ignored them. He wanted his players to feel like Premier players and a Championship economy trip to Europe would not have delivered that message. Everton had gone out there the season before and the trip was organised by Graham Smith (ex-Colchester goalkeeper) who was based in Ventura. He knew what was needed and the main game would have been against Mr Beckham's LA Galaxy but alas that fell through.

It was during this trip that we thought we had discovered the next George Best when a young South American lad, Fernando Guerrero, joined on trial. He was outstanding against Ventura. Alas when he discovered the cold, wet climate of East Lancashire was a million miles away from what he had been used to at home and in Spain, he wasn't quite so magical.

The whole squad was invited to a wonderful evening at the Beverley Hills Hotel by Frank Carroll and his wife Caroline of Cooke Oils, the club shirt sponsors. Barry and Sonya Kilby were also staying there, as they were big friends of Frank and Caroline. This was where all the big stars stayed. Owen felt really at home and started to walk like George Clooney – hoping to be recognised. This hotel was a real eye-opener, a glittering place where we were instructed not to bother any of the stars should we bump into any. Huh, we thought, have they never heard of Robbie Blake and Martin Paterson so we told them not to bother our stars. Alas we didn't see any stars. It must have been the one night of the year when the likes of Madonna, Jerry Springer, Nicole Kidman and Colin Waldron et al were out of town. The only thing we saw that made us laugh was Owen Coyle's new tattoo which he had done in LA at 'LA Ink' where they film the TV show. Maybe he was looking for an acting role?

Strangely, the build-up to the first game away at Stoke City was fairly quiet. It was as if we'd got all the traumas (and losing a friendly at Bradford City) out of the way and once the first game came, some semblance of normality and routine took over. But what a routine – Man Utd were due in a matter of days and don't forget whilst the game at Stoke was taking place, unknown to all the thousands of fans who made the trip to Stoke, another team of builders was manically working to get the dressing rooms altered back at Turf Moor. It was almost surreal. Before driving down to Stoke I was in those dressing rooms at 10am checking on progress. It looked like a forlorn hope that they would be ready in time.

As for the game, Burnley in the Premiership, that too seemed surreal. Again I couldn't help but see it through my own perspective of the ex-player, one of the last bunch that had played in the top division with Burnley 33 years earlier. It was tempting to go into the dressing room and make a little speech. I didn't. We viewed it as a winnable game with Stoke as a bottom half of the table club. So this we thought would be a good test. Hmmm, it was a reality check. They were bigger and stronger and disposed of us with minimum fuss. It was all a bit of an anti-climax. Behind the scenes the welcome and the hospitality was great. There was none on the field. Truth be told, they were an easy three points for Stoke who won 2 – 0.

I headed straight back to Turf Moor to see how the builders were getting on. They had just two full days and half of Tuesday to complete the job in time. There was an element of driving home with my tail between my legs. It was a chastening defeat and the run of games to come was utterly daunting. When we'd looked at the fixture list after its first appearance there was excitement and anticipation. Now as the games actually approached you just worried that there were some thumpings to come. We looked at the list again; to come were ... Man Utd, Everton, Chelsea and then Liverpool. Stoke had beaten us easily enough, what would these next teams do? Where on earth were the first points to come from?

I don't propose to go through every game played in the Premiership season. They are all covered in great depth in the Dave Thomas book, *Entertainment, Heroes and Villains*. But one or two do stand out and the images will remain for a long time. The home game against Manchester United left an indelible memory. The buzz around the game had built up to a crescendo. It was a complete sell-out. The changing room saga was completed with about an hour to spare before the team arrived. Someone had sneaked in with a mobile phone, taken a picture and sent it to the *Sun*. The Press painted a picture of us deliberately setting Man U up in dilapidated dressing rooms.

At Owen's request I rang up a local wine merchant and asked them to pick out a couple of bottles of quality Claret. It was a gesture of hospitality and goodwill towards Sir Alex. The local house wine from the fog-covered slopes of Bacup wasn't quite up to standard we felt. When the bottles arrived I gave them to Owen. Owen, a teatotaller alas knew nothing about wine at all and promptly put them in the fridge next to the Irn-bru. The story got out before the game and again it was seen as mind-games, with Owen serving his visitor ice-cold Claret.

For this opening home game I decided it would be nice to produce some special commemorative programmes. I looked back to when I was a player and remembered that I always used to keep the programmes from the really big games and clubs. So for this one I had the idea to individualise the programmes with each player's name on the front. So, for each player there was a personalised programme on his chair in the dressing room with his name on it, for example 'Burnley FC welcomes Wayne Rooney'. There was one each of them. Each was unique. It was a late-night idea (all my best ideas are). I thought the uniqueness might make them valuable one day so they could be auctioned for charity or donated to good causes.

Of course it was interpreted as more mind-games to soften the Man Utd players up. How daft can you get? Inevitably much later it came to be included in the list of my 'extravagances'.

And then Owen came in. He was a bit miffed and wanted one each for all his players and staff. I obliged. We had a special programme done too for the fans with a limited edition serial number. I thought £15 would be a fair price and produced just 100 with gold print on the cover hoping they'd sell. The club shop didn't open until 9am and there were fans queuing at twenty past eight to snap them up. I reckon if I'd printed 500 and sold them at £50 they'd still have sold out. But, in truth it was a heart thing not a money thing just to make the night and the occasion seem special.

Clubs parade their celebrity supporters. It might be Oasis at Manchester City, or rows of 'luvvies' at Chelsea. Burnley has Prince Charles and Alastair Campbell. The next King might well have a Burnley shirt under his robes when he is crowned. Burnley pennants hang or have hung in the unlikeliest places. There used to be one at the British Embassy in Tripoli hanging from the office door of Ambassador

Sir Vincent Fein an avid Burnley supporter. Maybe it still does. Former Prime Minister Edward Heath was a follower in the days of Bob Lord. So too was Margaret Thatcher's press secretary Sir Bernard Ingham.

It doesn't matter what or who you are though when you follow the same team. And superstitions are a great leveller. Here's how Alastair Campbell and I were involved in the build-up to Robbie Blake's stupendous winning goal. We will forever argue that Robbie's goal was down to us.

I was sitting not too far from Alastair and he was sitting almost behind his friend Fergie who was in the dugout. They're good friends because of their mutual political sympathies. The game was in full flow, the noise level deafening, the atmosphere cracking and I looked across to Alastair. We exchanged grins, what a night this was. Then he called out "Fletch" and beckoned to the way he was sitting. "Sit like this."

He was sitting in the most peculiar position with his right hand clutching his left knee and his left arm pulled across his body holding his right shoulder. "Sit like this," he motioned. So, I did. I copied the way he was sitting and looked at him again, momentarily distracted from the game. Then, just as I resumed watching, what happened next? Robbie Blake caught the ball with a sublime volley as it was cleared out to him in the angle of the box. His screaming shot hit the back of the net before you could blink. The ground erupted into scenes of pandemonium and ecstasy never seen before at Turf Moor, and believe me there have been plenty of great games under the lights at Turf Moor. What is it about floodlights that intensify the drama? They make great games seem even better. Here we were at this moment winning 1 – 0. I swear the stand roofs had lifted three feet. The celebrations subsided and we all resumed our seats and positions. Alastair and I were grinning like Cheshire cats at each other.

"Fletch," he said, right hand on left knee, left hand holding right shoulder, "Do you realise that 'we' made that goal happen because we sat like this."

The interior facilities of the Bob Lord suite had been refurbished. It seemed a good idea to refurbish corporate palates at the same time, or at least make the attempt. A season was in prospect where we wanted to raise the bar a little. Burnley wasn't all clogs, whippets and flat caps; in fact the last sighting of any of these things had been several years earlier. They are a disappearing species. But still it was the abiding image along with brass bands and cobbled streets. Send a Sky cameraman anywhere near Burnley and that's what they look for.

For years at Burnley there's also been an image of pie and peas.

Holland's are renowned pie makers and had been club sponsors. So at Turf Moor, Roy Keane could never accuse us of being the prawn sandwich brigade, but he might have said the pie and peas brigade. For the Man Utd games we did a very daring thing. We replaced the pie and peas with curry and rice. It was a decision that was on a level with changing your vote from Socialist to Tory.

The comments came thick and fast: "Where's t' pies gone ... what the hell is this ... this is bloody ridiculous ... ah know we're in't Premiership but this curry lark is just not on ..."

I knew what would be on the agenda at the next board meeting. And it was. It was back to the great pie debate.

Something had been going on in the background for a couple of weeks, something so sensitive that only Barry Kilby, Brendan Flood and me knew about it. You have to meet a lot of people whatever business you are in if you want to expand and grow and find new investment. I call it kissing frogs to find a prince. Or, you've got to be in it to win it, is another way of putting it. As ever there were some directors who simply thought it was all chasing thin air and wasting money. But, those who were realistic and didn't want to simply sit back in the comfort zone knew that any Premiership stay would be short-lived without more income.

There had already been the group of US businessmen expressing interest and that had come to nothing but then there was another intriguing show of interest. I was preparing to speak at a dinner in Burnley and a call came through to me late in the afternoon. It was from a football agent who asked if I would come and meet someone from China interested in the club. Nothing ventured, nothing gained, as the saying goes and I explained that I would be able to meet up before the end of the week. "Ah," said the agent, "my client leaves for China tomorrow. Can you meet before 11pm this evening in Manchester?"

On the basis that kissing frogs is essential in this job I agreed to get over there that evening as soon as I had finished speaking. It was after 10.30pm when I finally got away and raced over to the Midland Hotel in Manchester. So there I was turning up in my dinner suit wondering what it was all about and could this be the golden jackpot that we were looking for at the club. I have to say I was intrigued very quickly when I sat down to listen.

The Chinese guy represented a group of businessmen who wanted to invest in a Premier club and they were realistic enough to appreciate that they could not afford Man Utd or Arsenal. So, if they could hook up to a club that wouldn't be asking for the moon they would have a very cost effective way of promoting their brand. What they wanted to do was name their business 'Burnley' rather than just having the brand on the front of a shirt. On the front of a shirt the publicity is not 24 hours a day. But, if they named their brand 'Burnley' the exposure would be enormous, in other words every time the club was mentioned in the media. Brand and club would thus be synonymous. The guy also talked about youth development. We agreed to talk more.

I reported back to Barry that these people wanted to buy half the club and leave the present people running things. There wasn't a great deal of interest but Barry and Brendan agreed to go over to Hong Kong and discuss things further. For the moment it was to be kept quiet. We named it Operation Ping Pong. A couple of days before he was due to fly out Barry phoned me at home and asked me to do him a favour. He didn't really fancy the trip out to Hong Kong. Would I take his place? I guess his instincts were telling him that this might be a bit of a wild goose chase and there'd be no mileage in kissing this particular frog. Alas my wife was unwell, needed my support and I had to decline.

Barry therefore flew half-heartedly to Hong Kong. Having gone with little enthusiasm, he came back brimming with optimism for the place wishing he was 20 years younger so as to take advantage of all the opportunities out there. The Chinese people began to sketch out their plans and ideas. It centred on Burnley of course but to take advantage of the Premiership place it was also geared to youth and youth development across China.

Alas it all came to nothing but merely illustrated the lengths we were prepared to travel to find new investment. It was just another frog we had to kiss.

Meanwhile to our utter delight there was another great win in the Prem. This time we beat Everton 1 – 0 at Turf Moor. OK so there was a little stroke of luck as in the Man Utd game when Everton missed a penalty. Another full house, another ecstatic crowd and all of us stared at the six points we had won so far. I knew their CEO, Robert Elstone really well and we talked about their proposed new stadium in Kirkby which was to be part-funded by Tesco whose chairman was an Evertonian. It was another project that would come to nothing in these recessionary times.

Project Ping Pong had lit up our imaginations but something else was on the go. Brendan Flood's brain never sleeps. Now he was thinking of something truly original. The StadiArena plan was on hold; in fact any kind of stadium plan was on hold but Brendan began to think about what could be done at the opposite end of the ground in the Jimmy McIlroy Stand. Could a town of mill chimneys become a town of dreaming spires? Could we figure out how to initiate a

Football University at Turf Moor? It sounded a wild idea. 'Blue sky' thinking I thought. But that was also my kind of thinking too. It was the kind of idea that would be lampooned and scorned when it eventually became public.

But the university idea would not go away. Why shouldn't we do something along these lines? It would put Burnley on the map. It would generate income. The space was available. Universities today have business modules. Why shouldn't there be a module based on football business? The more we thought about it the more excited we became. Football is global but nowhere was there one place where all the disciplines to do with the administration and commercial side of the game were actually taught.

We talked and talked about it but it was clear that the board was not fully behind it. There would be no chance of the club itself investing in it and subsequently owning it which would have been the ideal scenario. Nevertheless I was really keen to proceed because I had come to Burnley not to push paper round a desk but to achieve something tangible and important. The new stand was clearly not going to happen but the university idea might. Again it seemed to me that opposition to the idea wasn't because it was a bad one, but more because it was Brendan's concept. I suspected some of the board still looked at him and saw risk. Some seemed uncomfortable and out of place in this new Premier land even though beating the likes of Manchester United and Everton had set the town alight.

Think about it we said to each other. You have media studies, management, stadium design, administration, sports science, catering and hospitality, commercialism and all kinds of other aspects. Why couldn't you have a situation where people from all over the world could come to one place and study all these things – in situ – at an actual football club? How good would that be for both club and the town of Burnley? At this point the ideas were literally on the back of an envelope. But what was also true that the trip to Hong Kong for Operation Ping Pong had been instrumental in generating this idea. It was a place that fired the imagination and we sensed a hunger for football over there and all its add-ons. It inspired a picture of overseas students taking up places.

And then the football side of things brought us back down to earth at Chelsea when Burnley were given a football lesson. It was painful to see them take us apart 3 – 0. There was no repeat of the previous season's heroics and night to remember. So far then, four games and two wins and it was all wonderful.

The home wins continued but it wasn't until November that the first away point arrived in a wonderful game at Manchester City. Burnley roared into a 2 – 0 lead against a team of galacticos and star names. And that was just on the subs bench. It was winter and a joy to sit on the heated seats in the directors' box. I had my eldest grandson, Morgan, with me and Mike Summerbee gave us a tour of the ground before the match. We had been at Burnley together for two years and did the after-dinner circuit together. The genius that was Jimmy Adamson had him playing full-back at Burnley. He reasoned if he could play as a winger and kick full-backs, he could play as a full-back and kick wingers. This he duly did.

Mike is famous also for his large nose and droll wit. I asked five different people at City exactly what did he do in his role as ambassador for the club. None of them had any idea.

Things were still going well when we played Sunderland and it was live on Sky. I was asked to be studio guest. I knew Richard Keys from my Coventry days (he was a big Coventry fan) and when he'd worked for Radio Lancashire he'd lived in Rawtenstall (not a lot of people know that). I was proud to represent BFC that day and also happy to donate my £1,000 fee to the Clarets Trust. It was another win against a club we always seemed to do well against and of course I thought back to the time I scored the two goals in a 2 – 0 win when we clinched promotion in 1973. I always enjoyed playing against Dave Watson when he was their centre-half. And another Sunderland legend had been Charlie Hurley who was then at Bolton when I was there.

The home wins came to an end against Aston Villa. It was a 1 – 1 draw that was never a true reflection of the football that Burnley played and the chances they made. When Emile Heskey equalised near the end of the game it was maybe the moment that the season changed and the struggles began. Away from home there had been heavy defeats against Liverpool, Tottenham and West Ham. Owen Coyle's last win with Burnley in the Premiership was actually on October 31st with a 2 – 0 win over Hull City. After that it was a procession of draws and defeats. The home defeat against Wigan Athletic cost the club dear. You could argue that the three points that Wigan won instead of Burnley that day cost Burnley their Premiership place. Had Burnley won it might well have been Wigan relegated.

Two of the home games, both 1 – 1 draws, could so easily have been wins with Burnley outplaying both Arsenal in one of the games and Bolton in the other. You can look at goals that should have counted but were disallowed for offside and point to them as being key factors in Burnley's eventual relegation. There was just such a one against Arsenal when Steven Fletcher's goal was wrongly given offside. It would have made the score 2 – 1 in a game when Burnley outplayed Arsenal.

It was after the Bolton game on Boxing Day that their chairman, Phil Gartside, annoyed us intensely as he left the boardroom. With hindsight it was another key moment in the story of the season and the club. The away fans had demonstrated against their manager Gary Megson. They called for Owen Coyle who had previous playing connections with Bolton. Burnley's football was as slick and creative as Bolton's was woeful. It was like watching thoroughbreds against carthorses.

The inevitable and the expected happened. Bolton wanted Owen. We'd beaten off Celtic after Wembley, but this had a different feel to it. In fact I felt uncomfortable during the game. There was an undercurrent that you sensed but you couldn't quite put your finger on. Had Owen and Phil been in contact before this game? We'll never know I suppose. Diehard Burnley supporters will always think so. I'd worked with Phil at the new Bolton stadium for two years and helped him get the chairman's job. I knew their chief executive Allan Duckworth and had arranged passes for his daughter and her fiancé (a Clarets fan). I'd even had contact with their chief investor Eddie Davis who up until now had allegedly sunk £100 million into the club. Whilst the Reebok was being built I was asked to show Eddie round the new stadium by a close friend and 'look after him'. He wanted a box but they had all been sold so I asked the builders would they add an extra one. It set him back £20,000. None of us knew then that he was a multi-millionaire after inventing and patenting the 'click' on an electric kettle.

After the game they all left quickly but Phil Gartside shouted across the boardroom to Brendan, jokingly we thought, "See you Brendan, we'll be coming for your manager next week." There was something all hale and hearty about the way it was shouted out. Yet I still felt uncomfortable that there was also something sinister about it.

We laughed it off.

We weren't laughing in January. They bloody well did come back for him. Unfortunately when I got the news I was sat on a beach with my wife, children and four grandchildren. I always take my family holidays just after Christmas, when it's quiet.

Quiet – how wrong can you be?

# 16

# A Year in the Life of Brian

It was January 2010. Brendan and Barry had two weeks to get themselves out of the mire of the untimely and upsetting Owen Coyle departure. The next league game would be away at Manchester United at Old Trafford. They had the choice of working fast and making an appointment as soon as possible, or appointing someone in a more leisurely fashion in an attempt to get it right, but that would have meant temporarily cobbling together something from the remaining staff as a fill-in. There was a rumour that Owen, along with other members of staff that he had taken, even tried to take the stuffed cat from the boardroom window ledge. Martin Dobson would have held the fort along with Terry Pashley; but Brian Laws arrived in time for the Old Trafford game. Martin can therefore claim to have an unbeaten record as a Burnley manager.

There was a choice of appointing one of two 'types' of manager. The first was the manager who was out of a job and would be instantly available. The second was the manager who had a job and would need to be prised away from his employers. The latter would be time-consuming and potentially messy. In other words the club could do to someone else what had been done to them. In this sort of situation another club would lose out and be angry, leaving strained relationships for what might be a long, long time. Everybody at Burnley had been hurt by the Coyle walkout and it affected the thinking behind the need for an appointment.

On behalf of Owen Coyle you could say he had done what was 'right' for himself and his family. He saw a better chance of staying in the Premiership with Bolton than with Burnley. But he had done nothing that was 'right' for Burnley, the team, the board, the fans or the town that had taken him to its heart. He left a devastated club behind him and many will never forgive him. In the dog-eat-dog world of football who wouldn't have taken that decision in his position? But I didn't think it was right to decimate his old club, by taking all the backroom staff with him.

All these things impacted on the decision made to appoint Brian Laws as the new manager. He was instantly available. Deloitte and

Touche analysed that in terms of available budget and success rate, he was very successful. Fans called it Deloitte and Tosh. Apparently, he had been first choice for the job when Steve Cotterill left but back then Sheffield Wednesday would not release him. One by one other candidates dropped out – Lambert, Grayson and O'Driscoll, or weren't interested. Steve Coppell was approached but talked telephone numbers. Thus, it came down to Brian Laws. But instead of offering him a low salary and a short contract, but a big bonus if he kept Burnley up; he was given a damned good salary and a long contract. It's hard to find a single supporter that didn't see this as a catastrophic mistake. It would cost the club dear a year later. I liked Brian Laws; he is a really nice guy. Do I think he was a good choice of manager after Owen Coyle? In hindsight no: he didn't have a chance.

I was mystified by the decision to appoint him. It is so important to feel continuity and as I sat on a beach 4,000 miles away with no real involvement in the process, I truly hoped the board would make the right decision. My phone rang several times from managers out of work, managers in work, and football agents. But, choosing the new manager wasn't part of my role.

The most surprising name put forward was Andre Villas Boas. He sent a very detailed and lengthy application for the job. Mickey Walsh, an old playing colleague of mine from my Blackpool days (he once scored 'Goal of the Season' for Blackpool), got in touch with me to describe Andre as being a real up and coming hot prospect. Mickey lived out there. At that moment AVB was managing in Portugal at Academica. Before that he'd been with Jose Mourhino including a spell at Chelsea. He was clearly something different and special despite his youth.

There are some fascinating things about him. Firstly his grandmother was from Stockport which is why he speaks such fluent English. His grandfather was a World War Two RAF pilot and Wing Commander. As a youth he lived in the same apartment block as Bobby Robson when he was managing in Portugal. He never ever played professional football. At the age of 21 he was manager of the British Virgin Islands. And his full name is Luis Andre de Pina Cabral e Villas-Boas. This is probably why he was never a professional player because you'd never have got that on the back of a shirt.

His CV and Power Point presentation was amazing. If you'd showed it to someone like Jimmy McIlroy he'd say, "Blazes, what the hell does it all mean?" Even by today's standards there was some complicated stuff in it; but also some very sincere stuff. Tommy Docherty used to say he never said anything to his players that his milkman wouldn't understand. I don't think any milkman would fathom the meaning of a lot of Andre's presentation. The language and jargon of football gets worse by the day. Villas-Boas uses a lot of it. His press conferences sometimes have the journalists scratching their heads. His command of English is so impressive he even makes words up, telling journalists that they must become "accultured" to new aspects of the game. Would Burnley players have ever understood what he wanted if he'd told them to "solidificate."

But, it's a fascinating thought, one of the many 'ifs' in football, that if Andre Villas-Boas had been made manager of Burnley's Premiership team; would he have saved the season? Burnley said "No" and Porto said "Yes" where he had a great run before joining Chelsea.

There's been a lot of talk since Brian Laws' appointment, that it was doomed to failure. Perhaps it was but when he led the team out at Old Trafford for his first game he received a huge and amazingly warm reception from the thousands of Burnley fans there. There was surprise at his appointment and he was the subject of huge debate in the media. This was seen as an appointment on the cheap. In fact it wasn't. The journalists who wrote stuff like that, or the fans who thought it, had no idea of the very generous salary that he was offered. Perhaps if they'd known, they would have been even more critical and cynical. It turned out to be anything but cheap when he was dismissed. Burnley played so well at Old Trafford that day and had chances been taken the score might have been very different and Brian would have been off to a flier and become an instant hero.

By the time I got back from holiday the decision was made and it was clear that whoever took over from Owen would be taking on a massive job. Alex Ferguson would probably have struggled to replicate the Coyle energy and enthusiasm. His sparkle and positivity was quite unique. It had got us to Wembley and the Premiership and had he stayed I'm convinced he would have inspired survival for another season. Another manager with similar characteristics or a bit more charisma than Brian might have done the trick. There was certainly no-one that was identical but it seemed to me that Brian Laws was so far different from Owen that the two of them were just chalk and cheese. And it wasn't long before I was getting that message from the dressing room too. We all had our favourites and the list bandied included names that you might describe as the usual suspects.

My own favourite was Iain Dowie. There is no saying that he would have succeeded but I would imagine the players would have at least respected the name. I worked with Iain at Coventry. He was no pin-up but he knew his football. When Barry Kilby announced, "Let the beauty parade commence," I half thought he had Iain in mind. He was there living in Bolton, as good as on the doorstep, was out of work and desperate to get back into football. Unfortunately he had lost a court case against Simon Jordan, then the chairman of Crystal Palace. Iain lost a little credibility because Simon Jordan had allowed him to leave Crystal Palace to be nearer his wife and family in Lancashire. Iain then popped up as manager of Charlton Athletic as good as on the doorstep. Jordan was not best pleased. A newspaper report suggested that the case cost Iain £1.4 million.

Anyway there he was, hungry for work, available, and desperate for success again. In my opinion he had several of the Owen Coyle attributes minus the George Clooney looks. His energy and enthusiasm was infectious. He was nothing like as dour as he can sometimes appear on screen. He was a big, family man whose boys were at school in Bolton. His wife and children were the driving force in his life. At Coventry he would leave Bolton at 5am and be at Coventry's training ground by 7am to have everything ready for his staff and the players by 8.30am. His training sessions were based on hard work and continual improvement. Every afternoon he would take a player on one side and hold a one to one session during which he built up a bond. At Coventry the players loved him. I know that because they told me so.

Unfortunately the £5 million-plus to buy players, that I had assured Iain was on the table for him never materialised. I felt that I had let him down badly. Even so he had taken Coventry to fourth place in the Championship and had just beaten Manchester united 2 – 0 at Old Trafford in a Cup game. It was at that point that I resigned my position at Coventry. Because of all the background shenanigans and the loss of so much income, generated by my initiatives in the first place, there seemed little point in me staying. I said my goodbyes to Iain reluctantly. He applied for the Burnley job but was never in the running. I felt that he would have made a first-class Burnley manager. Brendan met Iain but it was a rushed last minute affair and I felt at that time that Brendan's focus was being taken up by the problems he was having with Modus.

Brian's immediate problem was a shocked playing staff. Firstly they were stunned enough at the Coyle departure. The energy, vitality, constant optimism, the fun and buzz that he brought was immediately lost. Flatness filled the place and it was if a vacuum had been created. Brian was the last candidate any of them expected to be given the job. It's true to say some of them were simply stunned. From Owen Coyle who exuded a winning and positive mentality in came a man who had been sacked at his previous club for poor results and a bottom three position and never managed in the Premiership. To the players it was an unfathomable decision. It lacked all logic.

There were some grizzled old pros in that dressing room, some of them not afraid to say what they thought. Some of them had already clashed with Steve Cotterill in his final weeks. There was surprise at some of the players that Laws brought in, and on high wages. Leon Cort was a steady centre-half but no better than any of the existing players. Centre-forward Chris Iwelumo who arrived later from Wolves was another on the wrong side of 30 and in my opinion was well past his best when he was signed.

It always seemed to me that Brian modelled himself on one of his old managers – Brian Clough. He got on with the job but it wasn't long before the whispers from the dressing room reached me. Let's say that (as one player described it to me) whilst every day with Owen Coyle seemed to be sunny and bright; with Brian it always seemed to be rainy – "drab and dull". It's a sad reflection that several of the players celebrated when he left. One of them took a tray of cakes in I'm told.

Although I didn't try to interfere; there was one element of our play that was not down to 'opinion', it was down to fact. We seemed unable to score from corner kicks. There was I, once part of a team that was famed for its free-kick and corner-kick scams under Adamson, watching chance after chance go begging. It was a feature that dated back to Owen Coyle's time as well. In training there was never any drill or rehearsals. Owen believed that you improvised as and when the opportunities occurred during a game. And there was me, my head still full of all the ideas we used to use during a game played 30 years before.

So: one day I did point out to Brian Laws the lack of goals from corners. Still nothing seemed to improve. If during a game you had seven or eight corners you might expect to score from one. It was becoming a joke amongst supporters that we didn't. Burnley fans are not daft.

Over the previous couple of years, whenever in London, I'd meet up with Professor Chris Brady, ex Dean of Bournemouth University. I'd often heard Chris being interviewed on the radio in his role as a football specialist and he was extremely knowledgeable about many aspects of the game. But, what intrigued me were his quite original views and ideas about managers and set pieces during a game. Set pieces by the way were called free-kicks or corners in my day.

I met him one day at the Marriott Hotel in London at 5pm. We were still talking football at 9.45pm. Had I stayed longer, which I was tempted to do, I would have missed my train home. His philosophy was simple. It was so straightforward I wondered why every manager didn't take it on board. I became keen therefore to introduce him to Brian Laws and his staff but before doing this I tested him out using Colin Waldron, my dearest friend but nevertheless one of the 'old brigade' not entirely receptive to so-called football experts. If this guy can convert Waldo, I thought, he can convert anybody. Not only that, but Colin would take the 'defenders' and 'captain's' viewpoint on the 'Brady' theories. Over the years I'd kept Colin in the know about changes in football such as Prozone, pitch technology, new boots, balls, training methods, physiotherapy and even changes in goalpost design. In one of the lounges in the McIlroy Stand there is a photograph of square posts being used at Turf Moor.

By the end of the couple of hours Colin spent with Chris he was fascinated and said to me, "I've learned more in the past couple of hours about my centre-half position than I did in 15 years playing the game. That guy is incredible."

That was all I needed. We still hadn't scored from a corner, so I thought, "Right, next stop, Brian."

The Chris Brady theories were based on statistics. Amongst other things he is a mathematician and his findings were these:

A manager selects and purchases a player for his squad based on the player's ability. He then allows players to join his team in the knowledge that there are many things he cannot influence once the game starts and the ball is in play. He cannot tell the player how to control a ball, dribble, pass, shoot or defend. These are all rehearsed on the training ground but on the pitch in a real situation they are at the mercy of all kinds of events and situations. Some things can be practised but not fully taught because in a game instinct, instant reactions and individual ability levels are the key factors.

In contrast however, if there is a free-kick or corner, the manager can have real influence in the way the players are set up and instructed in their roles. These instructions can be based on statistics. For example suppose a manager knows that 66% of all goals scored from corners occur when the corner is 'in-swinging' and only 33% of goals come from corners where the kick is 'out-swinging' (these are current statistics). Once a manager knows this, why would he *ever* allow any player to take an out-swinging corner kick when the chance of scoring is reduced by half?

One night down in London again, Chris went into his ideas in more detail with specific reference to my old centre-forward role. In 16 years I lost count of the number of times I headed the ball over the bar. He explained why this was: "Paul when an out-swinging corner is taken, the trajectory and spin on the ball send the ball 'upwards' so that it is more than likely a downward header is more difficult; hence so many go over the bar." I was totally intrigued.

"By contrast," he continued, "from an in-swinging corner it is more difficult to head it over the bar because it is spinning downwards, so that you are more likely to head the ball downwards. Thus, more goals are scored from in-swingers." All this seemed such common sense stuff. I was desperate to tell Brian. There was always the feeling that in-swinging free-kicks and corners were more difficult to defend against, but Chris had the factual statistics at his fingertips.

Chris continued with his theses. "Paul, if you as a centre-forward break away from the defence and there is only the goalkeeper to beat, what would you do; dribble round him or shoot past him?" My answer was based on using instinct to tell me in a split-second what to do. In truth, real thought didn't come into the decision making process. It's a last second decision.

"That's fine Paul but what if I told you that in this situation 66% of goals are scored when the player takes the ball round the goalkeeper and only 33% of goals scored in this same scenario are when the player elects to shoot past him. Any player has a 50% better chance of scoring if he goes wide of the keeper."

Again I was taken aback by the simplicity of this. I had to agree, I would try to dribble round the keeper every time. By now I was beginning to realise that any manager who possessed these simple statistics would be able to 'tip the balance' in a game.

He continued this time focussing on free-kicks within shooting range: "Paul, how often do you see a player run up and blast the ball many yards over the bar?" The answer was simple – frequently.

"The player would be just as well handing the ball to the goalkeeper on most occasions. My view is that the ball should be aimed at the goalkeeper, as hard as possible. There is then the possibility of a direct goal, a deflected goal, the ball ricocheting to another player to give a scoring chance, or being deflected for a corner. Of course there is still the possibility of the ball going wide or over. But nevertheless the possibility of scoring with a low, hard kick with the goalkeeper himself the target outweighs the non-possibility. Keeping that ball low is the golden key.

"Next: what about free-kicks from out wide, from maybe 35 yards or more? They should be precisely planned. This is where a manager can give exact instructions. Free-kicks from the left should be taken by the right-back. Free-kicks from the right should be taken by the left-back. The 'target' is not a particular player (for example the centre forward) but the 'far post.' By using a left footed player from the right, the ball will curl inwards to the post; and likewise on the left with the kick taken by a right footed player. They are hell to defend. Again they are more likely to be headed downwards because of the trajectory. In a perfect free kick taken in this way the ball would bounce on the six-yard line before hitting the far post. Every day the two full-backs should practise this at least 50 times in a training session until he can hit the far post with a 90% success rate.

"Once the full-backs start to achieve this accuracy, the next job is to make sure the attacking players in the box position themselves so that, as the ball is struck, they will have run into the trajectory or curve of the ball. A glancing header aimed goalwards will result in a good goal-scoring chance if not a goal. Of all goals scored from this position either on the right or left, 66% are scored this way. On occasions the ball will go into the net without anyone touching it."

Chris expanded further and explained that the chance of a scoring opportunity increased if a forward could 'manufacture' a free kick from this position. Bloody hell! What's this all about?

"If you have a small forward, like Martin Paterson for example, you position him in the position where you want the free-kick. Again that might be out wide maybe 35 yards from goal. If someone is marking him tight then the ball needs to be played at head height so the defender wants to head the ball away. If the forward backs into the defender, then 50% of the time the referee will give the free kick to the attacker. You then have the free kick in the position you want it. You then implement the in-swinging free-kick routine to the far post."

In all my years in football I can't ever remember being given free-kick instructions based on statistics. We had a few set routines but often we ad-libbed, decided what to do on the spot and improvised. Jimmy Adamson was a mastermind at free-kicks but if you'd asked him which free-kick was statistically the most successful, he'd have had no answer. And for sure, Owen Coyle never had any rehearsed routines.

Chris continued: "Paul, creating goals from set pieces gives you such an edge over other teams. Stoke City are, or have been, the perfect example. If these edges you create give you seven or eight goals a year, it can be the difference in winning and losing, in success or failure, in relegation or staying up. They could win a team promotion; they could save a manager's job. If I were a manager these set piece rules would be non-negotiable. My players would obey them to the letter. If they didn't, I'd immediately substitute them and fine them. Alternatively, I could just sit back and wait for them to get ME the sack."

I took a phone call from Colin Waldron saying, "I've been up all night thinking about set pieces, free kick and corners. The bloke's a bloody genius!"

One Tuesday afternoon I brought Chris up from London by train; paid his ticket and picked him up at Manchester Piccadilly and we met up with Brian Laws, Russ Wilcox and Stuart Gray at Turf Moor. The focus of the discussions was to be corner-kicks and on the drive over to Burnley I warned Chris that he might not get the warmest of welcomes and his appearance might be seen as interference from me. He was, in fact, an 'amateur' amongst professionals. I wondered if he'd be given a hard time; but something needed doing. We hadn't scored from a corner for over a year!

Once all the niceties were out of the way I was impressed and amused by his opening line: "Brian, the hard fact is, if you want to *improve* performance at corners, the first plan is this. Tell the player taking the corner to simply kick it 12 inches from the flag and then every one of your players should sprint back into their own half. Not only have Burnley not scored from a corner for months, but on one occasion Burnley conceded a goal straight from one of your own corners. The retreat plan will stop that happening."

It was a risky start. But the pity was, it was not a joke, it was true. Chris had done his homework; we had indeed conceded a goal immediately after taking a corner. His 'retreat' plan would stop that happening again.

Eventually we got down to the statistics regarding in-swinging versus out-swinging corners and after an hour of debate the reception was still no more than lukewarm. But we did get an, "OK we'll give it a go next Saturday then."

And it worked. Over the next four games we scored three goals from corners. Brendan Flood and I had great fun in the directors' box watching them go in. It looked like we had turned a significant corner. Sadly this wasn't the case. The goals seemed to be put down to good fortune rather than planned statistical possibility.

The name of Chris Brady was never mentioned at Turf Moor again. As far as I know, he didn't even get a thank you email. That's football.

*****

Brian took over in January 2010. Very early came the game for which all Burnley fans clamoured for tickets, Bolton versus Burnley, with Owen Coyle now the manager of Bolton and so many of the Burnley staff had left with him. It was an utterly drab and dire game from both sides. Brian had another chance to become a hero but it was a 1 – 0 defeat, and there would be many more before the season ended. Abuse and scorn rained down on Owen Coyle before, during and after the game. Placards and banners expressed hate and contempt.

Most of the board that night refused to go into the Bolton boardroom. But I did. I knew football well enough to know that what had happened was just the way football operates. It doesn't make it right but you live with it. It may not go down too well with rank and file supporters but I shook hands with Owen, Steve Davis and Sandy Stewart. I also think that if Owen had stayed we would not have been relegated. But, what I did not like was Bolton chairman Phil Gartside asking me, "Fletch, when are *you* joining us?" If it was meant to be a joke I thought it was uncalled for. It seemed like rubbing salt in the wound. It was in poor taste. I think I smiled, but inside I was not. I felt thoroughly uncomfortable at the nerve of it.

Brian's first win came against West Ham on February 6th. The next one was not until April 10th. Yet even so, relegation was never anywhere near a cast-iron certainty until near the end of the season. Not until April 25th did Liverpool finally end the anguish with just two games remaining. For weeks prior to that there was still everything to play for. But games that we expected or hoped to win were lost. That was the tragedy. There were three home games in particular that should have yielded points, against Wolves, Blackburn and Portsmouth. It was heart-breaking to lose them and the supporters detected players who seemed to have lost their spirit and will. Some were accused of giving less than 100%.

There's a telling bit in Burnley goalkeeper Brian Jensen's book:

*"A lousy attitude affects the squad. We have too many who just spit the dummy out. They said Burnley's spirit disappeared with Coyle. But there was no Burnley spirit. It was a Coyle spirit and it evaporated with him. We could have done it if I could have got them going a bit more. We missed so many chances of points. A victory and a draw in the right matches would have saved us. "*

Owen Coyle's departure had sapped them of the extra yard they had previously put into a game. He'd had the knack of making them feel ten feet tall and told them constantly they were better than they really were. After a while of this kind of treatment, a player begins to believe it, self-confidence and belief increase, and his performance can improve even more. Take it away and all of it disappears as if it were an illusion. In some players disillusion set in. They felt let down, and felt even more let down by this strangest of appointments.

But Brian wasn't helped by circumstances. As if things weren't unsettled enough you don't need players being unavailable for selection. David Nugent was absent from the team for the Portsmouth game. He had been doing well and scoring goals. When the first part of the loan agreement was reaching its end, it was renewed; he was a popular player. He should have been available for the home game against Portsmouth but had a clause in his contract with them about his 'image rights'. It caused problems. It was apparently a clever legal way of some form of tax avoidance initiated by some smart lawyer somewhere to get extra money for their players. This of course was nothing to do with Burnley FC and was an issue between him and Portsmouth. We tried to get it sorted in time for the game on the Saturday, a crucial game I might add and a game we put down as very winnable. It wasn't sorted and he missed the game and we lost. Had he played who knows if we would have won or not?

The Blackburn game was lost and the goal came from the most blatant dive by a Blackburn player you will see. How can I grumble? We did it in my day. The great Burnley player and manager Harry Potts was famed for his dives into the penalty area. But when it happens against you in such as this one and decides the game, it's a heartbreaker. And on top of that, Burnley just didn't show up on the day anyway.

From an Owen Coyle team that rose to the heights of performance and adrenalin against the illustrious Manchester United and a reverberating 1 – 0 win that rocked the stadium to its foundations and nearly brought the stands down; this was a team under Brian Laws that sank to the very depths in an infamous display at home against the millionaires of Manchester City. On a night of torrential rain when you prayed that the pitch would be flooded; City ran amok and were 3 – 0 up after just six awful minutes. By half-time it was 5 – 0. I genuinely feared that City would get into double figures. The rain came down so badly we prayed for the referee to abandon the game. It was abject. There were dressing room rows; one player unbelievably walked out of the dressing room at half-time and went to a nearby bar a few hundred yards down the road. The club from top to bottom was shell-shocked. You could I suppose say that the second half was a 1 – 1 draw.

If only ... what would have happened if ... how often do we say these words in football ... be they from the players or fans? But Laws never appeared to have the full support of his senior players at the club. For a time following relegation the team flirted with the top six back in the Championship but supporters grew more and more restless and dissatisfied.

If there was one game, back in the Championship, that provided a high spot it was the 1 – 0 win over Bolton and Owen Coyle in the Carling Cup. For a game that might normally have attracted 5,000 at best, over 17,000 crowded in. Yet more disdain and derision was hurled at him throughout the game. It provided closure of a sort to the distasteful departure several months earlier. The boardroom was ecstatic and Brian was the hero of the night. It was a kind of comeuppance. I don't know a Burnley supporter who isn't delighted that they were relegated at the end of season 2011/12; not because they are Bolton Wanderers but because they are managed by the man they will forever say deserted them at the worst possible time in mid-season. Me: it's my old club and the club that set me on a career that has been so wonderful; so maybe I should have different feelings.

Brian was a hero for not much longer; his newly acquired status was temporary. The home game against Scunthorpe was the end for him. He had had several 'lives'. Some of the board had wanted him dismissed at the end of the Premier season, but victories against Hull City and Tottenham in the final games earned him a reprieve. Brendan Flood wanted to remove him seven or eight games before the Premier season's end before it was all too late, but by then Brendan was in business trouble and was no longer the power-holder. An away win at Barnsley over Christmas and a good performance left fans very much expecting a win over Scunthorpe but in a poor display they were given a football lesson by a team that had lost its last five games and were in the bottom three. The resultant boos and abuse were savage. His position was untenable. Barry Kilby was in New York but in a phone call he relieved Brian of his duties. A win would have put Burnley in the top six but supporters were out of patience.

If the loss of the Premiership place had been tame and spiritless; it could be argued that the Championship position was very much down to bad luck in some games when their play had merited more points. The line is so fine that separates success from mediocrity. A missed penalty, a wonder display by a goalkeeper in one game, the woodwork hit several times in the first couple of months of the season, poor referees' decisions all conspired to lose seven or eight points to add to the total. With those Burnley would have been in second spot. It was not to be.

Are some managers luckier than others? Are some managers able to inspire and motivate better than others? Are some managers natural winners and others not? Fans argued that Brian was an average, journeyman manager. Steeped in experience yes, even two promotions to his credit, but overall his 800-plus game win record was not the greatest. At Burnley his win record over the 12 months was very poor. Dismissal at Sheffield Wednesday for taking that club into the bottom three was always the millstone round his neck at Burnley. They had queried his appointment from the first. Me: I'd say that on far too many occasions he was let down by underperforming players and during the time he was in charge in the Premiership, there was an element that constantly undermined him, or was unwilling to respond to him.

And so the year reaching its end became truly an annus horribilis: the departure of Owen Coyle, relegation from the Premiership with barely a fight from several players; the appointment of an uninspiring manager, and just 11 wins over the previous 12 months out of 40 league games. Yet even so, when he was dismissed Burnley remained just two points out of the top six and with games in hand. It could still have been a promotion season.

My immediate thought again – get Iain Dowie. The team needed a motivator.

# 17

# The Year with the Eagle

There was one director at Burnley who I have to say I did not get on with. It's unusual for me to struggle with people but sadly Clive Holt was a rare example. Our differences surfaced during 2011 but I will always acknowledge that he eats, lives, breathes and sleeps Burnley Football Club. It was when Eddie Howe was manager that there was a perfect example of how differently we see things and it was all to do with pens.

My good friend Peter Thomson of 'Peter Thomson International' always maintains that any added extra little 'edge' you can add to your business will set it apart from other companies. An 'edge' may only be small, but add them all together and you build something special. (Barry Kilby introduced an 'edge' with 'The Chairman's Pledge', which persuaded a few extra people to buy a season ticket. This small edge helped us get back into the Premiership). Burnley FC is small, tightly-run and friendly. It tries to do things differently, or at least that's what I tried to do in my four extra years there. Just sometimes you want to add a little panache and class and just sometimes you can do that without running up a huge bill. I always looked for opportunities to do something extra that would set us apart. An example was 'the pens'.

One evening at a BOA (By Official Appointment) meeting at the club I came across something that immediately stood out as 'special'. Various businesses had an opportunity to set out their stall and information so that there was a chance for networking and business opportunities. BOA is simply a way of attracting as many businesses as possible to attach themselves to the club so that they can use the club crest and identify with Burnley FC. By doing that, the philosophy is that they raise their profile within the town. On one stand was a guy who made pens. He had a range of them all handmade and produced in his garage/workshop at home in Padiham. I looked at these pens and saw works of art, meticulously hand crafted in claret, blue and gold. Immediately I saw the chance to have a special Burnley FC pen that we could use in various ways to raise our profile and add that little touch of class; for example when a new player signed for the club or when an established player signed a new contract. After the signing, the special pen was a 'gift' to the player. For now more often than not we were using a £0.65p Bic. Using these special pens would add a small 'edge' and provide something a bit different to even a Chelsea or a Man U. A week later Peter Lyons delivered one beautifully made pen to my office at a cost of £60.

When Owen Coyle saw it he loved it. This was real Owen Coyle territory. Three days later we signed Chris Eagles and he walked out of Owen's office with a smile on his face and a brand new, handmade pen in a mahogany presentation case. He'd actually said to Owen, "This is something I'll show my grandchildren."

Many years ago Bob Lord's attitude to pens was entirely different. When Steve Kindon re-signed for Burnley after his stint at Wolves, he used Bob's lovely fountain pen to sign the new contract all laid out on the huge desk in Bob's room.

"Take my pen," said Bob. Steve thought he was giving it to him.

He had virtually named his own price but hadn't really intended to come back and only attended out of courtesy because he loved old Bob. But as the offer went up, and up and up, he succumbed and signed. And then assuming the pen was part of the deal he put it in his pocket. But oh no, it wasn't.

"And now Steve," said the old rascal, "I'll have my pen back."

So, when Chris Eagles was so obviously delighted with his claret and blue pen, Owen asked for half a dozen to be ordered. That season several players walked out of the office with a lovely pen. Brian Laws liked the idea as did Eddie Howe. On occasions if we had a visiting dignitary, or another VIP guest, we'd present them with a pen. We gave one to HRH Prince Charles.

Sometime in 2011 Clive mentioned the word 'pens' at a board meeting and I didn't really think twice about it. But, maybe 6 weeks later I got a phone call from Peter the pen guy asking if his bill could be paid. I checked with accounts, saw the cheque was ready to sign and again thought no more about it. Three months later Peter rang again to ask where his money was. Again I checked with accounts to discover that the cheque couldn't be found. I was informed that Clive had torn it up and he had expressed the view that we should order no more pens for players who have more money than sense.

Needless to say I invited him into my office and told him what I thought about him and his actions. There was a heated exchange. I suggested that if he had a problem he should talk with me about it first and discuss what to do having talked about the pros and cons. I explained that in the meantime a Burnley bloke who had worked hard and supplied these pens in good faith was still waiting for his money. I told him his behaviour had been unacceptable. My distinct impression was that he didn't care what I thought and that it was all water off a duck's back.

To be fair, when I asked at a board meeting some months later that each director should come up with an idea that might raise £2 million to £4 million a year he was pretty much the only one who managed to make a suggestion. I'd prepared and circulated a detailed paper regarding the serious implications of the proposed Financial Fair Play regulations and how they might affect Burnley. It was an important meeting and needed some real ideas to fill the gap once the parachute payments stopped. Prior to this Clive had proposed that the club should set up merchandise stalls and refreshment kiosks down Harry Potts Way. The problem was that the cost of staffing them would probably far outweigh any takings on the extra pies that might be sold.

Over the past decade the work done in the boardroom had developed great results without breaking the bank. The board did have the interests of the club at heart. But this was now a time of budgets in tens of millions and big, bold ideas were needed that were practical and operable.

I can't honestly say I had much to do with Eddie Howe's appointment. Brendan suggested Eddie Howe and Paul Lambert as 'the only two managers worth approaching' and suggested that we should 'work hard to get them.' He had previously suggested Lambert when Owen Coyle resigned and had met and spoken to him on a number of occasions, but others wanted a less challenging appointment – so we went for Brian Laws.

The more Lambert faded into the background, the surer Barry and Brendan became that Eddie Howe was the right man. They liked his youth and freshness. Yes he was young but he had some firm ideas and principles. His vision was for a young, hungry team that would respond to him, fed by a good refurbished youth system providing a conveyor belt of players. It was an echo of the past when Gawthorpe had once produced player after player. It sounded like a good plan.

He certainly faced problems when he came in January 2011. He faced supporters who believed that the season might still end in promotion. He faced players who had been disillusioned by Owen Coyle's walkout and that disillusion had grown, the more they had of Brian Laws to whom they found it very difficult to relate. It's not rocket science to work out that Eddie knew he had to change the dressing room mentality and average age. Several of the players who had performed miracles to reach the Premiership were now another year older – and another year slower. Graham Alexander later said he thought that Eddie had begun to break up the team too soon. But then Graham was one of the first to see less and less first-team football.

The evergreen Graham, along with Robbie Blake, was approaching that time of life and career when thoughts begin about what to do next. Clarke Carlisle was another one in this category and possibly Brian Jensen, although goalkeepers can prolong their careers a little more easily than an outfield player. It's a wonderful life being a professional footballer. But, it can also be a bit like the curate's egg, good in parts. Or it can be good while it lasts; good while you're playing or good if you have clear intentions and plans about what to do when you finish. I look at the young lads today coming into the game with mixed feelings. Some will make the grade. Others won't and will be heartbroken long before they're even 20 when they are released.

Or it can be 17% good and 83% bad. Let me explain: Some years ago I organised a seminar for the Professional Footballers' Association entitled 'Life After Football'. I asked the players to consider what life would be like when they retired and suggested they start to prepare for that straightaway, no matter whether they were 17 or 37. Forewarned is fore-armed being the philosophy behind it. A player can exit the game when he least expects it be it because of illness, injury, loss of form, or family troubles. Today, I told them, you earn exceptional wages, far different from when I was a player. We were on good money but nothing like the sums needed to retire at 35 and live on the proceeds.

There are clear benefits to being a professional footballer. So many of them are well paid, enjoy celebrity status, are paid to be extremely fit and healthy enjoying the best health benefits and care imaginable. While fame lasts all kinds of doors open, and when someone asks what you do for a living imagine being able to say, "I'm a professional footballer and I play for ..." It's a fair bet that heads will turn. Contrast that with saying I'm a bus driver. Your local restaurant will greet you with open arms, you can holiday in the most exotic locations and even if you are a lower division player it's hardly likely you'll live in a two-up and two-down and drive a second-hand car.

For the top players in the Premiership and the Championship, maybe even Division One, life will usually involve an attractive wife or girlfriend, a top of the range car, a very desirable house, membership of the local golf club and financial freedom: all that, of course, makes the basic assumption that you don't fritter it away. Benidorm becomes Bermuda and as someone once said to me: "You can order from the menu not the price list."

For many players being a professional footballer is like winning the lottery. At the top half dozen clubs a first contract wage of £5,000 a week is not uncommon long before the player has reached the age of 20. But it's a short career was the message I wanted to get across at the seminar. The 17% mentioned earlier represents the years from age 15 to 30 when commonly a lad joins a club then leaves the game. In today's terms that's just one sixth of your life. There's 0 – 15 childhood and early teens, 15 – 30 the football career, 30 – 45 the transition from football to some other lifestyle and job, 45 to 60 the middle years of whatever work you are doing, 60 – 75 final working days and then retirement and then 75 to maybe 90 the final years of retirement. Life expectancy now is so much greater. In my very younger days it was uncommon to live beyond 75. If a footballer, now, ends that career at any age between 30 and 35 that leaves an awful lot of years left over to fill and to lead a far different life. If you then consider that of the average 15 years as a player perhaps only seven or eight of those are at the very top in the first team, then that represents a very small percentage of a footballer's total life.

Let's suppose the money comes rolling in. Sadly a number of players have no financial acumen or self-discipline. Money is lost and wasted over a very short period of time. If you find earning half a million a year or more so easy, then the likelihood is you'll find it easy to lose it all one way or another. In the USA 78% of professional basketball players go broke within five years of retirement. 60% of American Football players are broke within two years of leaving the game. There are usually six main reasons: frivolous spending, misplaced trust with business partners, bad investments, divorce settlements, too many children with different mothers, and hangers-on. Celebrity divorces and settlements are expensive.

I set the players at the seminar a question: "Imagine having the best job in the world for maybe up to 15 years and then losing all your money and having the worst job in the world for the next years until retirement time. How will you cope? Better still what plans and decisions can you make now to avoid the problems that befall so many players after they leave the game and have enjoyed the life of plenty?"

My recommendation was simple. Think of a job no matter how basic that you think you might *enjoy* when you finish playing. If you enjoy fishing now, then why not work in a fishing tackle shop or plan to set one up. If you enjoy organising and managing and are sociable and enjoy company then why not manage a hotel. If you enjoy food and cooking, then you'll enjoy running your own restaurant. But, I said, don't jump into these things blind. Plan and prepare. While you are playing find someone at the club or a supporter who runs the kind of business in which you think you might be interested. People will be pleased to help. This is the positive way to cash in on your standing and status as a footballer. Ask them to teach you about their business. If you wait ten years until after you have left the game, you are by definition a 'has-been'. Help will be harder to find. 'Friends' will be harder to enlist.

Many ex-players will be persuaded to invest in a business, a restaurant, an apartment block even though they know so little about finance and commerce. Other people see footballers as an easy source of money and dazzle them with promises. Don't touch them I said at the seminar. A business card with your name on can look impressive but if you don't understand business plans stay well clear. The bigger the name, the bigger the offers and the bigger the potential losses can be.

And all this is before you even mention the word stress and pressure. The Gary Speed tragedy is well documented. Dean Windass filled the tabloids with his story of the money that went and the depression he felt. He experienced the ultimate glory of scoring the solitary winning goal for Hull City in a Wembley play-off final. What's the point of getting up in the morning anymore, so many ex footballers ask and then he became one of them. The ex-players who hit the bottle and battle addictions form an enormous group. It's a wonderful life while it lasts, I told the assembled group more than once; but one day it all ends, and you have to be prepared both mentally and financially. Lucky is the footballer who is level-headed with a gem of a wife who provides sound sense and stability. I think I might have said it earlier in this book, what footballers possess is an ultra 'competitive' gene. They are winners and battlers. The top players have all climbed their way up the greasy pole of competition and got to the top. Eventually they have made it. That achievement is praiseworthy. They have shown fight, determination, and dedication. They might well think it will last forever. But it doesn't. The problem then is that when they leave the game they are still 'blessed' with this gene. But now it becomes a curse for it is no longer any use in the normal life outside of football. Only a small percentage stays in the game coaching or managing and can continue to benefit from this 'magic' gene.

Whilst the footballer might have been holidaying in Dubai, riding around in a 4X4, buying Jimmy Choo shoes for his glamorous wife, his old school pals have had more mundane experiences. Maybe they've been stacking supermarket shelves, repairing cars, or selling photocopiers. Maybe they've worked to increase their qualifications and broaden their horizons. Some will have opened up and prospered in a business. They might not have had that 'winner's gene' but they will have learned how to earn a living in the real world. Learning how to take a (in-swinging) corner stands the footballer in little stead once you have left the game. It won't do him any good at a job interview. But when an ex-footballer wakes up in the morning as an 'ordinary' person, that winning gene still makes him want to be successful. But, if any sense of a lack of purpose sets in, that is when depression can start.

If I have one golden message to give to any young player, or older player about to approach the final days of his career, it is be prepared. In my extra four years at Burnley I looked at the young lads at the Centre of Excellence and felt a sigh of relief that they take academic studies alongside their football training. We never did that in the 70s. They have something to fall back on.

Read Roger Eli's book *Thanks for the Memories* for the picture of what happens when your day is done and you are of no further use to the manager. Roger had a couple of seasons of glory, but for his entire career battled with injuries and bad luck. His is the classic story of the little-known footballer that makes up a huge percentage of the game and who made no great fortune. He is now a director of Ventura Office Supplies, a thriving stationery business in Yorkshire. His book should be compulsory reading for all footballers. He says it took him three years to adapt to life outside football but today gets almost as much satisfaction from concluding a business deal as he once did scoring a goal. For him, the competitive gene still finds employment.

A football club dressing room, whether it is Chelsea or Charlton, Wolves or Wycombe, will have the complete range of characters. At least one will end up in the doldrums, probably on the dole, an alcoholic and a failure. In that dressing room there will be a cross-section of all types of person. Traditionally nearly all of them will be working class (if such a thing still exists) from the poorer end of society, from the rough side of town, and will not have any experience of higher education. In that dressing room there will be the gambler, the joker, the know-it-all, the family man, the womaniser, the drinker, the barrack-room lawyer, the moaner and groaner and the one obsessed with money and bling. It's amazing how young women find a grubby looking footballer so 'handsome' if he has a huge bank balance and a flash car. Those WAGS may well be the first to seek a divorce when the glamour fades.

Eddie Howe himself is the perfect example of how cruel the game can be. Injury ended his career prematurely. Today his competitive gene finds employment as a manager.

Regarding his time at Burnley so far (August, 2012), it's fair to say he has hardly torn up any trees. When he took over there was still a promotion winning position. As the season went on, it simply faded away. When the next season began, 2011/12, there was talk of this being a transitional year and that this was a team under construction. Results were mixed. Supporters seemed to grasp that this was an appointment for the longer period and that there was a rebuilding job. Eddie was accorded a patience that was never shown to Brian Laws. What supporters did find puzzling was that despite the parachute payments and a lucrative Premier season not much earlier, the AGM accounts declared a £4 million loss.

What they also questioned was the ownership of Turf Moor. The ground was no longer owned by the club, but by Lionbridge Ltd, a company registered in the British Virgin Islands. They had acquired it via the sale to them of Longside Properties. That company had once been owned by Barry Kilby who had used Longside properties as a vehicle to buy the ground and inject much needed cash into the club some years earlier when things were desperate.

The shock news was the announcement of the impending retirement of Chairman Barry Kilby at the end of the season. Barry revealed he was fighting prostate cancer. The better news was the advance of the youth team towards the semi-finals of the FA Youth Cup against Blackburn Rovers of all people. Pride and recognition grew as the young lads progressed through the early rounds and then disposed of two Premier academy sides, West Brom and Fulham, both away. For those who were long in the tooth, memories were stirred of a great night in 1968 when Burnley won this prestigious trophy with players like Dave Thomas, Steve Kindon, Alan West and Mick Docherty. Just being in the final four along with Rovers, Chelsea and Manchester United was magnificent enough; but I couldn't help thinking that just sometimes there is a wonderful symmetry in football and what an end it would be to Barry Kilby's chairmanship (he had announced his impending retirement from the post of chairman, but not as a director) if once again the youth lads could bring this trophy home. Nor was this an academy side. It made the achievement all the greater. Alas, Blackburn Rovers knocked them out.

At the same time, a 3 – 2 defeat at Watford in early March convinced most supporters that any chance of a top six position by the end of the season was now unlikely. It was a frustrating result. 2 – 0 up heading towards a win, the team then capitulated. It was the fourth defeat in five games. Such a run during Brian Laws' tenure would have produced disparagement. Under Eddie Howe the established mantra remained one of tolerant 'this is a work in progress'.

It was at the end of the 'Eddie year' that I decided my time was up at the club. I wrote for a match day programme in December 2011:

*I am sure you will now know that I am standing down as chief executive after a thoroughly enjoyable four years at Turf Moor. Looking back it's been an absolute thrill to have been part of this club during a wonderful time in our history. When I first came here four years ago it was in a development role. I had been offered the chief executive role on two occasions previously. I felt that my knowledge of stadiums would be very beneficial to the club so I eventually came back to build the new stand that had already been conceived.*

*Eventually, having had previous experience at three clubs, I was asked to fill the vacant role as chief executive and on the pitch it was a golden time for the club, culminating in promotion to the Premier League. I can't take much credit for that because Owen Coyle guided the team there; but equally we are a team off the pitch and everybody pulled together, which made me very proud to be at the helm.*

*Having said that, the real highlight of my time here was what followed. We had to do some serious work to the infrastructure during the summer and we were on target in every aspect until the moment I was lying on a beach and heard the news that Owen Coyle had left. I always go on holiday at Christmas time because that is the only time we can get away as a family. Suddenly I was being inundated with phone calls and texts from ex-managers, agents and newspapers, all on the managerial vacancy.*

*The chairman held the reins magnificently at this time. By the time I returned, the club had taken action and was on the verge of appointing Brian Laws. Hindsight is clearly a wonderful thing and maybe we will all question whether the appointment was a good one. But the decision had been made. We all got behind Brian, gave it our best shot and missed out by just five points.*

*I have to say that in my time here I've had a wonderful relationship with the chairman. I have tremendous respect for the owners of the club. Barry is probably one of the greatest chairmen that there has been here. He has seen it through the good times and the bad times and I like to think that he and Brendan Flood balance each other. I think the inspiration of Brendan coming in as a new director and the old head of Barry, who has been around for the past 12 seasons, is a perfect match. I also think it's still a great combination for the future of the club.*

*As chief executive, my role has always been to leave the player negotiations to the directors and my view is that what the club needs now is somebody who can take on those important roles and help Eddie Howe, not only to locate players but to sign them up and negotiate with the agents, rather than that burden falling on the directors. I would still encourage the club to consider building the new stand as quickly as it can. The reason behind this being that in football new buildings attract new investors – and this club needs new investors. If you look at the new stadiums I have been involved with, at Huddersfield, Coventry and Bolton, their major backers would never have got involved had they been playing at an old stadium. What I was trying to bring to Burnley with StadiArena was innovation; something new to a building that would otherwise sit there empty for 95% of the year.*

*If you combine that with UCFB, which is now starting to turn the corner and become a fantastic success, especially after winning an innovation award in Manchester, there are positives. Certainly UCFB is starting to become a real success and if it hits anticipated targets in the next two to three years, it will be significant to the club and the town of Burnley. The club has to continue to look for new innovative ideas like this because the next three or four years are going to be extremely difficult financially, especially when the new fair play rules kick in.*

*Burnley will be worse off because, although we are seen as a big club in football terms, we are not in turnover terms. As an example, Brighton, who have a new stadium and nearly 3,000 corporate seats every week, compared to our 500, have just had another planning application approved for another 2,000 corporates and another six or seven thousand seats.*

*I have a great love for this club and just felt I couldn't go any further. The time is right to move on and I eagerly await the new chief executive, Lee Hoos. I intend to give him all the help I can. I'm not leaving under a cloud. I'm doing this because I think it will benefit the football club and I genuinely say thank you for the time I've had here back at the club. I wish everyone here nothing but the best.*

*Paul Fletcher MBE*

# 18

# Harry Potts 1979 and 30 Years On

I'm proud of my Cup Winner's medal. Unfortunately it's not an FA Cup medal. It's an Anglo-Scottish Cup medal I won in 1979. I celebrated the 30th anniversary of this forgotten achievement whilst I was CEO at Burnley. Not many people remembered it, or mentioned it, or probably even knew what it was. It wasn't a tournament win that inspires a dinner or a commemorative DVD. Don't mock. I've got two medals to boast about; Colin Waldron only has one. I mention it too, because at the first leg of the Anglo Scottish Final, supporters experienced and witnessed the most violent scenes ever seen at Burnley.

Harry Potts had returned as manager to replace Joe Brown. Joe had replaced Jimmy Adamson 'sacked' in January '76. I therefore knew Harry well playing for him for two seasons and having also known him early in the 70s when he had been moved upstairs to the post of managing director, a meaningless role back then meant to keep him quiet, when Jimmy Adamson replaced him.

Whilst Jimmy was manager I'd see Harry wandering around the place always with a big smile but he never looked comfortable in the token job he'd been given. Then of course I got to know him much better when he returned as manager later in the 70s. We met again at Colne Dynamoes when I was commercial manager there. Owner Graham White had given Harry a job and a club car which made Harry feel needed again at a time when he was showing the early signs of Parkinson's disease and you'd notice his hands shaking. It was at this time that I suggested that Graham should have been manager at Burnley, then a struggling side. He was dynamic, a great motivator and had the best win record ever in non-league football. I actually put the idea to the Burnley board of which Clive Holt was a member. Frank Teasdale was chairman. The board's reaction was one of, "what a stupid idea, he's never been a professional player, how can he manage a league team?" Jose Mourinho might be able to answer that. My thinking was clearly well ahead of its time. Management is about selection, control and motivation. It's not about teaching how to play. Coaches do that. Burnley continued to struggle for several more years until Stan Ternent arrived.

What a lucky man Harry was to inherit the Turf Moor team he did in the mid 50s. There are those who say it was Alan Brown's team and indeed it pretty much was. But Harry was shrewd enough to leave it alone and give it just the one tweak by adding Alex Elder at full back. There's an old maxim: if it ain't broke don't fix it. Maybe the genius of Harry was to recognise that. What he also had was an almost bedside manner in the way he dealt with players and the young lads that joined the club. No end of them will pay tribute to him like a schoolboy fondly remembering an old teacher. Everyone except Colin Waldron that is; they never got on.

What a likeable man he was. How can anyone dislike a man who decided to change the days of the week? It was during the miners' strike when there were regular power cuts. Football was affected when it was obvious that evening games under the floodlights would be disbanded. With the possibility of games on Sundays Harry had a wonderful idea. It was pure Harry.

He decided that if we shifted the days along by one, we could make Sundays feel like Saturdays. He gathered us round and explained that we'd pretend Tuesday was Monday; Wednesday was Tuesday and so on until we got to Sunday and we would think it was Saturday and it would really feel like a Saturday. We pretended to be a bit gormless (not difficult for a footballer some would say) and asked him to explain it again. So off he started again telling us to imagine Thursday was Wednesday and we'd do on a Thursday what we'd normally do on a Wednesday, and the same on Friday, we'd do all the things we did on a Thursday. So when you get to Sunday it will feel just like a Saturday, a match day. We all looked at each other trying to figure this one out. At this point Steve Kindon piped up.

"But Harry that means that today is our day off."

"Oh," said Harry. His face fell and he thought for a minute. And then spoke again.

"That's right; you'd all better go home then." So we did.

But what a shrewd man he was as well. If critics say that he only rode on the coat-tails of Jimmy McIlroy and Jimmy Adamson in that great team of the late 50s and early 60s and was Bob Lord's yes-man; then what he also did, which kind of disproves that, was create another team in the mid-60s that included the likes of Willie Morgan, Ralphie Coates, Willie Irvine, Brian O Neil, Gordon Harris and Andy Lochhead; a team that came so close to winning the title again. But, one by one they were sold to pay the wages. Then at Blackpool as manager he took them to within a point of promotion to Division One.

What a brave and grateful man he was to return in 1977. His big strength was maybe his unflappability although to see him during a game in the dugout, you would never have thought that. If there was an earthquake during training, he'd probably have simply carried on playing five-a-side, telling you what a grand day it was to be playing football. Mind you he'd say that in the depths of winter when it was minus five and Pendle Hill was buried in snow.

"It's better than being in Switzerland," he'd announce warming his hands and smiling with pure pleasure. How could you not respond?

He was such a great bloke that you'd feel so sorry if you'd let him down. He had a successful record but never went around shouting about it. I can't recall any great impact he had when he arrived in 1977. In fact he was there already having been appointed as chief scout a little earlier because Dave Blakey had left. So there was no great fuss, he sort of just moved sideways and slightly upwards into a different office. But his appointment coincided with two things.

Firstly during a run of poor results he eventually asked us, "Has anyone got any idea what we should do, or how we should play?" We had got into a rut and he didn't seem to know how to get out of it. Ah ha, step forward yours truly. I've never had the slightest interest in becoming a football manager but maybe I should have done after this brainwave I had. I came up with what I called 'The Fletcher Plan' (don't mock). I should also add here that this was the 70s period when I sported a big bushy Mexican moustache. I cut quite a dash I can tell you. Birds made nests in it. I was the prototype for Juan Sheet. Regarding my plan, I'd seen something similar at Bolton as a kid under Nat Lofthouse when he called it the 'bag of worms'. In simple terms everyone in the team had to pull their weight and if anyone wasn't working hard enough the whole team descended on them until they picked up their effort.

The plan in some ways was very simple. What Harry had at his disposal was a team of workers (admittedly some of them nearing pension age) but no flair players. The flair players, or as we say in Bolton the flur players, had all been sold. What remained was a collection of bread and butter players (thick, white, and unsliced). So, the Fletcher Plan was simply this: if we couldn't do much WITH the ball, we'd be damned good WITHOUT it. We could run, chase, pressurise, intercept and force mistakes from any team that was better than us. (Let's face it; just about every team was better than us). But, with a bit of luck something might go our way before we all gave ourselves a hernia. Burnley fans lived on hard work and endeavour. So we decided to crank up our effort and leave nothing out there when we left the field.

And it worked.

In the very next game against Bolton Wanderers we ran round like proverbial headless chickens and won 2 – 1. There are two ways to look at this; either Harry could be discredited because he hadn't a clue what to do, or you gave him credit for being astute/genius enough to give the problem to the players.

Secondly he signed Steve Kindon. Before Steve arrived that season we really were heading for the drop but after his arrival the points mounted up. After 24 games we were still bottom but at last a win against Stoke lifted us up. After 30 games we were still in the bottom two but Steve was banging in the goals and like a steamroller he was flattening the opposition with regular frequency. It was like watching a big dog chase a ball. He always got it. Sometimes I used to half expect him to stand there, look at you and wag his tail. The groundsman was ordered to open the gates behind the goals whenever he saw Steve running down at full speed, so that he could run through the gates if he couldn't stop in time. Goalkeepers gave goals away because they were rooted to the spot, terrified, when they saw him bearing down on them like a giant steamroller.

At Christmas we were still in the bottom group but from then until the end of the season we only lost three more games. In March there were five straight wins the last of them being against Blackburn Rovers in a derby game that rivals anything elsewhere in the world. There was a sending off, eight bookings and violence on the terraces. I never use clichés (oh go on then), but we were over the moon and they were sick as a parrot. Harry was Bell's Manager of the Month. Pundits said we were playing the best football in the division. The revival was in fact quite amazing. My Fletcher Plan of course.

Suddenly Harry was in the limelight again. The media descended to interview him. There were features in the papers. I hovered in the background ready to talk about the Fletcher Plan. Funnily enough nobody asked. Peter Noble, by then about to apply for his bus pass, explained the transformation.

*"It's the boss. He never flapped, or put the lads under any pressure. And he has such a great knowledge of the game. All the boss did was to tell us we were First Division players at a great club. We were to continue playing our usual style (no mention of the Fletcher Plan you notice), give him 110% and go out and enjoy every game. If you'd gone to one of our training sessions, you would have thought we were leading the First Division, not dropping perilously near the Third."*

And it's true that every training session was filled with laughter and relaxation and Harry was instrumental in that. You rarely ever heard him swear until the day we were doing shooting practice. Several shots had gone over the bar and into the woods. Harry was in there fishing them out and booting them back. Suddenly with that wonderful telepathy that happens between naughty prank-filled footballers we 'chipped' all the shots into the hands of the goalkeeper, and he threw the balls over the bar into the woods. Twenty minutes later Harry obviously realised what was going on and emerged red-faced and apoplectic. "You f****g b*****ds," he went on, "Can't you f*****g shoot straight." On and on he went until he saw the funny side along with the rest of us as we lay on the ground heaving with laughter.

The reporters beat their way to Gawthorpe again after an interval of several years, praising the scouting system, the young lads coming through and everything else. The youth team had got to the semi-finals of the FA Youth Cup but were knocked out by Aston Villa. Pottsy said the club was on the up, youngsters he said were flocking to see him. There was a win over Tottenham to remind everyone of the great old days when fixtures between these two teams were the highlight of the football calendar. A 4 – 2 win over Cardiff City and the last two home games were both won. More than 11,000 people clapped and cheered Harry at the last game. The team that had been bottom of the division at the halfway stage of the season finished a creditable 14th.

He was never short of wonderful homespun advice of the arm-round-the shoulder variety. Steve Kindon tells the story that they were once driving through London on the coach to a game when he was just a young lad. Steve was drooling over all the classy cars and said something to Harry about them, something about how great it must be to have enough money to have cars like this.

"But Steve," said Harry. "You have a nice little car and it's paid for. None of these people have paid for theirs. Be happy".

The Anglo-Scottish Cup was in '78/79. By then my bones creaked like an old wooden door. My speed had gone. Mind you was there ever any in the first place? And looking back it's possible too that Harry was in the very, very earliest stages of the Parkinson's disease that would later affect him so badly. Leighton James returned to the club as well. He was still only 25 but seemed to have been around for years. Leighton by his own admission was temperamental and controversial. He was back just in time for the Celtic game in the Cup. But it was Big Steve Kindon's game. Burnley won with Steve's solitary goal. The Celtic riot it prompted was terrifying forcing us to leave the pitch.

The blame for the Celtic fans' terrible and violent behaviour was not hard to pinpoint. It was a reasonably straightforward journey from Glasgow via Carlisle and Lancaster using the available sections of motorway. Some Celtic fans had been drinking all day. Others drank copiously inside the ground. Some drank all day and then at the ground as well. Fuelled by drink, boredom in the hours leading up to the match and the lack of places to find something to eat, plus the natural belligerence associated with the Celtic travelling hordes at that time, it was all a recipe for disaster.

In September it was Sunderland who were the visitors, by now managed by none other than Jimmy Adamson. He and Bob Lord by this point loathed each other; a relationship that couldn't have been helped by the way Bob Lord had borrowed money from Jimmy. I remember a figure of £4,000 in a letter that Jimmy showed me from Bob, when Bob had paid the money back some years later. Sadly the grandchildren couldn't find this letter in Jimmy's papers after his death. The rumour is that Lord paid him back by increasing Adamson's salary. It's reasonable to assume that even the good natured and genial Harry by this time had no great opinion of Jimmy. Certainly the feisty Margaret Potts would have been keen to see Burnley win this game. The game however was a disgrace and it was Sunderland and Adamson going home well pleased. Surrounding himself with familiar faces Adamson had signed Colin Waldron, Mick Docherty and Doug Collins as well as backroom staff who had formerly been at Burnley. Sunderland fans used to joke that Adamson would have them playing in claret and blue before long instead of the famed red stripes.

*"A Kick in the Teeth for Soccer," wrote Keith McNee after the game. "Football reached a new, low ebb in this nasty, niggling, grudge confrontation which gave the game a dreadful kick in the teeth," he wrote.*

*"Professional," responded Sunderland player and ex Burnley man Mick Docherty afterwards.*

*"I am proud of my lads. I was sacked by Burnley so I get special satisfaction from winning," added Jimmy Adamson, after what McNee described as one of the most disgraceful masquerades of a match ever at Turf Moor. Even with two players sent off and three booked, Sunderland hung on to the 2 – 1 win. Much of the aggravation certainly stemmed from the bad blood felt by Adamson and the ex-Burnley players, and the bitterness they felt towards the club they had left three years earlier.*

*Harry Potts was incensed by everything he saw, although he didn't see the bitter confrontation between Adamson and Lord in the stand. "No team of mine has ever, or will ever, play like that," said Potts. "I would rather pack in with the game completely than sink to Sunderland's level. Sunderland just went for the man. As a match it was a shambles and I was disgusted at the way they went about it." Potts claimed that a Burnley player was even spat at.*

To rub salt into the wound, it was only when Sunderland went down to nine men that they scored the two goals, one from a penalty. Burnley pulled one back. Losing was bad enough, but for Sunderland to go down to nine men, and then score, made it embarrassing.

If the Sunderland game did one thing it showed yet again that calm and serene that he might have been on a weekday, Harry could certainly lose his rag during a game on a match-day. We used to call him 'The Mad Hatter' and there were no end of incidents involving him 'losing it' during a game. His head used to be marked with cuts and bruises from when he had jumped up in the dugout, angry at something, and banged his head on the overhang. In his time he'd grabbed linesmen, thrown cushions at the referee and in the infamous European Reims game had even gone onto the pitch to move the ball at a French free-kick. Whoever was the nearest Burnley full-back to him would regularly suffer endless shouts.

Never the greatest coach in the world (probably the thing that began to irritate Jimmy Adamson the most) his most famous instruction was to tell the midfield players to aim for the Burnley Building Society. It was Colin Waldron who asked him, "Harry what the f***k do you mean, aim for the Burnley Building Society?" Harry explained that any pass landing in the vicinity of the Burnley Building Society advertising board alongside the pitch would be perfect for Steve Kindon to run onto. It actually made perfect sense.

The final of the Anglo-Scottish Cup in 1979 was over two legs. The first was at Oldham on an icy pitch and we won 4 – 1. The return game at Turf Moor we actually lost. But a medal is a medal. And Harry thought it was wonderful, just as brilliant as playing in Europe.

There was this thing known as the 'Harry Potts way'. It was to do with how Harry thought that life should be lived and the game played. Always do your best and give 110%, know what's expected of you and conduct yourself properly, care for others and always remember you represent the club. It meant that just about every person who ever met him remembers him with affection, smiles at his memory and describes him as a gentleman. Four words might sum him up. Football was his life.

I was privileged to be asked by Harry's widow, Margaret, and her family, to say a few words at his funeral. I decided to make it into a humorous celebration of his life and achievements rather than anything sombre. I used my own memories of him and what a lovely person he was without an ounce of malice or cunning in him. He thought the best of everybody. I checked with Margaret that she was OK with the idea of me telling of the funny things that had happened. I never kept the notes I made, more's the pity, but Margaret told me later that I'd got it just right. I was happy with that. He was such a good man.

Bob Lord died in September 1981. Harry and Margaret were at the funeral. Harry died in January 1996. Jimmy Adamson died in November 2011. These three figures are integral to any history of Burnley Football Club. The story of their close early relationships with each other and then how they changed over time and across the years into bitterness and recriminations is a fascinating one. Ultimately, Jimmy Adamson had no contact with Bob Lord. Harry had little or no contact with Bob Lord once his second spell as manager ended. There was certainly no further contact between Harry and Jimmy in the final years. The way in which three men once so close became so bitter towards each other, was so terribly sad, providing another of football's heartbreak stories.

# 19

# Tribute to Jimmy – The Boss

In January 2011 we opened the Jimmy Adamson Suite in the Jimmy McIlroy Stand at Turf Moor. I'm proud to have played a part in that; proud that Jimmy was able to attend the event and saw and heard the crowd at the game paying him homage with cheers and applause. At the time of the event he was not in the best of health and had moved some time earlier into a care home. His wife, May, and two daughters had died earlier leaving him alone other than his grandchildren. The way that Jimmy spent the final years of his life is a heart-breaking story. He'd had no interest in re-visiting the ground since he was last there as manager of Sunderland in the late 70s. The bitterness he felt towards Bob Lord simply would not go away. Colin Waldron and I had tried to get him to attend a game at Turf Moor many times and at last when there was a Cup-tie against Liverpool, he agreed. Colin and I picked him up, walked him up into the boardroom, handed him a programme and waited for other people to arrive. With supreme irony the heavens opened with a torrential downpour and the game was postponed. By 7.45pm he was back home with his wife May. So the next visit some years after that was for the grand opening of the suite named in his honour, lined with glass cabinets filled with his memorabilia. In November of 2011 he passed away.

The story of Jimmy Adamson at Burnley Football Club is inextricably entwined with the story of Chairman Bob Lord. If Jimmy's managerial career ended on such a low at Leeds United then that doesn't concern me, except to say it was a crying shame and a sad end to such a distinguished career in football. Truth is it was actually Bob Lord who effectively 'broke' Jimmy Adamson several years earlier and some of the evidence is there to see in the following article. From the minute he left Burnley Jimmy was never the same. The rough draft of the article was found in Jimmy's box of football paperwork on his death. Whether it was ever published I don't know. There is no indication of the co-author. But, what is clear is that it dates to shortly after he was 'sacked' by Bob Lord in January '76. There is enough in it to show just what a despot Bob Lord was and the effect he had on those people he employed. The players saw nothing of this. From him we had the best of everything. He treated us well. That is to say as long as we were in the first-team and delivering the goods. You could argue too, that Bob Lord 'broke' Harry Potts, Jimmy's predecessor. Bob was ruthless and demanding. There are stories about him that are good and bad. The following piece may be short but the insight it provides is enormous. The old typing paper is creased, stained, yellowing now and faded. The contents are almost harrowing. This was the man who was a revered coach, produced one of the finest ever footballing Burnley teams, was admired and visited by Bobby Charlton a self-confessed disciple, had been assistant England manager, and then invited to take the post of full-time manager of England. The article is reproduced courtesy of Jimmy's five grandchildren Katie, Jennie, Sarah, James and Sam. I have got to know them well over the last four years and their contribution to the Jimmy Adamson Suite has been immense.

*"Bob Lord created for himself the image of being the most feared man in football, blasting his way to the top by a constant bludgeoning of people and principles. Nobody escaped the lash of his tongue, including the man groomed to be his right-hand man, Jimmy Adamson.*

*"I lasted for six years under Lord after expecting to be Burnley manager for a lifetime," reveals Adamson.*

*"To be fair Lord treated me well until I started disagreeing with him. Then our relationship went sour. We lived almost in each other's pockets. I planned Burnley's future on the playing side and Lord did the rest. At one time I thought we were a great team. We both made mistakes but I thought our future was healthy until the day Lord retired from his butchery business and took up football as a full-time job. Then things started to go wrong. I spent more of my time filling in forms and listening to Lord rather than concentrating solely on the job I was paid for. Not that I'm blaming Lord entirely for the lowly position the club was in when I left last January. But his interference didn't help.*

*"I expect any chairman to be fully informed but don't think it's right to devote the majority of the working day to the chairman's whims. And he had many of those. He ruled the club with an iron fist demanding attention most of the time.*

*"My wife used to dread weekends especially when we were playing at home. Sometimes she didn't feel like going to the game but it wasn't just a case of opting out. She had to ring the chairman's wife and report the fact that she wouldn't be there. Too many excuses were frowned upon.*

*"Even after a game Lord needed his men around – to play snooker! We'd troop down to the local Conservative Club, discuss the game while Lord popped in the colours and got results World Snooker Champion Ray Reardon*

*would have been proud of. Most of us were reasonable players but somehow we always seemed to miss a crucial pot.*

*"That was only the start of the weekend activities. Most Sundays we were summoned to the Lord household for lunch and hours of chatter. I didn't mind the ritual but my wife hated it. But we kept going, kept eating the roast beef and the Yorkshire Pud, and swallowed the rest just to keep Lord happy.*

*"There's nothing worse than Lord when he's upset or angry. Conversation is restricted to a grunt or a sharp blast and he seems to surround everything with a dark, depressive cloud. The consequences can be disastrous as I know to my cost. He starts what I term the 'pressure' system forcing people to the limit until he gets the result he wants.*

*"He started with me picking up on every point, scrutinising then trying to provoke an argument. This went on for months until our FA Cup defeat at Blackpool. Obviously this was the last straw in a disappointing season for Lord. Nobody likes going out of the Cup at the first attempt especially to a Second Division side. Burnley were no exception. While I was out of the dressing room there was a heated exchange which finally exploded into a flare-up between skipper Colin Waldron and my chief coach Joe Brown. I eventually got into the dressing room and sorted out the row. It was just one of those instant flare-ups and I knew there would be no recriminations.*

*"Lord missed the Saturday snooker match for the first time in ten years and I spent the whole of Sunday in bed. I was shattered from working a 12-hour day and suffering from an overdose of Bob Lord. I was no better on the Monday morning. I decided to take the morning off – my first in 12 years. But I didn't get the sleep I needed. A director called, examined the facts, and then said: 'Would you be willing to resign if Mr Lord paid up your contract?' Lord had the final word of course. The following day he sent for me to sack me for 'not reporting the Blackpool incident and not turning up for work'.*

*"The pay-off of £25,000 softened the blow somewhat as I became another of Lord's victims. I'd almost walked out on him 12 months earlier after an explosive bust-up at London airport. The club's tour of Madeira had started off badly for him. Somebody had forgotten to pick up his luggage and he had to carry it to the taxi himself. The strain must have been too much. He was grumpy for all the train journey to London and his mood didn't improve when another taxi spilled his luggage into a London street.*

*"I'd arranged to meet the party at London Airport and Lord was in vintage form even for him. The red cheeks had exploded into a deep crimson. The chest was heaving and the hat was tilted. The old war-horse was ready for battle and London Airport suddenly inherited a new tannoy system.*

*"It's your bloody fault that my luggage was forgotten. You ought to arrange things properly," he bellowed. I just turned and walked away. I didn't get far. Another director stepped in and calmed me down. It took hours for Lord to*

*regain his composure and to grunt his apologies.*

*"All my troubles with Lord seem to come from tours or holidays. A couple of years ago I was lying in the sun enjoying Majorca when I got a phone call from our groundsman. He was upset and complaining bitterly that Lord had ordered him to work from 8am until 6.30pm with only an hour for lunch and no tea breaks. I didn't want to lose a highly qualified groundsman and I asked him to hold on until I returned from holiday.*

*"I found that the groundsman had apparently upset the Lord family over the growing of tomatoes. In his spare time the groundsman was paid for looking after Lord's garden. On one of his weekly visits he found that two tomato plants had died through lack of water. The following day Lord informed him that he didn't want him at his home again. Whatever I said didn't matter. The groundsman eventually left and we had problems. It ended with me and my family manning the mowers to cut the grass at Turf Moor and at the club's training ground at Gawthorpe*

*"But we didn't mind. We thought Burnley was a family club, a place of spirit and warmth. It was – until Bob Lord blew through and froze me out."*

The picture painted of Bob Lord is pretty horrendous. By late 1976 when I guess the article was written, Lord was ageing and increasingly cantankerous and irritable. Joe Brown when he took over as manager did not last long. It was no surprise that after Brown, Lord turned to the ever reliable and the still faithful Harry Potts. It's not rocket science to suppose that Lord turned to Harry because he knew he was compliant and amenable. He was well practised in enduring Lord's whims and demands. He would never have dreamed of sending Lord out of the dressing room as Jimmy Adamson once did.

But, as Jimmy Adamson wrote in another article published sometime in 1988 in a booklet produced by me to raise funds for the club; 'It's fair to say that Bob Lord helped build up one of the finest club set-ups in British football.'

This he certainly did and no-one can take that away from Bob Lord and the work he did for the club in the 50s and 60s through until season 1974/1975. But that date is significant. It was the season that Martin Dobson was sold. Players had always been sold to pay the wages, but it was this sale, when the club were riding high and in with a real chance of lifting the First Division title, that marked the beginning of the end for the club that Lord and Adamson knew.

Jimmy called his piece for the booklet *BFC and Me, Who Sold McIlroy?*

*When I joined Burnley in the late 40s I had no idea I would be spending 27 years with the club. Those years contained incredible happiness and periods of great sadness, both as a player and a manager. The downfall of this great club began with whoever made the decision to sell Jimmy McIlroy. There is no doubt in my mind that this disastrous decision was made by Chairman Bob Lord, the club's megalomaniac dictator of the day. I do not want to say anything that will sound like sour grapes because the club has given me far too much pleasure for that but I think it's fair to say that Bob Lord helped to build up one of the finest club set-ups in British football AND THEN DESTROYED IT.*

This is just a small part of the article in which he goes on to cover his own career in a few hundred words. One thing he said to me when I was a player has always stayed in my head. It was the occasion of the club trip to the races at the end of the season. I asked Jimmy what he thought might happen the following season and how we might do in the league. "I don't know," he replied. "I want to build a team but the chairman wants to build a stadium."

Oddly enough years later I can identify with that aim of Bob Lord's. The problem was that the old Brunshaw Road Stand was in a terrible state of repair and I learned some time ago that a report commissioned to examine it, as good as condemned it. The steelwork was buckling and rusting. Barbara Lord, his daughter, revealed that he had sleepless nights over the state of that stand. It was in urgent need of replacement. Old Bob was responsible for the building of two new stands. His argument was that if you bettered the facilities you got a 'better' and happier supporter. I've based my own stadium building principles on that very same philosophy.

In his article Jimmy also paid tribute to former manager Alan Brown. It was a significant thing that whilst Jimmy heaped praise on Brown, there was not one mention for Harry Potts, the man who took Burnley to a Division One title, and into Europe, not once but twice. Journalist Brian Glanville who had unlimited access to the team at that time is still adamant to this day, that the achievements were less to do with Potts than Alan Brown, and the outstanding presence of Adamson and McIlroy. It was a sad fact that the relationship between Potts and Adamson certainly soured over the years. The more I think about it today, the more pointed it seems, that Jimmy ignored Harry in his article. In a piece he wrote in 1963 Jimmy wrote glowingly about Potts. By 1988 he couldn't mention him even once.

Hugely significant too, is the lengthy tribute to Jimmy that Bobby Charlton makes in his autobiography. He devotes quite a few pages to him. He was there at Jimmy's funeral as well. It was on the 'plane home from Chile following the '62 World Cup that they sat together and talked. Jimmy had been assistant manager. Not only did they talk on the plane but Charlton also reveals that he visited Jimmy several times in Burnley driving over the moors to see him. He saw in Adamson a man with the capability to impose a new style of professionalism on the England team. Talking to Adamson, Charlton realised that a new and stronger form of leadership was required if England was to progress. Winterbottom was almost the 'amateur' in his approach, donnish and schoolmasterish. Adamson convinced Charlton that an altogether different approach was needed. Had he accepted the post, Charlton thought that Adamson would have been a brilliant choice.

Adamson on that long journey home talked about responsibility, teamwork, professionalism, togetherness, expectations, effort and performance. Charlton saw him as a realist, grounded in what life was really like and the practicalities of earning a living on a day to day basis. In Chile one of Adamson's roles was to drill into the players what their roles and responsibilities were and how to take those onto the field of play.

As the years went by, he and Charlton went their different ways but it is clear that Charlton was deeply influenced by Adamson whom he described as a 'visionary'. The basis of his philosophy was that he thought that every player should have their specific role but within the team ethic. It was from 1973 to 1975 that this was best illustrated by his beautiful 'passing' team. The team was the sum of its parts, not 11 separate individuals, brilliant though they may be, simply doing their own thing and assuming that the results would come. Each individual had to fit into the group and obey his instructions regarding roles and functions. Maybe it was for this reason that an individually mercurial and brilliant winger like Dave Thomas would be sold at a stage when the 'team' was emerging. The brilliant Brian O 'Neil was another one to be sold, ironically at the beginning of the season that Burnley were relegated. Was it that the impish Brian was too much of a free spirit for Jimmy? The bullish Steve Kindon was another to be jettisoned. All three of them were tremendous players and still had much to give but clearly didn't fit with Adamson's mould.

In November 2008 a historian at the National Football Museum at Deepdale Preston, now at Manchester, contacted Colin Waldron. He was keen to learn why Jimmy Adamson was never selected to play for his country. This was odd as Adamson was voted Footballer of the Year in 1962 and was regularly called up to the squad. They had been trying to contact Jimmy for some time and had got no response.

They asked Colin if we could visit Jimmy and ask him the question as they had found out we went to see him every Christmas Eve.

So we decided to call up one afternoon in early December and get him talking about the Team of the 70s, BFC, Bob Lord and then we would casually drop in the question: "Boss, how come you never got selected to play for England?"

His answer was very clear and understandable and a stark contrast from football in the 70s when we played, or with the current England squad. Jimmy told us: "I was a bit mystified myself. The Manager Walter Winterbottom always wanted me to take the training sessions and work on all the free kicks and set pieces, which was odd as I was only in my late 20s. For the match he wanted me sat next to him in the dugout and he would discuss the game with me as it progressed. On a number of occasions at the pre-match meetings when he announced the team, I sat there waiting for my name to appear but it never did. In those days nobody ever questioned the manager. When he left the position he recommended me as England manager, but I turned it down. I've often wondered why he didn't pick me in his team."

There is very little written by Jimmy himself that explains why he turned down the England job other than to say he wanted to carry on playing and that he still had a life left as a player. He was linked with the managers' jobs at Norwich and Ipswich. One thing he did write in 1962 was: 'At this moment I am just not interested in team management. On top of that I feel my future is with Burnley Football Club. I have been at Turf Moor for 17 years now. I started my professional career there – and I would not mind finishing it there. My wife, our children and I like Burnley ... and here is where our future lies'. His wish did not come true and the parting was brutal.

It is also reasonable to assume that when Bob Lord heard of the interest he might well have said to Jimmy that there was a job and the eventual managership at Burnley for him if he stayed. Maybe even promised? But one obscure journal he did write regularly for was the *Times of Malta*. It was in this that he wrote about the need for any footballer to be adaptable and to be able to play in any position in which he found himself during a game. In this respect he was envisaging 'Total Football' long before the Dutch and Rinus Michels invented it in the 70s.

His initial appointment to the manager's role had raised eyebrows amongst supporters who at that time, great player though he had been, were less than impressed with his coaching and assistant's role under Harry. There is a school that thinks without his meddling the team of 1966 would have won the title. When he did actually become manager, he was soon under the cosh and being criticised for the poor football and the lowly position in the table. Adamson splashed £60,000 on me in March 1971. Relegation was near. Bolton needed the money, Burnley needed a striker.

"This is a great move for me," I told the local Press. This was the period when he was supported and backed by Bob Lord to the hilt even following relegation in 1971. The following season the grumbles aimed at him by supporters grew and grew. There were angry scenes after several games when he was abused and jeered. Lord announced that he would remain as manager. The angry accusations and letters to the *Burnley Express* subsided however, by the end of the season. Something was beginning to blend and the 1971/72 season ended with six straight wins and entry into the Watney's Cup. Confidence grew and all of us had no fears about the new season.

The promotion season of 1972/73 was magical, not the least of which was the £5,000 bonus that most of the team got. That was a small fortune back then. Mind you, a large chunk of it went in tax. I'd just bought a new four-bedroom detached house in Rossendale for £9,850.00 so the bonus was a good start to married life. Everything clicked, great football, some tremendous wins but one of the things I remember best was a home defeat against Orient 1 – 2. They were way down the bottom and we were comfortably up at the top end. The Orient centre-half was advancing with the ball and Colin Waldron was taunting him mercilessly as he approached. "Shoot... shoot," he kept mocking him fully expecting him to blast it 10 yards over the bar and we'd regain possession. The centre-half obliged and scored a blistering goal into the top corner from something like 35 yards. Waldo was utterly gobsmacked.

August, season 1972/73, was the start of three golden seasons; was it possible that his claim that Burnley would be the 'Team of the Seventies' would be achieved? No: the last of them was marked by fading fortunes in the final few weeks as the steam ran out following the sales of Martin Dobson and Geoff Nulty. In March of that season, 1974/75, Burnley were second in the table, but the team simply lacked the strength and depth to maintain that position and maybe do even better. It was also the season when non-League Wimbledon knocked Burnley out of the FA Cup at Turf Moor in one of the great football shocks of the decade. Nevertheless, it was in those three seasons that Jimmy's reputation as coach and manager was cemented. He would never surpass them. After that things deteriorated both on and off the field so that by January '76 it was quite possible that Bob Lord was simply waiting for the excuse to sack him. He grabbed the opportunity after the Cup defeat at Blackpool against Harry Potts' side. Harry Potts was jubilant. For him it was a win over Jimmy Adamson the man who had manoeuvred him out of the manager's job, and over Bob Lord who had given Harry the axe, albeit with the sweetener of another job within the club. All of this is covered in great detail in the Dave Thomas book, *Harry Potts Margaret's Story*. Harry was devastated and Margaret revealed that he had gone home crying; "Bob, Jimmy, Bob, Jimmy, what have you done to me, what have you done to me?"

What Bob Lord saw as a possible dream-team, Jimmy the on-field manager, and Harry the behind the scenes genius recruiting players, never happened. For some years before this Harry had been manager and Jimmy chief coach. Harry after the change round was marginalised, was made to feel unwelcome, and maybe even told to stay away from the training ground. Whereas it was once Harry who was the son that Bob Lord never had, now it was Jimmy; and Jimmy simply didn't want Potts around, so that eventually in '72 Harry was paid off and dismissed. How sweet it must have been for him to win that Cup-tie. Margaret Potts had no sympathy whatsoever for Jimmy Adamson, when the fate that had befallen Harry, then befell Jimmy.

But my story concerns Jimmy the Burnley coach and manager, and how close to success and maybe even greatness we came with him. Colin Waldron wrote about him in *Burnley FC and Me*. He begins by outlining how his request to open a restaurant was not well received by Lord and Potts. He was dropped from the first team and stripped of the captaincy:

*"Many years later I was given the club captaincy but this time under the guidance of Jimmy Adamson. He was without doubt the greatest coach or manager I have ever played under. His coaching technique was outstanding and our tactics often proved so successful that over a three or four year period in the early seventies, players who had left the club often found themselves being asked in coaching sessions, 'What would Burnley do here?'*

*"Adamson's coaching had a passing theme which was always reflected in our play in the First Division. We became known as a passing side. On one occasion after my retirement from football I spoke to former West Ham and England captain, Bobby Moore. He said to me, 'We always hated playing Burnley because we were always chasing leather.'*

*"Adamson managed the club in handcuffs knowing that at the end of every season he would have to balance the books by selling one or more of his star players. A classic example of this problem followed the promotion year of '73. Queens Park Rangers and ourselves both gained promotion to the First Division and by Easter were many points ahead of the pack. I felt we were a better side than QPR; we just needed our side strengthening with a few players. In the summer QPR bought two top players. Burnley sold two. In*

*our first year in Division One we finished tenth. QPR finished second.*

*"When Bob Lord's personal ambition and dictatorial rule began to destroy the empire he had built, he finally pulled the rug from under the club's feet by sacking Jimmy Adamson. The decision lacked any logic as Adamson was the only man capable of keeping Burnley in the top flight. The club has yet to recover from this tragic mistake."*

That was written in 1988. The club did recover eventually in 2009, but in between came years and years of near bankruptcy both on and off the field. As Bob surveyed the scene from his seat in the stand until he died in 1981, all he could see was decline, near administration, unpaid bills, and yet more decline. All he could hear was the anger and criticism of the supporters who saw the club heading only one way as he stubbornly held on to the chairmanship. We will never know what his real thoughts were as he eventually watched Fourth Division football at Turf Moor, instead of the years of glory in the early 60s. Jimmy Adamson was right. Bob Lord built the club, and then destroyed it.

Jimmy Adamson never had a prayer of sustaining the work he did in building that team of which I was a part. If he was a great manager in that period there was one simple reason. He was in love at that point with Burnley Football Club. When he left, wherever he went, it was never the same even though he tried to surround himself with familiar faces. He maybe wasn't the greatest ever manager at Burnley but at Burnley he got the mix right. It's an essential football secret; in fact it's no secret at all, if you get the right blend of players, youth and experience, flair and workers, you'll fit a team together that will gel. It's like a jigsaw puzzle. The pieces have to fit. Owen Coyle did it in 2009. Jimmy Mullen did it in 1992 although they were Frank Casper's players, Stan Ternent in 2000. Jimmy didn't want 11 star players; he just wanted 11 team players who could play together. The team ethic came first. It still binds us together to this day as our pensions approach.

Several games have left great memories and one of them was at Chelsea. It's what Jimmy said that left an indelible impression. We were losing 3 – 0 at half-time to a good Chelsea side. A hammering seemed on the cards and as we trooped off we expected a hammering from Jimmy as well for the way we had played. To our amazement all he said was not to worry and go out for the second half and treat it as a training session with our training boots on. Out we went for the second half and the game ended 3 -3, with me scoring the equaliser. Absolutely delighted we went back in at full-time and Jimmy was beaming. We looked at him bemused and told him we'd expected a bollocking at half-time. "I'd have been relieved if it had only been 6 – 0," he said. "Chelsea were outstanding. What else could I say to you other than something to try and relax you?"

I didn't score for Burnley until my sixth game but got great support from Jimmy and the supporters. Nat Lofthouse used to tell me that supporters were people who worked hard all week, and therefore expected nothing less from the players they watched. "They don't expect you to be brilliant every game," he would say, "but they do expect you to give everything you've got. Most, if not all of them, would give anything to be in your place." Jimmy Adamson was much the same.

Being dropped from the team, if it happened, was a massive blow. There was no squad rotation where you expected to miss some games. The team was much the same every week. The best players played week in week out. There was the inevitable period when I wasn't playing well and I expected the worst, especially when coach Joe Brown came to me to say that Jimmy wanted a word with me later that day. It could only mean one thing. I was out.

It was a beautiful sunny afternoon and when I met Jimmy he was standing in the middle of the wooden bridge at Gawthorpe that spanned the river between the changing rooms and the pitches on the other side of the river. It was a beautiful spot. He was deep in thought and was throwing dandelions into the river below, clearly contemplating the news he had to give me. I looked glum and despondent. "How are Sian and the kids?" he asked. "Claire must be about three now and Daniel must be nearly walking." He talked about the holidays and his family and Burnley and how lovely the weather was, clearly getting me relaxed before he gave me the bad news. But there was no bad news. This is what he said:

"Paul, of all the players I've brought to Burnley you are my best signing. I love every aspect of your game and each week you give me everything you have. You are still young and will get better and better. On Saturday I'm expecting you to have the best game of the season so far. I totally believe in you. If you don't score, don't worry, it's my problem. Just keep trying, that's all I ask. And on the way home, pop in the dressing room, there's a bunch of flowers for Sian and some chocolates for the kids. Give them my love. See you Saturday."

How's that for man-management? Can you imagine how I felt as I drove home? I was expecting a bollocking and the axe and here he was telling me I'm the best. If he'd asked me to jump off the Town Hall roof I would have done. All I wanted was to get out on the field and play my heart out. Only once in the next ten years was I dropped from the team. It never wore off.

My loyalty to Jimmy Adamson is based on gratitude but at the same time there's a lingering admiration for Bob Lord despite all his curmudgeonly failings. Of course we can find terrible things to say about him but I prefer to think of him as the man who put this club on the map, in fact not just the club but the town of Burnley. On my achievement scale he is one of the greatest ever club chairmen. What he built is still here. It still exists. He kept the club in the top flight far longer than any supporter had any right to have expected. I prefer to remember him as an iconic figure rather than look under the carpets for the dirt. I still adhere to his maxim; that if you have a quality stadium you will have quality people in it.

So, where did it go wrong for Jimmy? Clearly it was well before the infamous Cup-tie at Blackpool in January '76. And what is his legacy?

There are two schools of thought. The first sees him as a great coach and manager who should never have been sacked. The other sees him in a less kindly light, that whilst as a coach he was a genius, as a manager he was not everyone's cup of tea, to quote Colin Waldron in an article following Jimmy's departure. Colin was an Adamson disciple and reveres him to this day but was realistic enough to see that others did not have the same feelings. As a general rule, those players who revered Harry Potts did not have the same feelings for Jimmy seeing him as aloof and even arrogant. But is that not human nature? If a manager does not retain you, you are hardly going to have warm thoughts towards him?

What I think is simply this: that he was a great coach, that for me he was a good manager, and I had the best years of my career under that management. I visited him every Christmas Eve until he died. The Jimmy Adamson Suite at the club is a wonderful tribute to him with the glass cases filled with memorabilia and pictures. And: whereas some managers from the club's past will barely be remembered, if remembered at all, Jimmy's achievements will be there forever.

On the day of Jimmy's funeral the cortege drove along Harry Potts Way passing pavements lined with people paying their respects and appreciation. There was spontaneous loud applause as is the growing custom these days. The funeral was attended by the 'greats' of the football world, Bobby Charlton, Eddie Gray, Jimmy McIlroy amongst them. Many members of the 'Team of the Seventies' were there including myself. For me it was a hugely personal day as images and memories of great times with him came back.

At the game against Leeds United on the 19th of November we stood on the field before the game started and joined in the applause that rang round the ground. How ironic it was that the game was against Leeds for that is where he ended his managerial career and connections with football. The Leeds fans joined in with the rest of us, even though his time there was not the best. Probably, too, it was the place where his great 'Team of the Seventies' started their decline in 1974 after the injury to Frank Casper.

He played 486 senior games for the club, scoring 18 goals. He was one of only two players to lead the Clarets to the ultimate success in winning the Division One title before it became the Premiership. He was a superbly elegant player, a thinker, and was 'Footballer of the Year' in 1962.

He changed my life and I will be forever grateful. I think of him still and will do so for a long, long time.

# 20

# Bob Lord's Tours and the 'Hundred Greatest Clarets' Spoof

I'm addicted to jokes, April Fool stunts and pranks. Maybe it's being a footballer. A lot of us are like this. It's difficult to grow up in the football world where there's a fourth form school mentality that lingers. The jokes people play on you are endless, the banter merciless, the ribaldry continuous. Bawdiness reigns supreme. On a good day, if he was in a cheerful mood, physio Jimmy Holland used to put bubbles in the bath after a game. This meant you never knew if someone had done something nasty in the bathwater. Whilst he was out of his medical room we'd put a bucket of water above the door so that he'd get a soaking on his way back. Everyone checked their shoes in the dressing room as a matter of routine.

On the road trip in the USA Sandy Stewart asked me about my most embarrassing moment. I seem to think Brendan and Barry were asleep at this point in the reclining seats in the back. I liked Sandy Stewart a lot and we exchanged a few good stories about our time as footballers and our afterlife once we had retired. Dear God there were so many embarrassing moments, so off the top of my head I told him about the time at the Dunkenhalgh in the 90s when Colin Waldron and I were regular visitors to the Fitness Club (don't laugh) there. We'd arrive at seven in the morning, work out, swim; have a sauna, and then eat breakfast at about eight before driving off to work. Over the five or six years we went there a few others joined us, including Mark Bowie and Keith Bennett who ran a car firm in Nelson, plus my close friend Kevin Collinge, and John Haworth, the latter known to all of us as Bobby Blue after he wore a ridiculous suit on one of our race days. He'd also been club secretary at Burnley and Blackburn Rovers amongst others. Then there was Brian Lee who ran a textile firm in Blackburn.

The atmosphere and camaraderie was not unlike the dressing room days in the 70s at Turf Moor. We'd had some great fun one week when I'd got Bobby Blue's car keys and while he was in the gym I'd hidden a raw kipper under a mat in his car. Every day for the next week both he and the car reeked of kippers and he couldn't understand why.

Now in this game you immediately beware of retaliation so before Bobby had time to even suspect it was me, I retaliated first, as Danny Blanchflower once said. Whilst we were all working out in the gym I excused myself to go to the loo but instead went into the changing rooms, found his clothes, and then rubbed a large dollop of 'Deep Heat' into the part of his underwear that would come into close contact with the most tender part of his anatomy. After training, we showered and then I watched as John dressed and awaited the reaction. There wasn't one. Whoops, I'd put the stuff in the wrong underpants.

Now into the dressing room had come a rather 'gay' looking bloke. He'd presumably stayed at the hotel the night before and my mouth dropped as I watched him put the underwear on, into which I'd liberally applied the 'Deep Heat'. The reaction isn't always immediate with 'Deep Heat'; I hadn't the courage to tell him and headed up to the breakfast room as fast as I could. How do you explain something like that to someone you've never met before? How do you tell someone you suspect is 'gay' that you've had your hand in his underpants? I've wondered ever since, I told Sandy, at what point did the ointment kick in? Was it sitting at breakfast eating a kipper? Was it halfway down the M62 on his way to his next appointment? And if so did he veer off the motorway in agony wondering what he'd got up to the night before? Colin Waldron was also a merciless prankster and nor was he ever embarrassed about taking the mickey in any situation.

There's a massive difference between a pre-season tour and an end of season tour. In May a hard season is over. The league position is finalised. A new contract offer has just plopped through the letter box. The sun is shining. It's good to be alive. A pre-season tour is in total contrast. It is part of the build-up to the new season. You have to get on the scales, check your weight and lose the extra flab. It was often stressful and demanding. The intensity could leave you exhausted. With Jimmy Adamson we took it very seriously.

It's not rocket science to work out which kind of tour we enjoyed most and I can tell you now we had some cracking end of season trips. This type of tour was a thankyou from the club and in particular Bob Lord. Say what you like about him he treated his first team players well. At the season's end we let our hair down, had a few drinks, the drinks that we had denied ourselves during the season. But we were always well behaved. We mixed well with the staff and guests wherever we were. We did not wreck our bedrooms. As an additional thankyou there was always an envelope under our pillows from Bob Lord with some cash in it to help us get through the arduous weeks wherever the tour was heading. They were wonderful days.

Bob Lord loved these trips, but he would never stay in the same hotel as the players (he probably didn't like playing bingo every night). He was always somewhere nearby in a hotel that had a couple more stars than ours. But we didn't feel slighted by this at all and got on with the serious job of having a good time. Our wives meanwhile were left behind with the kids, the washing, ironing and dusting, not to mention keeping the grass cut. Our wives were never WAGS; they hadn't been invented in the 70s. Magaluf was a favourite and Jimmy Adamson used to tell us of his trips in the early 60s when the plane actually landed on the beach at Palma Nova. They went to Mauritius as well one year on an old prop plane that took about 18 hours and several stops for refuelling. Every so often it was sprayed with DDT. By the time they got there they could hardly walk.

We soon moved up a peg or two as we started to have more success on the field. Next it was Madeira and then Bermuda. But there was always a problem with these trips; we had to play a game. The reason for this was seemingly down to taxation rules at the time. A free holiday was a taxable event, so it was important to play a 'game' and even provide the evidence. It didn't seem that we had to play someone like Barcelona, Real Madrid or even Magaluf United, as long as we played a game of some description. So: we would play against some ragged little team that was always assembled from the hotel waiters.

Normally this was a stress-free event so we could stroll around, not work up a sweat, use minimum effort, rattle in six goals, and then get back to the beach. But one year it seemed more serious. Bob Lord sent a message from his top hotel up the road that he was bringing some important guests to watch the game, so could we please put on a special performance. By this we wondered did he want us out there in fancy dress or do a bit of Shakespeare at half-time (or even should I take out the ukulele and sing while I scored?)

It looked pretty straightforward as we weighed up the dishevelled set of assorted misfits that Brian Miller and Jimmy Holland had assembled from the hotel bars, kitchens and dining room. Some of them didn't look as if they could walk, let alone run, let alone play a game of football. Miller and Holland handed them some kit, we pulled on our claret and blue jerseys over our pink, sun-reddened bodies and we kicked off in 90 degree heat on a bumpy, threadbare pitch that wouldn't have passed a test at Towneley Park. To add to all that, one of the waiters, believe it or not only had one arm. To make it fair Peter Noble our ace full-back put one arm inside his shirt and tied a knot in the sleeve. And so we kicked off.

The one-armed waiter was called Mario and it soon became clear that even with one arm he was a bit of a Super Mario. He ran rings round Peter. In fact they all ran rings round us and rattled up a half-time score of 3 – 1. Bob Lord and Jimmy Adamson sat open-mouthed. Keith Newton in particular was having a hard time in the heat and exhaustion was setting in for a few of us. Jimmy Adamson rollocked us at half-time so that we put as bit more effort into things, and managed to score two more goals with Frank Casper getting the equaliser. Taxis whisked away a far from pleased Bob Lord and his guests. We never did find out who they were. And we got on with the serious business of enjoying the holiday.

On another occasion we played a game with a Burnley supporter in our team, Dave Burnley. None of us knew him from Adam at the time but we'd seen this scruffy looking bloke wandering up and down the streets near the hotel, all dressed up in what looked like claret and blue rags. When we turned up to play the waiters and got off the coach into the open-air oven, there he was again by the touchline. We've since learned that Dave has never missed a game since the mid-70s, devotes his life to travelling the world watching his beloved team, and for this game in Majorca he was dossing down in an old burned down hotel in the town and was literally living on scraps.

On this occasion we beat the waiters 7 – 2 and Dave came on at our invitation as a sub for Leighton James and he scored twice in the 7 – 2 win. He split his shoes (old golf shoes) scuffing a shot, so Steve Kindon gave him a pair of his trainers, and after the game we had a whip round and gave him the equivalent of about £25. Seeing as he'd only come out to Majorca with about £20 in his pocket, he did rather well then and went home in profit.

Early in 1975 we heard from Doc Iven, the club doctor, that Bob was to have an operation on his ears. He would not be able to fly again; or if he did he was warned he would be in serious agony. We were disappointed as we wondered if this would be the end of the trips abroad. The thought of a coach trip to Inverness didn't quite have the same appeal and perish the thought we'd have to play a game against a bunch of kilt-wearing, one-armed, Scots waiters.

But: one day we were called to a meeting. It was a Thursday afternoon and we all assembled in the Turf Moor dressing room. We were mid-table and were told Bob Lord wanted to see us. I'd been at the club about four years and we'd no idea what it was all about. We knew that the club was always selling players to pay the bills and wondered if it was news about something like that. For sure we thought it must be something serious as he never spoke to the players as a group. Was he even going to retire maybe? Was he going to stop the Christmas turkey that we were all given every year? This was a tradition that went back years to the days of when even Jimmy Adamson was a player.

What was hilarious about the turkey that all the first teamers and the management were given every Christmas was that the size of it depended on your seniority and how much old Bob liked you. We'd gather round and compare sizes (turkeys that is) and whoever got the biggest presumed that he would not be sold that year. And some of them were so big you'd find they wouldn't fit in the oven when you got it home. Whoever got the smallest went away very worried. But Bob was a crafty old sod. He loved the generous chairman image and always cultivated the idea that they were a gift from him personally of course. But I learned years later that he always stuck a large bill in at the club for them. So dishing out 30 turkeys every year was a nice little earner for him and his business.

Anyway: there we were sat waiting in the dressing room and in came Bob Lord. He had a face like the Churchill dog in the insurance advert. He spoke. "You've probably all heard I've had an operation on my ears so I'm not allowed on aeroplanes. So, we've decided that this year we will be goin' on a boat." He did not elaborate on the boat or what sort of boat but he did add, "You'll need a black suit for dinner and a white one for when the weather changes. So I'll let Jimmy give you all the details.

"We're goin' on a boat." And that was all he said.

Without any more ado off he went out of the dressing room. What he didn't tell us was that this would be a three-week tour of the Caribbean, visiting New York, St Lucia, St Thomas and Martinique. The dinner jackets would be needed in the five-star Queen's Grill Restaurant, at that time voted the second best restaurant in the world.

And by the way, the 'boat' he talked about was only the world's most luxurious liner of the age, the QE2. The life of a footballer, how lucky I was; things like this were organised for you and all you did was turn up, sit back and enjoy the ride and play against a better class of waiters.

It was aboard this floating palace that Brian Flynn became the victim of what we thought at the time was the prank of the century. He was only 17 and was with us on this QE2 cruise round the Caribbean in 1975. As a rule we would all get together at around 4pm to play bingo in the Queen's Ballroom and we would gather in 'Mick McNally's' Bar on the second tier of this fantastic ship along with another 500 holiday makers trying to win the first prize which amounted to the equivalent of £1,000 in today's money. So: not to be sneezed at then.

On this particular afternoon Waldo did not get one single number and the game was nearly up. So, in frustration he left, but not before he filled in all the numbers bar two, handed the card to Brian Flynn and asked him to keep an eye on it. Brian was anxious to please, he was only a kid, resembled a cherub, and Colin was a god (well he thought so). Little Brian took over while the god went to the loo.

At this point I wouldn't really say that Colin Waldron, who really did think he was incredibly handsome, had airs and graces; but in a magazine where players were asked for their favourite this and that, he'd been asked what his favourite meal was. Now, most players said beans on toast, or egg and chips but not Colin. "Steak au poivre," he said.

"You pretentious knob," we called him and made merciless fun of him for days. If he'd said steak and chips it would have been OK, but then knowing him he would probably have said, "Steak avec pommes frites."

Anyway, the bingo: Colin told Brian Flynn that he was going to the loo (but hid around the corner to watch the spoof unfold) and asked Flynny to keep an eye on his bingo ticket. Hugely excited, not easy for him because he's only 5' 2", within minutes he had filled in the missing numbers when they were called out. I remember them to this day, 15 and 28. Today if we hear those numbers and Brian is around we all shout "HOUSE." He was so excited and bounded down to the front holding the card high in the air, well as high as he could, and dashed up onto the stage. The room erupted into cheers for him because nobody thought he was more than 12. In fact now I think about it, it was a long spiral staircase that he had to go down to get to the centre of the ballroom. On the way he signed autographs for those who thought he was the Burnley mascot and at last was greeted by the caller, who just happened to be a Burnley fan. You couldn't make this up could you?

He was interviewed for several minutes and Brian thought he was the bees' knees picking up the £1,000. But there was one small detail. The caller had to check the numbers. He took the card ... one by one he read out the numbers to the checker and you can guess the rest ... 7 – no, 13 – no, 26 –no, 38 – no, 44 – no, 62 – no ... as the no's got more frequent the laughter from the audience got louder and louder. The caller said, "Sorry Brian, it appears that you haven't got all of the numbers called. You've only got two of them." Brian's mouth dropped as he cottoned on to what Waldo had done.

It could well be that the bingo win was Brian Flynn's most embarrassing moment ever as he crawled back up the spiral staircase to rapturous applause, especially from his team-mates. But, I said to

Sandy, who amazingly was still awake in the car, what a player Brian was, a perfect example of the old saying, "It's not the size of the dog in the fight; it's the size of the fight in the dog."

We still hadn't finished with Brian on the QE2 and persuaded him because he was so small that he was perfect for a joke we wanted to play on Jim Thomson. The plan was to dress him in a white sheet, put him in one of those laundry skips that they wheel round a ship up and down the corridors to collect the dirty laundry; park it by Jim's cabin door, knock on the door and when he answered Brian would suddenly jump out of the basket in the white sheet and shout BOOOOO. What a joke, what a prank.

So Flynny got in the basket in the sheet and we closed the lid. But, deliberately, we didn't park the skip outside Jim Thomson's door, we carefully put it outside another door and we'd no idea whose room it was. We knocked on the door and it all went to plan perfectly. Except when the door opened it was an elderly couple standing there. Flynny in a startling performance flung open the lid, leapt up dressed in the sheet, and shouted BOOOOOO as loud as he could. I swear the woman's teeth dropped out and the old man's toupee lifted up six inches. They went as white as the sheet and we thought they were about to have a heart attack. They were absolutely terrified. It wasn't a stunt we ever repeated.

It was on this wonderful boat that we also played what we called bedroom golf. Mind you, we played this game in every hotel we visited. I found this written by the late, great Keith Newton in my little book *BFC and Me*:

*"What do I remember about my time at Burnley Football Club? Great goals, great games, promotion, foreign tours, no it's none of these. Believe it or not the thing I remember most is THE GOLF. No: not golf course golf but bedroom golf.*

*"I arrived at Burnley on a free transfer from Everton and found myself in the middle of not just a great team, but an incredible bunch of characters who were to provide me with a most enjoyable and successful eight-year stay. After signing for the Clarets I was introduced to my new room-mate, Peter Noble. On our first trip away we played in London and stayed at the Great Western Hotel in Paddington.*

*"'What do you normally do after dinner?' I asked Nobby.*

*"'Play golf,' was his reply. 'Can you play?'*

*"At the time I was playing off a seven handicap at Pleasington Golf Club and like many professional footballers had become addicted to the game. But the idea of playing at 8.30 in the evening, in the centre of London, the night*

before an important game seemed ridiculous. 'Where do you play?' I asked.

"'In Paul Fletcher and Alan Stevenson's bedroom,' came the reply.

"I must admit I was intrigued to find out about bedroom golf but absolutely flabbergasted when the door opened to the Fletcher/Stevenson room. There they stood both completely naked except each was wearing a jock strap, rubber golf shoes, golf glove, a flat cap, and Alan Stevenson was pulling a Jack Nicklaus golf bag – on a trolley – with one club, a putter, in it.

"'What the bloody hell is going on?' I asked Alan Stevenson as he did a few warming-up exercises like golfers do. So he explained that 12 months earlier he had bought a second-hand hickory shafted putter from a shop in Praid Street, across from the Great Western Hotel. When he got back to the room he and Fletch started putting on the carpet in the hotel room.

"They would have a contest to see who could hit the 'pot' (the toilet) and flip the ball into the waste bin, in the least number of shots. Then another few 'holes' were added. And then the etiquette and correct dress developed. They called the game 'Pot Bin' with hole number one always the dog-leg down the room and into the bathroom. The last hole was always the bin. The game was played as a Stableford with all four 'teeing off', then each team picking the best 'drive' and then playing alternate shots.

"Great tournaments were played, always named by Stevo: The Great Western Open, The Swindon Post House Masters, the Norwich Moat House Classic, the Bermuda Medal and the QE2 Celebrity. Stevo and Fletch challenged every pairing at the club. Apart from myself and Nobby, there was Waldron and Collins, James and Ingham, Thomson and Rodaway, even a Miller and Holland pairing tried their luck. And nobody else ever won mainly because Stevo and Fletch were the biggest cheats I have ever come across. They always had some trick up their sleeves. You would find the bath full of water when your ball went in. 'Water hazard, one shot penalty,' Stevo would shout.

"'How is it there was no water in the bath when you were in here,' I would ask.

"'There must have been a storm,' came the reply from Fletch.

"On another occasion in the middle of a tense game we rang down to reception to get coffee and sandwiches. The young maid nearly dropped the tray as she walked into the room with all four of us wearing only our golf attire.

"'Just put the tray on the fourth green and mind you don't step into the bunker,' said Stevo as she placed the tray on the bed. He was the perfect gentleman but couldn't resist nipping her bum as she ran out.

"We may have acted like children but one thing is for sure, it was great for team spirit. The fun and laughter we had off the park gelled us together as a team when we got onto the pitch. We read about other teams away on tour smashing up hotel rooms, insulting the guests but in our case I don't *remember even a glass being chipped.*

*"The club gave me a new lease of life which lasted 8 years. I will never forget this great club, the wonderful supporters, and the bunch of idiots I shared my time with. And I certainly won't forget the golf."*

What wonderful, rollicking times we had. I sometimes wonder if the likes of Balotelli, Silva, Toure and Aguero, have the same kind of dressing room bond and banter that we had. Will they still be in contact 40 years from now? I somehow doubt it.

And then, there was my master spoof. It is reproduced in the picture section. In terms of the responses it got, ranging from the incredulous to the furious; in terms of the response it provoked on the hugely read Claretsmad website and in particular the messageboard, it surely must be the greatest prank I have pulled off. Let's just say there was never any such thing as the 100 Greatest Clarets Award at the Grosvenor Hotel in London.

From a Burnley FC history book I just pulled out 100 names. Some of them I'd never even heard of. Some of them went back to the pre-war years. A number were the well-known star players from the 60s and 70s. I ranked them 1 – 100, allegedly as the result of a non-existent Burnley fans' poll. I made up something about the Football Association Heritage Committee inviting all clubs to participate in polls for their own clubs. I then published the 'results'. To give it immediate authenticity the top three were Jimmy McIlroy, Jimmy Adamson and Leighton James. Nobody could grumble at that. You might have expected someone like Martin Dobson to come fourth in a genuine poll. In mine I put him 64th. At somewhere like Man Utd it was like putting Bobby Charlton at 50th. My great pal Colin Waldron without a doubt one of the best centre-halves ever at the club I put at 90th. And so it went on. I put lesser known players quite high up and some real stars only midway or even low down. And no one knew how to react to the published results. Was it really serious? Surely it was a joke. But yet it had a superb ring of truth and authenticity to it with headed paper, and fancy titles, and formal, official language.

But like all good spoofs or April fool jokes there has to be something in it somewhere that is there to be spotted and give the game away. So for this although the letters were dated 6th, February, 2009; the awards ceremony would be on 01. 04. 2009. And the whole thing was sponsored by Daehbonk International along with official groups such as the FA, Nike, Dulux, and McDonald's. Look closely and you see that 01. 04. 2009 is April 1st (April Fools' Day). Look closely and you see that Daehbonk is Knobhead backwards. The giveaways were clearly there.

It was announced with a big splash on the club website and a fans' site. I sent copies of the four-page letter to all my mates in the team of the 70s. Eleven letters went out. God were they taken in. Martin Dobson and his wife were quite aghast at his lowly position. "How on earth can people say that Chris Pearce (at 50) is better than you?" Carole exclaimed, "Or Roger Eli (at No 36)?"

And then there were the prizes. The top ten would win an engraved gold Omega watch valued at £2,586. But Martin's position only entitled him to a limited edition club scarf (players voted 51 to 100). "Well I'm not going to London just to receive a f*****g club scarf!" he grumbled.

"And Fletch, you've won yourself a gold Omega watch that's worth £2,586," he humphed. I'd put myself in there at number 10 ha ha ha! They all went apeshit! Result!

It was a ridiculous £135 per ticket to attend. There was another giveaway. There was dancing until midnight to the Batchelors. It was the wrong spelling. Anyone who turned up at the Grosvenor would have been dancing to a tin of peas.

He won't thank me for saying so but Dave Thomas (an ex headmaster who once upon a time used to be intelligent) was completely taken in and fired off disbelieving emails and responses to various fans' websites where there was general incredulity at the 'results'. Dave is still laughing about it. "How on earth can people vote Paul Gascoigne at number six when he barely played half a dozen games?" he wrote to one message board. "And Steve Kindon is down at 87."

Don't worry Dave; Steve Kindon wasn't too pleased either. You can't believe how much pleasure I got from stitching up my old mates. Looks like I stitched up a few Clarets fans too ha ha!

# 21

# The Recent Years, an MBE and the Boys From Burnley

My partner in crime at many dinner events is Steve Kindon. I've known him since the early seventies. He is just about the most irrepressible guy I know. Years ago he played for an England representative XI that was sent out to Egypt to spread the soccer gospel. The temperature was in the 100s all the while they were there. The locals hadn't seen rain for 50 years. In these terrible conditions the England X1 lost something like 0 – 4. Highly embarrassed, from the game back to the hotel they travelled in a sort of ancient truck with a canvas roof sitting on long hard benches. They bumped and rattled along the stony road and the sweat poured off them. In short, they were down and out. Steve thought this is no good, let's cheer them up a bit, as they sat with their heads in their hands and were nearly passing out in the sweltering heat.

"Hey ladsh, 'aven't we been lucky with the weather," he piped up.

He has won the award for Best-After-Dinner Speaker more than once. His unique style makes use of something that other people might try to hide or mask. He has a speech impediment. How can someone with a speech impediment be a famed after dinner speaker you might ask. The answer is simple; he milks it all he can.

In his opening moments he thanks his parents: "Ladiesh and gentlemen you may notishe one thing – I have a shlight shpeech impediment. Now, my parents when I was born could have called me many thingsh. They could have called me David, or Richard or Mike. But what did they call me? (He pauses for effect and glares at the audience. "They called me Shteven. Of all the names they could have chosen. They called me f*****g Shteven." And thus the mood is set for 40 minutes of mockery, self-parody and raucous anecdotes. I have never known any audience not roll about in shtiches, sorry stitches.

During the 80s and just after we'd both retired from the game, Colin Waldron and I were keen tennis players and we would often travel over to Huddersfield on Wednesday evenings to play in an indoor court against Steve and whoever else he could find to be his partner.

In those days he was working over there and on the odd occasion, like me, would go out onto the after dinner circuit at various venues up and down the country. Once he finished working in Huddersfield he decided to go on the circuit full time and eventually established himself as one of the great speakers. At its peak there was a market for him to appear five nights a week, 10 months of the year. The other two he would recharge his batteries and disappear on holiday.

Apart from the tennis, we'd bump into each other on the odd occasion but in the main we went our separate ways both very busy with work and speaking. Things changed sometime around 2006 when Steve rang and asked if I fancied doing a 'double' act with him. A Manchester agent was looking for something different. Steve is very good at volunteering people and he knew that I played the ukulele and said that I should be happy to include this in a performance doing George Formby impersonations at the end of our speeches. It was my dad who had taught me a few strums as a kid and on the coach at Burnley after a game, or on a tour somewhere we'd always had some really good sing-alongs. But, a sing-along in a bar in Benidorm is far different from performing at a posh after dinner 'do'.

So, when I heard what Steve had in mind I declined the ukulele bit although the speaking double act sounded good. "Hmmm, too late," said Steve. "They've sold all the tickets and we're down as the Boys from Burnley and you're on the ukulele doing George Formby."

Steve had me by the short and curlies and I had to agree on condition that I could use a George Formby backing track to make me sound better. We then decided to include a fair selection of 70s and 80s music as a quiz because that was the period when we had our fame in football. Quizzes had played a big part in our football lives when we were travelling. There was no shortage of questions.

"Ok then, where is this appearance?" I asked. I assumed it would be some small low-key affair not far away.

"Er just up the road, a few junctions up the motorway," replied Steve.

I believed him.

It was the first time we would make this double act and we started to prepare. We bought some PA equipment and speakers so we could have a decent sound system and have our own control over the show. The day came and we set off for what I was led to believe would be a small luncheon group somewhere not far up the M6. Steve picked me up early ready for a leisurely drive and to give us plenty of time to set up the equipment. I wanted to practise a few songs as well.

"So where are we going?" I asked.

"Hilton Hotel," was the reply. "There'll be about 750 there plus Dave Mackay, John McGovern and Bernard Manning." Steve fell silent and waited for me to pass out. For five minutes I couldn't speak. I wanted to. I wanted to say, "Turn this bloody car straight round and take me home." At last a few strangled, stuttering words came out.

"Bloody hell Steve! I thought it was a small gig."

"Well it is small. The Glasgow Hilton can hold even bigger events," he replied.

"Glasgow ... f*****g Glasgow!" I moaned. "All Scots ... they hate the English. They pinch our sheep. We beat Celtic in the Anglo-Scottish. They'll never have heard of George Formby. And I want to go home."

Steve grinned. "Don't worry Mr Formby – Turned out nice again, hasn't it."

I needn't have worried. It went down a bomb. The music quiz, the speeches, 'The Boys from Burnley', 'When I'm cleanin' windows'. The standing ovation at the end was truly special. As we drove home the next day Steve rang the agent to ask did he want to book any more 'Boys from Burnley' shows. He called back several days later. Because the Hilton had gone so well he wanted to book a whole series of shows. Steve rang: "Fifteen lunches, this December, we start in Aberdeen and finish at the Grosvenor Hotel in London a week before Christmas Day. So get the bloody uke' tuned up."

This was the big-time. So, we hired a small people carrier, threw in all our gear and suitcases and on 1st December set off on tour of Aberdeen, Edinburgh, Glasgow, Middlesbrough, Sunderland, Leeds, Manchester, Birmingham, Belfast (flew in and out the same day), Milton Keynes, Bristol, Bournemouth, Southampton, Torquay and London. We did all this in the three weeks before Christmas coming home every Friday evening for the weekend. Not only did we have a great time working with the likes of Dave Mackay, Martin Bayfield, Matt le Tissier, Lawrie McMenemy, Jim Watt, Gareth Chilcott, Pat Jennings and many other famous sportsmen, but we made so many good friends and established 'The Boys from Burnley' as a top act. It continues to this day. More than anything, we really enjoy it and enjoy each other's company.

On our journeys of course we re-lived the old times. Steve was never too impressed by the way Jimmy Adamson sold him, and still isn't. Steve was originally from Warrington with a strong rugby background, both League and Union. He had uncles who were internationals and never, himself, kicked a football until he was 15. I used to tell him I could always tell that when I played alongside him. The England World Cup win in 1966 inspired his interest in the game and remarkably, two years later he was playing for Burnley against West Ham. His development and rise to the Burnley first-team was meteoric. His impact in the 1968 Youth Cup Final for Burnley, when they won, was huge.

As a teenager in the team he was as strong as a bull and if anyone tried to take the mickey out of him in training he would actually lift them up over his head and spin them round until they were dizzy. On one occasion Brian Flynn, who was an apprentice at that time, was responsible for putting out Steve's kit. It had to be immaculate but alas the boots hadn't been cleaned properly. Punishment was par for the course back then. Steve took hold of Brian and dangled him over the bridge at the Gawthorpe training ground, holding him by one of his ankles 15 feet above the river. Brian was certain Steve would let go. After that, the boots were always immaculate.

Steve's speed was legendary. For a big man he was a fantastic sprinter. His stamina was awesome so that when we did a series of 100 yard sprints he'd be going just as strong at the end and would breeze past us with a big grin and quite often casually whistling. Today his speed might have gone and he's gone from the 'fastest' ever Burnley player to the 'fattest' ever Burnley player but you ask him any question about kings and queens of England, presidents of the USA or emperors of Rome and you'll struggle to catch him out. It passes many a mile away on our trips up and down the motorways.

His problem, our problem in fact, was with Leighton James. Boy could that guy play. On his day he was as good as the legendary George Best. That was our problem with him; with more application he could have been better than George Best. There we were the grafters and workers, making every best use of our limited talent and there was Leighton quite often a genius with the ball without even trying. His gifts were God-given, his talents instinctive, and his skill sublime. We felt he should have been at Manchester United or any of the really top teams. Steve was about speed, effort and enthusiasm. He was quite literally the 'bull-in-a-china-shop'. Leighton was all about finesse. For a spell they vied for the same position. Jimmy Adamson preferred Leighton. But in our opinion Leighton had another level he could have got to. It frustrated us to see it unfulfilled as he moved from club to club.

Taffy's other problem was that he could be very opinionated. Sometimes it didn't go down too well. Jimmy Adamson used to tell us to make all the friends we could on the way up; "Because you'll need them on the way down." Alas Leighton was sometimes quick to voice an outspoken opinion. Maybe it cost him a lot of friends. It possibly lost him the Burnley manager's job at one time and I suspect it cost him the Welsh manager's job after winning nearly 100 Welsh caps.

I've met at least three queens in my time. First there was the one that Stevo hired when we closed Wembley. Then there was the one at the Ricoh when they did a concert. And then there was the real one at Buckingham Palace for the MBE.

One morning in November 2006 when I was opening the mail I saw a letter from 'the Prime Minister's Office'. "Huh, another bloomin' mailshot and waste of paper," I thought. "It can go on the rubbish pile, no point in even opening it." But for some reason (probably serendipity) I did open it after I'd first of all started to tear the envelope in half as you do with junk mail. The letter, with the original tear, is now at home in my office, framed. It was from *'the Prime Minister's Obedient Servant'*, Mr William Chapman. It began:

### IN CONFIDENCE

*Dear Sir,*

*The Prime Minister has asked me to inform you, in strictest confidence, that, having taken the advice of the Cabinet Secretary and the expert Honours Committee, he has it in mind, on the occasion of the forthcoming list of New Year's Honours, to submit your name to the Queen with the recommendation that Her Majesty may be graciously pleased to approve that you be appointed as a Member of the Order of the British Empire (MBE).*

*Before doing so, the Prime Minister would be glad to know that this would be agreeable to you.*

*If you do agree, your name will go forward and if the Queen accepts the Prime Minister's advice, the announcement will be made in the New Year's Honours List.*

*I am Sir,*

*Your obedient Servant,*

### WILLIAM CHAPMAN

What a wonderfully composed letter and you may rightly assume that the words gob and smacked sprang to kind. It also crossed my mind that it could be a spoof letter from my old mate Mr Waldron. But then he couldn't spell obedient.

I learned later that two years earlier in 2004, some of my old work colleagues, George Binns at Huddersfield, Ken Heathcoate from Bolton Health Club and Ken Sharp from Coventry, all ably assisted by my daughter Claire, had proposed me for a Queen's Award. As I began to read, I nearly fell off the chair. "Come on," I thought, "I'm just a lad from a council estate in Bolton."

I was just a bread and butter footballer who jumped as high as he could, fell over a lot and never even made a full England appearance. I'd had failed businesses, made numerous mistakes building stadiums and nobody knew me outside Rawtenstall. Surely this was a mistake.

But then I began to think. Maybe this award was indeed significant and a reward; not for being special, gifted or talented, handsome (don't laugh), rich (you must be joking), or a leader or a celebrity. Maybe it was the very fact that I was just an average guy from Johnson Fold Estate who had made good; had done something with his life and shown that from very ordinary beginnings a person can strive to become better and achieve something. All through my life I'd been a listener, whether it was to Nat Lofthouse, Jimmy Adamson, Ken Heathcoate, Dale Carnegie, George Binns or Tony Stephens – and more than anyone else, my wife Sian. They were the ones, amongst many others, who had guided and cajoled me to make progress with my life and career. And then I began to think something else; that in some kind of way this award was aimed at any 17-year-old in Bolton, Burnley or Rawtenstall who had the will to succeed and get out of the rut. This was an award that I could use to inspire other young lads; that it isn't always the super-talented that win and pick up the trophies, sometimes it's the triers and the persistent; and sometimes the ones who get out of their comfort zone.

The problem came at the bottom of the letter. It said: 'This must be kept in strictest confidence until an official announcement is made'. And so I had to sit and wait for the New Year's Honours list to be published before I could tell a soul – except Sian who I knew would be able to keep the secret. She deserved a medal herself for putting up with me over the years.

Five minutes after midnight, on the 31st of December I sat down in the computer room at the Mango Bay Hotel in Barbados. This is a holiday we take as a family every year at this time, come what may. Sian was fast asleep in bed with our four grandchildren all around her. My daughter Claire, husband Andrew, my son Daniel and his wife Wendy were out on the town, probably in the piano bar on First Street, Holetown. I could hear the music. The black pioneers who had landed here no doubt fleeing from slavery had built their homes in the area – hence the name First Street. And here was I, with the sound of the music from the piano bar seeping into the room, linked up into the ether and the internet, trying to see if I had really and truly been awarded a gong.

There it was. It was under the 'F's'; Mr Paul John Fletcher MBE, awarded for services to football.

It was hard to keep control of my emotions that evening as I sat alone in a computer room in Barbados. I couldn't help remembering things from the past. There was Granddad coming home from work with his face covered in coal dust after a long day stoking the fires at the mill. Most days his Bolton programme would have been curled up in his pocket. There was me as an eight-year-old coming home at dusk after managing to get a game with the teenagers who played at Moss Bank Park. There was my dad cleaning my boots for me when I played for Bolton Lads Club; my mum always with him watching whatever team I played for. I saw a 17-year-old Sian at the Beachcomber Night Club in Bolton, the woman who was at this magic moment curled up with our grandchildren round her; and John Ritson, the guy who persuaded me to go for a drink that night thus enabling the chance sighting of Sian – serendipity or not? Nat Lofthouse telling me to "hang in the air and head with my forehead," and Jimmy Adamson teaching me all the ways to control a ball so much better than I ever did. I felt the warmth of friendship from people like Colin Waldron, Steve Kindon and little Aussie Ken Sharp. Then there was George Binns the man at Huddersfield who taught me "how careful we are with money in Yorkshire." I remembered collecting the award for 'Building of the Year' with George in 1995.

Then I wondered what was happening at that moment in the Trades Club, Haslingden. I'd arranged for the landlord to have a bottle of champagne ready and to invite my mum and dad down with the message in the letter I'd left for him to read to them. Both Mum and Dad, like their parents, had worked in the cotton mills of Bolton when they were first married to give me this chance.

Some weeks later I received another letter but this time it was the official invitation to Buckingham Palace. It was strictly three guests only. All ten of us went down even though only Sian, Claire and Daniel could see the actual ceremony. We all travelled down the day before and had a wonderful few days in London. The protocol at the ceremony was terribly rigid so that something like 35 of us were given instructions on how to walk, turn, bow, receive our medal, walk backwards three paces, then turn and walk away. We were told not to begin any conversation with HRH the Queen, but were permitted to speak if we were asked something. If we did speak we had to address her as "Ma'am."

So, myself, Sian, Claire and Daniel sat there waiting for my turn. I was with the other nominees and could see them through a gap in the curtains as they went in one by one. The announcement was made: "Her Royal Highness Queen Elizabeth the Second." What a moment when the medal was pinned on. There were real butterflies in my stomach. Suppose I tripped up, fell over, said something stupid, stammered or made a fool of myself with everyone watching. It was worse than speaking to 1000-plus people at the Grosvenor Hotel.

I looked at the other people receiving honours. Mine paled into insignificance when I saw people from the Armed Forces, some with terrible injuries. Theirs was real bravery. Their lives had been at risk. All I'd ever done was head a football. But, how proud I felt. The medal now sits in the trophy cabinet at Turf Moor. Without Burnley Football Club, there wouldn't have been a medal. For days I kept saying "Paul Fletcher MBE," not out of vanity, but in astonishment. My mum and dad were utterly beside themselves with joy. It's on the front of this book, not out of conceit but out of pride.

It's funny how the name Nat Lofthouse kept coming into my head at this time, but he really was one of the inspirations in my life, at a critical time too when because of a health scare I was on the sidelines for several months. He picked me to make my debut as a 17-year-old. Nat made his at the age of just 15 years and 207 days in 1941. Believe it or not in his early days he was not a fans' favourite but by 1950 he had his first international cap. He scored twice in a remarkable debut. It was the beginning of a glittering international career and in 1952 he became known as 'The Lion of Vienna' with two more goals in a 3 – 2 win against Austria. In the 1954 World Cup he scored three goals in three games. In '55/56 he was the top scorer in the top division with 33 goals. At the end of 57/58 he won an FA Cup winners' medal and scored twice. It was the game where he clattered into the back of goalkeeper Harry Gregg and scored a controversial goal as he bundled him and ball over the line. Today it would probably earn a red card for violent conduct. Later in '58 he won his final England cap and scored his last international goal in a 5 – 0 win over Russia. Injuries dogged him in the later stages of his career so that in December 1960 he called it a day as a player. The club appointed him assistant trainer and in 1967 he became chief coach. He enjoyed a spell as manager (although according to Jimmy McIlroy enjoy would probably be the wrong word) for a couple of years. That was when the long-serving Bill Ridding had stepped down. Jimmy McIlroy became Nat's assistant. Two seasons was enough for Nat who was never comfortable in the role. He became a sort of general manager and eventually Club President. A fund has been set up to commemorate his status with a statue. I can still picture him at the club when I was a young player. Few centre-forwards can say that they were coached by the great Nat Lofthouse. I'm one of them. I owe him such a lot. Maybe a bit of the MBE belongs to him.

In 1997 when I re-joined Bolton Wanderers as chief executive at their developing stadium at Horwich, Nat was still there and a legendary figure around the town. I always felt in that respect he was almost a sad figure around the place and he had never really recovered from the loss of his wife Alma in 1985. He was still Club President but it was a position that carried few real responsibilities or roles. He was simply a figurehead. By the time he died in 2011 he had spent over 60 years at the club in a range of jobs that included player, assistant trainer, chief coach, caretaker manager, manager, chief scout, administrative manager, executive manager and finally Club President.

In the 1980s he had a short spell working in sales for a local businessman who idolised him and said: "I don't want him to work. I just want to pay him a good wage for all the pleasure he gave me." But it wasn't long before he was lured back to his beloved Bolton Wanderers. You can't imagine something like this happening again in today's football world, where people like Nat at Bolton, Tom Finney at Preston, Jimmy McIlroy at Burnley, and Bobby Charlton at Manchester United served just one club as a player. Gary Neville, Paul Scholes, Steven Gerrard and Ryan Giggs are probably amongst the last of this dying breed. But Nat's record is unique – 60 years in total at just the one club. Giggs' record is astonishing though, 900-plus Premiership games for just one club. It will never be repeated.

I had a fair amount of direct contact with Nat when I returned to Bolton. He would sit in his office all day waiting for someone to 'roll him out' to meet anyone visiting the club. He kept a close eye on his pennies and one day asked me to help him, telling me he had a train to catch down to London and he needed to book a taxi. Would I help with the taxi? To make a bit of conversation I asked him what he was doing in London to which he replied he was doing the FA Cup draw.

"Hmmm," I thought and asked him, "How much are they paying you?"

"Nothing," he replied. "They just send me a train ticket and pay my taxi fare."

I was astonished that he received nothing for performing this iconic function in front of millions on TV. I'd done a few appearances by this time in various places and always negotiated a fee for time off work, travel, accommodation and so on. But I'd never done anything on the scale of a live FA Cup draw. This was something for which he certainly merited payment. I asked him for the name of his contact and suggested I get in touch and try to get him a small fee. At this he was surprised and embarrassed thinking that no-one gets paid for doing this kind of work and that it was all part of his role as Bolton Club President and figurehead.

So: we sat in his office, had tea and biscuits and I eventually managed to get in touch with the producer of the show that was live on TV. The conversation went something like:

"Hello Mr Johnson, I'm Nat Lofthouse's commercial agent and I've just taken over his affairs. I understand he's booked to appear live on TV this coming Thursday with Geoff Hurst and Alan Ball. Please can I ask what the fee is?"

"Er well," he replied, "I'm sorry but that's confidential information."

"Well," I went on, "I understand you are paying him no fee at all. I also understand there is no contract for this appearance just an invitation. He has just been asked to appear at a Sportsman's Dinner in Manchester where they will be paying him quite a large fee. I'm sorry but he won't be able to appear at the FA Cup draw unless we can make some kind of arrangement."

I could sense a bit of discomfort at the other end of the phone and after a brief silence the reply was: "But we have never paid Mr Lofthouse any kind of fee."

By now I had the bit between my teeth. "Well I'm sorry but this man is a legend. There aren't many footballers of his standing out there. It's a little unfair that you don't pay him anything but I imagine you do pay the other people for appearing. I'm so sorry but Mr Lofthouse won't be able to attend unless you do pay him a fee."

"But it's been publicised that he will be appearing at the draw. Everything is arranged." By now the producer was becoming more than a little flustered.

"Sorry but unless he receives a fee he won't be coming, get back to me if you wish." I said again firmly and put the phone down.

The producer began to backtrack and agreed to speak to his director and get back to us as soon as he could. He and I knew that time was running out. Over the next few hours we had three more conversations. At each one a fee was suggested and each one had got a little higher but I kept rejecting it. Not until the fourth call did I agree.

I got Nat his taxi organised, which I paid for, and early Thursday morning waved him off having simply said I had managed to get him a fee as well his travel expenses. I knew when he saw the cheque he would nearly pass out. I wasn't disappointed. When it arrived some days later I put it on his desk. When I went to his office later that day to ask how he had got on, he was wide-eyed. "Bloody hell Paul, £525 for a day in London, I can't believe it."

I told him to look more carefully at the cheque. "No Nat it's for £5,250 and you deserve every penny of it." He was utterly amazed. It led to a conversation about how much he (and me) had earned as players. Never had he earned anything like this. Even at his peak it was five times more than he had ever earned in a full season. In fact in the days of the maximum wage of £20 a week he hadn't earned £1,000 a year because in the summer they earned less. They had £4 knocked off when they weren't playing.

Tommy Docherty tells a story about it. At Preston he went to see the manager to ask, "Why is Tom Finney getting £4 more than me?" "Because he's a better player than you," was the reply. "He's not in the summer!" answered Docherty. Probably every old player in the game tells the story and subs his own name.

Nat had helped me so much as a young player that I was delighted to be able to help him now that he needed a bit of a shoulder. Eight months later he helped me. I'd promised to take one of Bolton's first-team players with me to open a new ward in Bolton General Hospital's stroke unit. I asked Nat if he would come with me as well. Everyone at the hospital was delighted when he arrived. Many of the stroke victims were elderly of course and could remember Nat from many years ago when they had seen him play. After the speeches, unveiling of the plaque, a champagne toast and prawn sandwiches, we were just about to leave when a nurse hurried towards one of the specialists, whispered something in his ear, and then came over to us.

"Paul," she began, "one of our patients had a bad stroke four years ago and hasn't said a word since. Before Nat goes would he come and meet him. He's over there with his wife and daughter – *and he wants to say something to Nat.*" The patient was in his pyjamas and dressing gown and was clutching his wife's hand. In his working days he'd been a plumber. He took deep breaths and his wife looked very apprehensive. Her husband wanted to try and say something. Nat walked over and shook his hand. There were maybe 100 people in the room and all of them fell silent as the retired plumber, who had never spoken a word for the last four years began a conversation with the Lion of Vienna.

His mouth opened but no words came out. He tried again. The strain on his face and in his eyes was immense. He tried again and then managed to speak:

"I ... I ... I ... m mend ... mend ... m mended ... y y ... y y your ... w washing ... m m machine."

The effort clearly exhausted him. The room erupted into applause. His wife had tears running down her cheeks. Nat was open-mouthed at this superhuman effort. But then the old plumber started again. Slowly, painfully, stuttering and stammering, struggling and striving, his eyes now closed with the effort and strain he added:

"And ... y y y you ... n n n nev ... never ... f f f ... f fucking ... p p paid m me!"

The room exploded with laughter. Nat embraced the old chap. His wife and the whole room were beaming with smiles and tears. The plumber was exhausted with effort and his wife propped him up. The power of football, the power of meeting an old hero, was never better illustrated. Many tears were shed that afternoon and some of them were mine.

Nat was made a Freeman of Bolton and was awarded the OBE. He was 85 when he died in 2011. His final few years were marked by Alzheimer's. It was so terribly sad.

When Barry Kilby announced that he would retire as chairman at the end of season 2011/12 for health reasons, probably every supporter was stunned. The *Lancashire Telegraph* published my thoughts:

*"He is a rare breed of chairman. I've come across many in my time who are egotistical and put themselves before the club, but Barry is the opposite. He is never looking for the limelight. He treasured his position as chairman, which is an unpaid job. My only hope is whoever takes over is a Burnley fan – someone who walked through the turnstiles as a child – because those people make judgements with their heart more than their brain. All the board members are fans of the club, so if it's one of them the club will be well served. He is handing over a great club, in a great position on and off the field. We're sitting nicely in the Championship with a great manager, a great set of supporters and an excellent squad – all that can only point back at the chairman. He vies for the position of the best chairman that Burnley's ever had. It's a close contest between him and Bob Lord. Although we were champions under Bob Lord, Barry's tenure can be measured against that for keeping Burnley in the position he has."*

Over the years the previous three Burnley chairmen, Bob Lord, John Jackson and Frank Teasdale all did valiant work for the club, but each one of them eventually became the target of grumbles and criticism for varying reasons. But chairmen are brave men. They stick their heads above the parapet. They do a thankless job. When things go wrong they are the second target, after the manager, for the inevitable abuse and catcalls. Sometimes they are the first. Lord, Jackson and Teasdale, in different ways, did massive jobs at the club but left with derision ringing in their ears and were the targets for some vicious personal attacks. For them it became a thankless job. But somehow, Barry Kilby, despite something like 14 years in the job faced his retirement with a giant thank you banner at the back of a stand and no end of tributes. It's a remarkable achievement.

# 22

# The Seven Go£den Secrets of a Successful Stadium

On my first day at Turf Moor as development consultant I was bursting with ideas and energy. I couldn't wait to start. The chance to help in the construction of a spanking, state of the art, new stand was mouth-watering. This was my old club and I owed it so much. I wanted to repay it. I arrived with a string of awards under my belt: The McAlpine Stadium of the Year 1995, the Reebok Building of the Year 1998 and the Ricoh Arena Venue of the Year 2004. In addition I had been awarded the MBE for services to football. I was confident in myself and my ability and determined to abide by the teamwork principles that had served me well so far. I was raring to go especially as on the day of my arrival there was no hint of the world's financial troubles to come.

Wherever I had been so far I had always felt that I'd been warmly welcomed. Alas, it seemed to me straightaway that this was not the case at Burnley of all places. Maybe my appointment was seen as too much of a fait accompli. Brendan had only discussed my appointment with Chairman Barry Kilby (as they were the two largest shareholders). That made me a 'Flood' man and Brendan had already ruffled a few feathers. There's no question that from some quarters I felt not so much the warm hand of friendship but more of a cold shoulder and even a touch of suspicion as if to say, "what's he doing here?" There might well have been politeness and smiles but it was not universal. There were occasions when I felt like an intruder. Nevertheless there was a job to do and I was desperate to do it.

It struck me straightaway that there was one man I had to get onside and this was Clive Holt. Clive was the director with stadium responsibility. He had been there during the construction of the two newest stands – the James Hargreaves and the Jimmy McIlroy. He had been there for years and had been a director on that traumatic day in May '87 when Burnley had to win to stay in the Football League. He was an established figure with a great deal of influence. I cannot recall that he has ever spoken to me about stands and stadiums over my 'four more years period'.

I'd already had the experience of greeting Clive some years earlier at my home to discuss joining Burnley. I hadn't forgotten how it seemed to me at the time that he gave the impression of being relieved to have found me too expensive to employ.

It's reasonable to assume that cost and sheer economics determined the basic design of these two newer stands at Turf Moor but unfortunately they are examples of how not to design a stand. The biggest, the James Hargreaves Stand, contains as its corporate area what is basically a huge open long corridor from one end of the stand to the other. It can seat up to 400 people at a function such as a dinner, but in truth the design makes it a frustrating experience for anything more than 150 because most of the people are so far away from the main action area. Plus, their views are obstructed by pillars. The design could have been far better. Bars and entrances should have been located at the ends of the room so that the full depth in the centre was available for tables and an audience. At either end there should have been four or five self-contained permanent executive boxes, mini rooms in fact. What happens today is that the executive 'boxes' are temporarily created with low screens. Because of the rectangular overall shape of the stand no banqueting suite would have been perfect but if the central area had been better utilised more people would have a better view of whatever event is taking place.

Numerous speakers and comedians I know on the circuit describe the James Hargreaves corporate area as a terrible room to work in. "50% can't see the top table and there are pillars everywhere."

This banqueting area could have been the best and biggest in the area and given real competition to the Dunkenhalgh Hotel that gets much of the events trade. Over the lifetime of this stand there has been, and will continue to be, a massive loss of revenue from conference, banqueting and courses. It could well add up into millions eventually. It represents the purchase of players.

In 'executive box match day mode' the concept is far from first-rate. Wooden screens do not give privacy. They do not provide small room spaces on weekdays that are ideal for small meetings. Again there is a loss or revenue on weekdays. Sadly, the James Hargreaves Stand at Turf Moor does not provide multi-purpose facilities and multi-purpose is the key buzz-word these days. It's more of a multi non-purpose. Don't get me wrong; on match days the room is alive. But on non-match days it generally lies empty and unused. The key to successful stadium design revolves today around utilisation at least five days a week. But I suppose hindsight is a wonderful thing.

The Jimmy McIlroy Stand is the smaller stand behind the goal.

There was a void inside, the complete length of the stand, which lay empty and unused for 11 years. After that time the Community Sports Trust took over the building with Burnley declaring losses of around half a million during their tenure. It was suggested to me by a highly respected official at the FA that during the Premiership season a similar amount was lost in "missed grant opportunities".

Dave Edmundson eventually did a fantastic job and sourced around £1 million of grant funding for a complete refit of the space. I liked Dave Edmundson, he was a good operator and as straight as the day is long.

Modesty stops me from saying that I doubt that anyone knows more about stadium design than me after all the years I've spent in the business; but let's just say I know enough to have put a 330 page book together, *The Seven Go£den Secrets of a Successfu£ Stadium*. It's a sort of autobiography of stadium development is how Tommy Docherty described it.

It could be called 'Stadiums for Dummies,' wrote Professor Chris Brady (cheeky sod).

I liked what Tom Watt wrote (ex East Enders and now football writer):

*I met Paul at the old Wembley Stadium in 1999. As I was catapulted backwards over a table when trying to sign an autograph with the 'exploding pen' he handed me, our friendship was sealed for life. I love a good joke and a good book, and this is one. I remain fascinated by football, its players and its stadiums and have written myself about the subjects. But I've never come across the word 'verisimilitude' before. This is one of the many lessons the book has taught me.*

"His knowledge of stadia is legendary," wrote Pete Winkleman.

The essence and message of the book is simple: stadiums must be in operation at least five days a week if not seven, to pay for themselves and then become profitable. What is the point of spending millions on stands that lie empty six days a week and are only used on match days? Secondly if a project is driven and dominated by architects, you run the risk of having a stadium that is an architectural masterpiece, a wonder of the age, but a match-day functioning disaster.

As the book title suggests there are seven areas, or needs, in stadium building.

S E N S E Sound common sense.

S M A R T Good designs, teamwork and motivation.

S O U R C E Potential revenue streams.

S U S T A I N Knowledge of successful existing stadiums.

S P O N S O R Sponsorship and commerciality.

S T A D I A R E N A The StadiArena concept and its potential.

S E E I N G Future needs and trends.

The purpose of the book is simple: to show how to plan, build and operate a sustainable stadium venue.

Football doesn't want trendy, arty designs. It wants atmosphere, passion and close-up spectators who feel they are involved in the action. It doesn't want white elephant buildings that now litter the world in places like Athens, unused and litter-filled, weeds and debris accumulating by the day. I have been involved in building four stadiums and advised on 30 others. It breaks my heart to see the ones that are empty now, victims of over- ambition and failed Olympic legacies. Ken Sharp was co-author of the book and a huge help. Here's one thing he wrote:

*Paul has a clear vision, leads from the front and has a wicked sense of humour which also makes the job so much more interesting. We worked together on the Ricoh Arena Coventry for a five-year spell in mid-2000 and ended up sharing a flat in the centre of the cathedral city, as Paul's wife and family were 120 miles north in Lancashire. But he made sure he was home every weekend. If there is one person who knows and understands every aspect of a new football stadium it is Paul Fletcher. He has fought and won most battles with builders, architects, planners and town councillors to ensure a fine building is delivered for what he describes as his 'most important clients', the football spectators.*

How right that is. It is the spectators and their needs that should be the driving force behind any design. Paramount are the basics such as access, shelter from weather, sight lines, facilities, comfort, ease of exit, and catering. All of that comes ahead of any need for the building to be an architectural landmark, or a city status symbol. Should it really be necessary to mention shelter from the weather? Sadly it is. How many people buy their seat under cover of the stadium roof, and still get a soaking in bad weather? Sadly, one of the wettest is at Burnley; the Jimmy McIlroy Stand behind one of the goals.

I can't possibly give you a detailed analysis of what makes a good stadium in just this one chapter or cover even a fraction of what is in the book. My introduction to the stadium book sets the scene and sums things up:

*The best stadiums in the world are not the ones that look good. They are the ones that feel good. Football stadiums are venues for supporters of a club to watch their team. If their team has performed well over the years, the stadium, irrespective of its condition, becomes a shrine, which will seduce the supporter back for the next confrontation. Memories of past victories will echo round the place, it feels good. It feels like home. It's where the heart is. But does it really need to be where 'art' is?*

*Architects, builders or project managers when they write books about football stadiums explain to the reader what the stadium building should look like, which direction the pitch should point, what materials it should be made of and how 'its form fits its function', which in turn 'ensures its symmetry is both sympathetic and warm with its environment'......*

*Seven Go£den Secrets is different. It is written by a 'client'. This is someone who commissions these specialists to design and construct his stadium building. Once the building is officially opened, the band of architects, builders, structural engineers and project managers hand over the keys. The client, and the others who follow him, then have the job of operating this building for the next 50 to 100 years in a desperate attempt to perform against a business plan, to make a profit, or find alternative revenue streams to service the debt created by the new stadium.*

*I am a client. With others, I have designed and built four of these buildings. One won the RIBA Building of the Year in 1995; another won the BCI Building of the Year in 1997; another won the 'Venue of the Year 2004'; another is now owned by a local authority and charitable trust with the football club merely a tenant struggling to make ends meet.*

*This book pulls no punches. I am a lover of fine design but also a critic of stupid concepts. Someone once described me as 'The Prince Charles of football stadium architecture'. My book tells you both the pitfalls and the joys of designing, building and operating a new stadium. The journey can best be described as a 'Grand National Race'. You have choices; find a way round, find a way over, or fall at the fence – and then the race is over. Somehow I've managed to stay in the saddle for four races. Seven Go£den Secrets is the story of how I did it and the people I got to help me.*

I was once asked what the top ten aspects of my favourite stadium were, and what was the stadium? My response was:

Commercially successful building that does not require subsidy from the football club or local authority and allows the football club to fulfil its ambitions.

Commercially successful building that allows the football club to attract external investment.

Iconic building where every square foot of usable space has been carefully designed to 'sweat' commercially.

Provides great views, easy movement and safety and because its commercial success provides fair pricing for supporters.

Close connection between the spectators, seating and the pitch, which creates an electric atmosphere.

A multi-purpose building that can be used extensively by the community on non-match days.

Comfortable and well finished but not expensively done.

Iconic, but looks more like a modern football stadium than the Starship Enterprise.

Efficiently operated, clean and welcoming.

Old Trafford, Manchester.

There are good architects around who know of the relationship between appearance and revenue. I know who they are. But there are a whole stack of architects out there whose concern is for appearance only. Their list of needs would be different than mine. As a solution, I recommend to all architectural practices, that they employ as part of their team, a commercial stadium consultant, if they are involved in a stadium building project. It would be the job of that particular consultant to advise both 'client' and 'architect' on the opportunities and the risks that a new stadium can create and advise on its sustainability.

Someone once wrote that if you can't write your business plan on one A4 sheet of paper, then the plan will never work with 1000 sheets. Essentially there are three starting points that are basic: How much will the stadium cost? Where will the funding come from to pay for it? And what profit or loss will it make once it opens? There is another basic question that underpins them. What comes first, beauty, function or revenue? The answer is revenue for without it there can be none of the other. A stadium that makes money allows the club to move forward. A building that loses money takes the club backwards. These are commercial buildings that need to make money. It is a recurring theme. If a stadium has a lifespan of 50 years, then if it is only used on match days in effect it is empty for 49 of those years. This is absolute folly. This is why now, today, any new stadium, any new stand must be viewed as a money-maker. Then it becomes self-sustaining. In short, I'd rather have a plain, multi-purpose stadium built in the right location that is in use seven days a week and is therefore profitable, than an award-winning, spaceship stadium that looks fantastic, but drains away the cash and is only in use maybe not even half the week.

Building a stadium is a long, long process. It needs teamwork and motivation. Both these things are close to my heart. In the motivation courses and workshops I do around the country I make use of one of the finest speeches I have ever heard. It's the speech in *Any Given Sunday* that Al Pacino makes in the locker room at half-time when his football team are losing. It has become quite iconic. It could be used to cover any occupation or project that is dependent on teamwork and striving to do that bit extra – to go the extra inch. There isn't the space to reproduce it but it's worth googling.

How do you respond when someone asks, "how are you?" How do you answer? Do you say, "Not bad ... fair to middling ... fairly average ... surviving ... I've been better." You might think those are perfectly acceptable responses. True they are better than Mr Doom and Gloom who might say, "Oh not good, I feel really fed up at the moment ..." Boy what a start to the day that is for both of you.

Try this. Say, "I'm magnificent, how are you?" And say it with a big smile. Exude confidence. Sound as if you are in control of your life and successful. Sound positive. It might just become contagious. I used to try it on the original Mr Gloomy. Very often, and footballers will confirm this, the most long-faced person at a club is 'The Groundsman'. They are miserable because they love their pitches and their grass but not anyone who walks on it. I have this theory that most groundsmen hate footballers. They come along every Saturday afternoon and kick lumps out of the pitch and make skid marks and scuff up great divots. Why else would they have signs that say KEEP OFF THE GRASS? And so it was at Huddersfield in the early 1990s that the groundsman was Ray Chappell and boy was he an example of this. I'd breeze past him, and chirpily enquire, "Morning Ray, how are you?"

Most times he wouldn't even look up but he'd just grunt and reply, "How's they?" (This is Yorkshire for, "How are you?")

To this I would reply, "Magnificent."

It took four months for the penny to drop with Ray. Once again I asked him how he was and his answer knocked me for six. "I'm cooking on gas, how's they?"

*****

I used to think it was impossible to fund a new stadium from scratch that could self-fund and pay for itself but then re-appraised that view. I can use the example of Tim Parsons a big fan of Aston Villa. Before he sold his business for many £ millions, he was the founder and managing director of MCP, Midlands Concert Promotions, which in the 80s and 90s was the most successful rock concert promotion business in Europe. In my early days at the McAlpine Stadium, Tim agreed to bring one of the world's most famous rock bands, REM, to

Huddersfield. Tim and I had a few 'run ins' during the build-up to the event and we seemed to argue about everything. At the end of it all we became very great friends, only after he told me, "Don't take it personally, I was always trying you out, you were a naïve client." Hmmm, I'd heard that before.

A few years later I invited him to a Burnley versus Aston Villa game and as we dined before the match I asked him how he was enjoying his retirement. He replied:

"Strangely Paul, I have more opportunities and I am earning much more money now that I've retired. It's because I have *thinking* time. When I was with MCP it was a hectic schedule and I led such a busy life, but I didn't have time to think through what I really wanted to achieve."

I tell that story because writing the stadium book has given *me* thinking-time. It's given me the opportunity to reflect on my time in building football stadiums. I've analysed and researched the numerous attempts at new stadiums around the world. I've also had chance to revisit my evaluation that it's impossible to build a football stadium that can pay for itself.

This thinking-time has led me to a fresh conclusion regarding the profitability of a new football stadium in the UK. I now believe that it IS possible to construct a new, 30,000, 40,000 or even a 50,000 seater stadium that will pay for itself within three years, without any subsidy from the football club's gate receipts, or a local authority. It's quite simple really and the answers were all out there, staring me in the face, waiting to be discovered and pieced together. It was a little like a Rubik's Cube, the correct colours just needed matching together.

There are seven key components all of which are mentioned somewhere in the *Seven Go£den Secrets* book. If these are put together it is completely possible to fully fund a new stadium from the revenues they generate. If and whenever Burnley want to build extensions that will be profitable and move the club forward. I'll be ready and willing to help.

# 23

# Serendipity

I love this area, the Rossendale Valley, the hills and moors around Burnley, the people, the honesty; Rawtenstall and Ramsbottom, two local names to get your tongue and teeth round. The old mills have gone so it's an area that's trying to re-invent itself. But old values and traditions haven't disappeared just yet even though new industry, regeneration and refurbishment are the bywords. Promotion to the Premiership inspired the Premier Plan for the town. The council saw that the name of Burnley would become globally known. The win over Manchester United was reported as far away as China. It's changed so much since I was a player in the 70s. It still has its social and economic problems but they might not be as bad as news programmes would have people believe. The news programmes still like to find a cobbled street and a chimney to film; oh and a bit of brass band music. But now, cobbles and chimneys belching smoke are not that easy to find in Burnley.

On the porch of the old, cosy shed that I use as an office, in the corner of my garden, I have this wonderful old rocking chair. It isn't one of those huge, farmhouse, 'grandfather' type things. It's smaller than that; and special because it once belonged to the great Harry Potts. It's the chair he'd sit in beside his coal fire at home and the one I love to sit in on a warm summer evening. It's where I can sit and think and muse, and remember all the good things – and have a few regrets as well. When I resigned as chief executive of course there was immense disappointment at what I had not achieved. But I hadn't quite left the building and slipped quietly over to the Football University end of the club.

I so badly wanted to make a difference at Turf Moor, to establish revenues from a new stand that would set them up for many years to come. I've looked into so many things – like the Italian club where at one end of the ground you can have your infant christened – and at the other you can hold your funeral. At Swansea they have a ladies' hairdresser salon next to the ticket office. So, thank goodness I've left the CEO job with the university up and running. But I do sit in Harry's old rocking chair and wonder if anyone at the club other than

Brendan and I can see the huge revenue potential of it. When it is fully subscribed it could be generating £3 to £4 million of annual profit. And to think, this university exists because the Stand project fell through. When Brendan first discussed the concept it immediately grabbed me.

But just sometimes I'll sit in this old chair and chuckle at some of the things I've done. The 100 Greatest Clarets spoof still makes me smile. I chuckled too when Dave T told me that on eBay a Paul Fletcher 1970s footie card only fetches 99p. He said what a great book title that would be for this book: *'Only 99p on eBay'*.

And then there was what I did to old Jim Thompson. Prince Charles came to the club in February 2010 and as part of his tour the plan was he would walk across Turf Moor and up into the James Hargreaves Stand on the far side of the ground. Then as he was leaving he would meet and say goodbye to selected people who were to line up at the top of the stairs. Problem: who would be first in the line, the plum spot, and who would be at the end? It was a classic bun-fight, jockeying for position moment, but was eventually sorted.

Except: I had plans for old Jim, a lovely, lovely man, he had worked at the club for over 60 years in all kinds of roles. His wife Violet used to be one of the laundry ladies and footballers wherever they are and whoever they are always have a soft spot for the laundry ladies. Jim, in fact, won a Football League special long-service award at a glittering ceremony, not too long ago. He was there in the finance department when I was a player. Boy did we have fun back then with secretary Albert Maddox and fund-raiser Jack Butterfield kidding them we knew where all the money went and we'd shop them if they weren't nice to us. Albert used to go pale.

Anyway, on the day of the visit I told Jim to stand by me; all smart he was in a new suit and tie, and thick jumper, for a good view of the proceedings. People like him are the salt of the football earth at the centre of what makes up the heart of football. Jim stood by me with no idea of what I'd planned. Suddenly as HRH got closer I grabbed Jim and stood him at the very front of the line to be introduced. The look on his face was priceless. Prince Charles chatted away to him for about three minutes (the ones at the end of the line might get 30 seconds) and the photographers were shooting away. Jim still talks about it to this day. You get magic moments in my job. This was one of them.

Sometimes I'll sit in that chair and think back to where I came from. If ever I see a coal fire my mind takes me back many years to Teal Street. The centrepiece of the small living room was a brown and cream tiled fireplace that housed a wonderful coal fire that burned all day long and for much of the night. Just sometimes the embers were still glowing in the morning. Granddad got his coal cheap because of his stoker's job in the mill. In this tiny space there was a dining table, two chairs, a mahogany dresser and a large wooden wireless. Granddad listened to the news and football. Beneath the rug that almost filled the little room was a stone floor. The flowered wallpaper was bright and cheerful and so was Grandma Ethel's permanent smile that lit up the room as much as any fire. She loved me dearly and I always knew that it was the kind of love that was unconditional and forever. As I got into my schooling years and moved across to the council house, I would only see her at weekends. But she always had a half-crown for me. How quickly we forget the old coins that weighed down our pockets all those years ago. Back then the half-crown was a fortune. There were eight of them in a pound and when I was small you could do half a week's shopping with one. Next door lived Aunty May and in the nearby streets were three more uncles and aunts. Luxuries were few and far between but it was an age of extended families, unlocked doors and neighbours helping neighbours.

In front of my granddad's house was a high wooden fence and behind it, the monstrous Great Lever Cotton Mill. At the bottom of Teal Street on the corner was the local shop. Grandma Ethel would frequently ask me to nip out to do an errand. It had a gable end and some space in front. On the end someone had painted some white goalposts. I'd spend hours kicking a ball against the wall. Years later I learned from Jimmy Mac that this is how he honed his skills as a small boy in just the same way in his little village of Ballyskeagh. And the shop inside was magical. You rarely see shops like this now. I watch Ronnie Barker in repeats of *Open All Hours* and I'm back in Bolton outside the shop where I bought sweets for me, and bread or sugar for my grandmother.

I've referred to Dale Carnegie many times. There's no question that the discovery of this way of life and thinking changed my life. If it was the Dale Carnegie course that I attended with one leg in a pot, in fact I first came across it many years earlier. I was 17 and my football career seemed to be going nowhere. I was still stuck in this outside-right role; my heading wasn't yet discovered. My father Frank, and my mother Lilian who gave me so much support saw the doldrums I was in and decided that I should seek advice from Alan Ball senior, the father of the famous Alan Ball and the one who didn't even sign my pot as I lay on that hospital bed and he told me he needed the insurance money. We knew that Alan senior did football coaching and he seemed to know how to get the best out of his lad.

So: off I went with my dad to see Mr Ball at his home in Farnworth just outside Bolton. It was the briefest and strangest of meetings. He sat and listened as I told him of the problems I was having and that I didn't seem to be heading anywhere. "What should I do?"

At the end of this chat he simply took a piece of paper and said, "My advice to you is to go to W H Smith's in Bolton and buy this book." He took the paper and a pen and wrote something down. He passed it to me and wished me good luck. And that was it.

Neither dad nor I knew what to make of this bizarre meeting. He'd never mentioned the things we expected, fitness, speed, skill, dedication or how to improve ball control and passing. All he'd done was advise me to go and buy a bloody book. We decided it was all a complete waste of time and petrol and never thought any more about it.

It was probably 12 months later that I asked could I borrow dad's car. So I cleaned it because I needed it for the weekend. As I cleaned the inside what should I see but the slip of paper that Alan Ball senior had given me earlier. I picked it up and was about to put it in the bin when I noticed the words written on it; *"How to Win Friends and Influence People."* For a minute maybe I cast my mind back to the strange meeting I'd had with him. By this time my career anyway was improving. I'd been moved to a centre-forward role, my heading was being tutored by Nat Lofthouse and the washing line was about worn out. The future seemed brighter, I had developed a little confidence and I didn't throw the slip of paper away and in fact, went to Smith's and bought the book. To my surprise I enjoyed it and read it again. All this of course was long before I joined Burnley and long before I ever attended that fateful Dale Carnegie meeting at the end of my career. Was this not serendipity? And believe me 'serendipity' is a word I use a lot and I'm pretty sure it has got me to where I am today. It's to do with happy accidents, chance discoveries; stumbling upon all those good and useful things that you're not even looking for at the time.

So I was 18, getting fitter, faster, heading the ball like a young Nat Lofthouse and starting already to put some of the Carnegie principles in action. I taught myself to be a good listener; look people in the eye whilst shaking hands, encourage team-mates rather than criticise, and meet people halfway in arguments. Never try to win an argument, it advised, meet halfway.

And then 13 years later there I was in that hospital bed looking through a magazine feeling sorry for myself and I got to the small ads at the back. Lo and behold what did one of them say? 'Enrol on a Dale Carnegie Course, Bark Street, Bolton'. It was three weeks later when I hobbled into that room, left there by my wife Sian, little knowing what the result and the impact would be. Serendipity, there's that word again.

The Beatles have played such a part in our lives. 13-year-old Sian saw them 'live' in Bolton. I shall be eternally jealous of that. Their songs played a large part in our courtship. They sang about boy meets girl, girl meets boy, breaking up, and making up.

*Help, She Loves You, Something, Yesterday* and the wonderful *In My Life*.

They wrote and sang about so many emotions; emotions that Sian and I went through, our children have been through, and that will face our grandchildren. Part of our grandparents' job now is to prepare them for all those emotions that they will meet when they are older.

Sian and I not only have a dog called Jude; we each also have a tattoo on our bottoms of the "LOVE" logo from the magnificent Cirque du Soleil that we saw in Las Vegas In 2007. Too many drinks that evening and we both woke up with a tattoo on the butt. That was a show we enjoyed so much that the whole family went, all ten of us, even little six-year-old Alfie.

And I often think what would have happened if I hadn't gone into The Beachcomber for that drink:

*When I was just seventeen and you know what I mean, and the way she looked was just beyond compare ... So how could I dance with another when I saw her standin' there ... Well she looked at me, and I, I could see ... That before too long I'd fall in love with her ... Well my heart went boom, when I crossed that room ... and I held her hand in mine ... And before too long I fell in love with her ... Now I'll never dance with another ...*

My family is everything. You could say serendipity brought me and Sian together all those many years ago. You could certainly say that serendipity provided me with the inspiration for one of the most magical moments I've had involving other family members. I've met kings and queens, prime ministers, celebrities, stars, World Cup winners and Olympic champions. But none gave me better advice or a more wonderful moment, than a little white-haired old lady in bright red shoes.

I was working away in London on the Wembley project. It was 2001, about a month before my daughter's 27th birthday. On one occasion I was in the city centre for a meeting and as always my wife Sian was thinking well ahead. She rang my mobile: "You've got a busy month ahead. Maybe while you're in town today you could pick up a present for Claire's birthday at the end of the month."

It was late, about 4pm on a Friday afternoon and I had just a little spare time as I walked down Oxford Street's splendid shops. I estimated that if I caught the 5.30 train to Heathrow I would be ok to catch the later flight to Manchester. I had plenty of time. As ever though the mobile went again so that by the time I'd taken a couple more calls walking along the street it was now nearer to 5pm and I hadn't seen anything suitable. Ok then, I thought, I can get a later train and a later plane. But by 5.45 I was getting nowhere and the shops within minutes would be closing down. Panic began to set in. There were the usual things I could choose such as perfume or jewellery but that would hardly be original. What about an expensive watch I wondered as I began to get desperate.

And then the heavens opened and I had neither coat nor umbrella.

So, there I was standing in a shop doorway sheltering from the downpour looking at bracelets with little enthusiasm until a small, old lady joined me in the doorway. She wore a shiny yellow raincoat, a plastic 'rain-mate' head cover that tied under her chin, and she was wearing bright red shoes. So there were the two of us stranded until the rain eased.

"You seem to be looking for something," she said with a slight smile, as if she was a mind reader.

I returned the smile and said that yes, I was looking for a present for my daughter for her 27th birthday but was having trouble and was running out of time before I had to dash off to catch the train.

The old lady looked quizzically at me and then spoke again. "Why don't you give her the greatest gift she has ever had?"

"Pardon," I replied, somewhat mystified by her question.

She said, "Why don't you give her the greatest gift she has ever had?"

"I'd love to, but what on earth would that be," I asked her.

"Something so simple, but so unusual – a memory jar. It's so simple. Find some ordinary little shop or a Woolworths, go into the household department and find a nice glass jar. It doesn't have to be fancy or expensive. Then get a small notepad and when you can, start to write down on separate pieces of paper all the memories of happy times you have had with your daughter. Fold each one up and place it in the jar. Then find a nice label you can attach to the front of the jar and write 'Memory Jar' on it. Wrap it up and present it to your daughter on her birthday."

She then reached out and gently touched my arm. "I promise you it will be the greatest gift you can give her." With that, and the rain having ended, she slowly walked away with a smile on her face.

In all honesty I thought the situation was almost surreal and weird. I'm not a user of words like spooked, but I actually did feel as if I'd been visited by some kind of unreal person. The whole situation had a strange kind of eerie feeling to it, and yet in no way frightening. I checked my watch; there was no time for any kind of proper shopping now and I hurried away. I did manage to buy a jar however from a small shop I passed. Sian was waiting for me when I got in and eventually asked: "Did you get the present?"

"Yes I have," I said (well there was a grain of truth in that I thought). "It's a surprise and I'm not even telling you what it is. But I can promise you it will have you talking for hours."

By the time I flew down to London again I'd made a nice label and had started to scribble down a few ideas on small squares of paper that I then folded and placed in the jar. If it did one thing, it certainly made me think. I needed as many as possible to fill the small jar, and day by day I added more until the jar was about half full. In fact I became quite obsessed with the challenge of bringing back all the wonderful memories of special occasions and events we'd enjoyed as she had grown up. Things like:

*Do you remember our first dog Gizmo ... what about the time we rode on camels in Tunisia ... and do you remember the night you brought home your first boyfriend ...*

But then a little bit of panic set in. The jar was only two thirds full and my memory began to go blank. I could remember many things but the trick was to find those that were truly magical. It was then that I started to realise how time had flown by and my little girl was now little no longer. She was married and planning her own family. How precious time is. How precious memories are. Of course the things that I recalled invariably involved Sian and there were times that I became quite misty-eyed.

Still there was space in the jar and I had a brainwave. Why not stick small pictures of family, pets and friends on the pieces of paper? So, that's what I did next with captions on the other side such as:

*Do you remember Uncle Maldwin ... I wonder what happened to your first horse Banjo ... was it you who built this snowman ...*

It was time to organise the next step, the actual presentation of the jar. I neatly wrapped the jar and I booked a meal for three at our favourite Italian restaurant, 'Nino's' in Rawtenstall. On the night I dropped them off at the door and told them I would park the car. But I didn't join them. As they waited for me a parcel was delivered to the table for them. With it was a note to say that the evening was just for the two of them and to open the present and share some memories.

They arrived home just before midnight still talking about the jar and the contents with all the memories of great moments in our lives.

They had both been in floods of tears. As Claire left to go home the next day she hugged me and said: "Thanks Dad that was the greatest present I have ever had. It was just magical. It was special." Today, over ten years later that jar still sits on her dressing table at her home. Since then I have often wondered would jewellery or perfume have given her so much joy. I somehow doubt it.

I'm sure that little old lady was real but just sometimes I still wonder if I imagined her appearance in that doorway on Oxford Street.

Chance plays such a part in our lives. It has certainly shaped and guided mine. Chance, serendipity, good people, a wonderful family, and being willing to step outside of the comfort zone have made me what I am.

Oh, and not forgetting.

I could once head a football.